D1522272

PISTOLS

AT

DAWN

PISTOLS
AT
DAWN

A HISTORY OF DUELLING

JOHN NORRIS

First published 2009

The History Press
The Mill, Brimscombe Port
Stroud, Gloucestershire, GL5 2QG
www.thehistorypress.co.uk

British Library Cataloguing in Publication Data.
A catalogue record for this book is available from the British Library.

ISBN 978 0 7524 4710 0

Printed in Great Britain

CONTENTS

To Chris Lay and Dave Biggins,
thank you for all the great times together.
Here's more to come

ACKNOWLEDGEMENTS

I would like to extend my sincere gratitude to Her Majesty Queen Elizabeth II for granting permission to use material relating to Frederick, Duke of York's duel. I am grateful to Pamela Clark the registrar at the Royal Archives at Windsor Castle, the staff at the Jersey Heritage Trust, the States Archives Trust on Guernsey and Simon Hancock and the staff at Haverfordwest Museum in Pembrokeshire in Wales; they have all been most helpful. My thanks in particular to the 41st Regiment of Foot re-enactment group for taking the time to recreate a duel. My gratitude also goes to the many other museums and archive sources, including the City of Portsmouth Museum, for their capable assistance in putting this work together. And special thanks to Pat Farey for additional photographs. Finally, as ever, I would like to thank my wife Elizabeth for accompanying me on my visits as we stood in fields and cemeteries in fair weather and foul, and helping take essential notes and remembering details.

INTRODUCTION

The term 'duel' as we understand it today can be traced back to medieval times and is derived from the Latin word *'duellum'* meaning war between two. In its most basic form the duel is a contest between two opponents in a form of ritualised combat, examples of which can be found in the pages of history dating back to ancient Greece. At the ten-year-long siege of the city of Troy where Hector kills Patroclus, the legendary Achilles challenges Hector to a personal fight to answer for killing his friend. This act of single combat between the pair of warriors was witnessed by the opposing armies who watch as Achilles slays Hector. Such engagements were more about revenge than resolving differences of opinion or seeking restitution. However, over the centuries the resolving of disputes in such a combative manner came to be seen as the ultimate means to finally settle differences between two people.

In the medieval period the right of a nobleman to defend his honour gained universal acceptance, and challenges to personal combat were usually issued by a knight throwing down his 'gage'. This was a token gesture and could take the form of a glove or a hat and meant to challenge the accuser to retrieve the item for the fight to take place. It was the Church which eventually intervened to try and limit the practice, but in the end it only succeeded in seeing it survive, albeit in a modified form. This was the joust, which was a form of personal combat without the judicial aspect, and this turn became the tournament which, even though governed, could dissolve into mini-battles as old scores were settled between rivals. In those days of knightly chivalry it took many years of training to perfect the use of sword, mace or lance. It was a brave man who stood foursquare against an opponent of equal courage and experience. All of that changed, however, with the development of gunpowder weapons. There was no longer any requirement to stand in close proximity to inflict mortal wounding, as gunpowder weapons lengthened the range of engagement in battle.

With the introduction of gunpowder weapons it was claimed that gunpowder made all men equal. Certainly, after the rise of such weapons the armoured knight of noble birth was equally at risk from being killed as the humble foot soldier. In the early fifteenth century Gian Paolo Vittelli of the Italian Condottiere illustrated the contempt with which he held troops who used gunpowder weapons by ordering that on capture they be blinded and their hands cut off. This severe treatment towards handgunners was continued into the sixteenth century by the French commander Pierre du Terrail, Chevalier de Bayard. Times were changing but he remained traditionally of the old order, having engaged in single combat, a form of duel, many times and as a consequence his bravery was unquestioned. Nevertheless, his ire towards handgunners was worse than Vittelli, and the Chevalier de Bayard ordered that all captured handgunners be executed. He declared them to be 'cowardly and base knaves, who would never have dared to have met true soldiers face to face and hand to hand'. It was ironical, then, that the Chevalier de Bayard was killed on 30 April 1524 at the Battle of Sesia with his spine shot through by a handgunner.

Challenges to engage in duels were invariably fought out by opponents using swords of some description, such as the claymore, cutlass or sabre, and this practice continued well into the eighteenth century, by which time handguns had been in use for some 450 years. Men may have fired on one another across the battlefield using muskets and pistols, and some personal disputes were settled with pistols on occasion. For the most part, though, swords were the preferred means of defending one's honour when a man's reputation was called into question.

Then a remarkable transformation took place and pistols became the duellists' weapon of choice. There are examples where duels were conducted between opponents quite literally 'armed to the teeth'. In Ireland in 1759 Colonel Barrington met Mr Gilbert in a mounted duel, with each man armed with pistols, swords and daggers. Both fired and missed, so they went at one another with swords during which Gilbert's horse was killed and he was thrown to the ground. The mêlée must have more resembled a medieval tournament than a dispute between two so-called gentlemen. Lying prostrate, Gilbert was unable to defend himself. Taking advantage of his opponent's vulnerable state Barrington moved in and presented a dagger to Gilbert's throat. It would have been all too easy to have made the fatal thrust, but Gilbert saved himself by conceding defeat. The affair was deemed concluded and the two men became firm friends after their deadly encounter.

Duels still continued to be fought with swords but they required skill to wield while a pistol could be used after the minimum of instruction. Certainly by the eighteenth century swords had all but given way to pistols as the preferred weapon in duels. This gave rise to a period, which some sources have identified as being between 1770 and 1870, when matters of personal honour were settled by two men armed with pistols facing one another across a remote field. The historian Harold L. Peterson places the date when pistols began to be used in duels as early as 1650, and certainly there are many examples of firearms being used in duels during the mid-seventeenth century to bear out this statement. Not all duels were conducted on foot and there are many accounts of where the exchange of fire took place between mounted riders, a practice which continued until possibly as late as the second half of the eighteenth century.

Duels could sometimes take months to unfold and reach a climax as insults, either real or imagined, were examined in notes to various parties, and efforts were made to conclude the affair before shots were exchanged. Sometimes a duel could be fought and concluded in a matter of moments. In 1808 two officers serving in Ireland entered into a disagreement; within the space of 20 minutes the argument had become a duel and the men had exchanged shots. The surviving officer was later arrested and hanged for the murder of his fellow officer. It was a cautionary tale but one which did little to deter duelling. During a dinner party in Los Angeles in 1859, Colonel John Bankhead Magruder and Dr William B. Osborn fell into a dispute at the table concerning over whom each of them considered to be the greatest man in America. Not unnaturally the two men disagreed and Dr Osborn, who by all accounts was the worse for drink, challenged Colonel Magruder to a duel. The colonel as the challenged party had choice of weapons and he selected 'Derringer pistols across the dinner table'.

Events were unfolding fast and the poor doctor must have felt distinctly uneasy at how quickly things had got out of hand. The Derringer pistol was a short weapon usually between 4 and 9in in length but with a large calibre bullet which could be up to .51in. A pair of these compact weapons was brought to the men and on the command 'Ready' the nervous doctor fired without waiting for the correct order. The colonel, despite the closeness of the range, was unharmed. At a range of barely a few feet the colonel aimed at the, by now terrified, doctor. Fearing for his life Osborn fell to his knees and begged for mercy. Colonel Magruder showed leniency and spared his opponent's life. What the poor unwitting doctor did not know was that the pistols had not been properly loaded with lead bullets. The incident serves to illustrate just how quickly matters could get out of control, but not all encounters ended with embarrassment being the only injury inflicted.

Duels did not always end with one man dead. Sometimes things could go awry and onlookers became the innocent victims, and other engagements would be conducted in conditions which belied the seriousness of the encounter. It was the steadfastness which allowed a man to hold his weapon in an un-quivering hand. In the nineteenth century an anonymous author who identified himself only as 'A Traveller' wrote a treatise entitled *The Art of Duelling*, which appeared in 1836; from the date we may conclude that the author could have witnessed a number of duels, but it is not known whether or not he participated in a duel himself. 'Traveller' claimed to have studied the results of almost 200 duels and concluded that if a man is hit the chances are 'three to one against his being killed'. This would appear to be a better than average rate for survival, but a series of trials using an unrifled pistol of 1790s vintage was conducted in the 1970s that showed at a range of 85 yards a firer could hit a man-sized target three times out of four. This goes to prove that nothing could be taken for granted when it came to duelling, and experienced military men on the field of the duel could just as easily fall victim to the untrained civilian who held a pistol for the first time in their life.

From the records available to us it would appear that duelling with pistols was the preserve of the gentry, politicians and officers in the army or navy. However, this was not the case; it is simply that duels between gentlemen of high standing made for a better story in the newspapers. Elements of the working classes would also have fought their own forms of duels but these would have been less formalised and very much of the rough and ready nature. Not all members of the higher echelons of society were upright, stalwart pillars of their class and some could show a base side to their nature. The difference between the two lifestyles lay in the fact that, within the working class, if a dispute was resolved with the use of a pistol it tended to be a drunken brawl and as such little more than murder. Men of a higher class, on the other hand, were usually expected to conduct the affair of settling any argument concerning honour in a more formal manner, like some deadly appointment for an interview. But even in these upper limits of society there was to be found an element who were little more than blackguards; even so, they could demand satisfaction in a duel. For example, Mr Butler from County Kilkenny, and Captain Bunbury fought their duel in an Irish tavern in the presence of customers who were drinking. The incident took place in 1784 when the two men in the company of their seconds entered the tavern and ordered food and drink, which appeared quite normal. At that point the two men fired at one another, which left Bunbury hit in the mouth by the bullet and Butler lying dead. Exactly what caused the duel is not clear and as to why the men should choose to fight in a tavern is not understood either. It may have been the drink and a hasty choice to fight as soon as possible, but the incident does prove the point that consumption of alcohol could lead to an argument becoming a duel. The writer Jean-Jacques Rousseau rather succinctly noted in his work 'La Nouvelle Heloise' in 1760: 'A scoundrel only needs to fight a duel and he ceases to be a scoundrel.' There was much truth in this statement, because after a duel a man's social standing among his peers was greatly elevated. He was now a duellist with a reputation and it was a rash man who did not countenance an experienced duellist. Of course, that is unless he was tried for murder and hanged.

Like the gunfighters of the American 'Wild West', such as 'Wild' Bill Hickok, Wyatt Earp or William 'Billy the Kid' Bonney, duellists were held in awe and seen as special people and not to be meddled with lightly. Such people had stared at death and by participating in formal duels or gunfights had shown they had the courage to stand, pistol in hand, to face down anyone who doubted their veracity. This reputation could stand them in good stead, that is, until someone brave enough and with a better aim ended their career with a shot from a pistol. Experienced duellists could be self-opinionated and this was observed by Benjamin Franklin who noted: 'How can such miserable worms, as we are, entertain so much pride as the conceit that every offence against our imagined honour merits death?' At the height of its fashion there emerged a saying on the subject of duelling. It ran to the effect that if two Englishmen were stranded on a desert island they would soon find something to gamble on; but if two Frenchmen were stranded on a desert island they would fight a duel.

Duels could only be conducted between two people of equal standing and in *The British Code of Duel* of 1824 the definition of a gentleman was quantified as being: '… the lowest distinction of civil nobility yet in character assimilates with the highest'. This wording identifies gentlemen, such as merchants and bankers, and means they could indulge in duels on equal terms. Over the years during which duels were commonplace, various codes of conduct were compiled, but they were unofficial and meant only as guidelines. The content of these codes have a significant bearing on this work and they shall be used to intersperse the narrative with supporting remarks.

This book does not set out to detail every single duel of any significance that was fought with a pistol; that is an almost impossible task, because each duel has a bearing on the history of what is surely one of the most peculiar aspects of social behaviour. What this work does endeavour to do is explain the circumstances leading up to a duel, the consequences of the affair and the results which followed. For this purpose only a select number of incidents can be highlighted to serve as examples, and a duel which is seen as being very important to someone with an interest in local history may not necessarily be of enough significance to use an expression of example.

This, then, is a history of duelling with pistols rather than duelling with swords. Each form had its own set of codes by which the engagements were conducted. Sometimes duellists did resort to swords and daggers but it was usually the pistol which decided the outcome. Many famous personages fought duels, some of whom should have known better than to engage in such acts of recklessness. These include the victor of Waterloo, the Duke of Wellington, William Pitt the Younger and Andrew Jackson the President of America and a host of many other politicians, military men and businessmen. In fact, so many prominent figures took their stand on the duelling fields that one could almost believe that duelling was their sole preserve. This work will examine the codes by which duels were fought, the outcomes and the reasons why men faced adversaries with loaded weapons as they prepared to keep their date with destiny.

1

CAUSE AND EFFECT

What is the Duel?

Over the years there were literally thousands of duels fought with pistols, but only a fraction of those encounters were believed worthy of being actually recorded. Certainly the principals if they were noteworthy, such as politicians, officers or characters of public standing including town mayors; then the incident became the subject of newspaper accounts and even cartoons of the day. A number of so-called duels fought between lesser notable figures would have passed unnoticed and unrecorded unless, of course, it was reported that one of the participants was killed. In such cases a murder enquiry and trial would be convened. Statistics compiled from the same period can be ambiguous, but one set of figures examining some 200 duels fought in Ireland, Scotland and England tells us that only some 10 per cent of the participants came to trial. The historian Victor Kiernan states that duellists, '… could kill each other and go scot free, when a poor man could be hanged for stealing a few shillings'. This is, of course, entirely correct with English courts sentencing transportation to the colonies as an alternative punishment for such trivial crimes as stealing a loaf of bread, and public executions, even of young offenders, for stealing a sheep. The Italian 'Lothario' Giacomo Casanova fought a duel with Colonel Xavier Branicki of the Polish army in March 1766 as a result of being called a coward by the officer, even though duelling was illegal in Poland. The colonel shot Casanova in the hand but in return received a wound which entered his right side and passed through his abdomen. It was serious and it appeared that the officer was mortally wounded. In his shocked and weakened state Branicki, believing himself to be dying, uttered words of advice to Casanova by suggesting he make haste away, 'as you are in

danger of the gibbet'. The great womaniser was apprehended but spared
the hangman's noose by the personal intervention of the King of Poland.
Colonel Branicki somehow survived his awful wound and made a full
recovery. It was a close call for Casanova, who despite his reputation as a
lover and seducer of women was no coward. The fact that the case against
him was dismissed shows how unbalanced the judicial system could be
when it came to hearing the cases of duelling.

Over the years duels have become romanticised due to novels and, more
recently, films and television; dramatisations of romantic fiction have added
to the perception that duels were invariably fought over affairs of honour.
These modern depictions have been stylised to suit mass audiences and
invariably show two men attempting to resolve their differences by engaging
in a duel. The vision these recreations present is erroneous because they
show honour being restored after an argument or insult. In truth there was
nothing honourable about killing a man or maiming him for life. Death
in a duel was very rarely instantaneous and the mortally wounded victims
could linger for hours or days in the utmost agony – all for the sake of
honour. This question of honour was either to preserve one's own social
standing in society or to defend a lady's honour. Furthermore, the question
of honour, like the insult itself, could be real or imagined. It permeated
through society and affected some more than others who felt as though they
had something to prove if they believed they had been insulted. The author
Sir Walter Scott held the opinion that duels in Scotland were common
during the 1730s because: 'the gentry were at once idle, haughty, fierce...'
Certainly they had much time on their hands and with their days filled
with gambling on cards and horses, betting on boxing bouts and hunting,
it was not surprising they took to duelling to settle differences of opinion
arising from such matters. In Ireland the populace were equally bellicose
and apt to hotheadedness, leading the landed gentry to indulge in duelling
with pistols to the extent that it was almost akin to other forms of sport.
Albeit a deadly interest, this sport was almost exclusively the preserve of the
well-to-do for it was they who had the most time to spare in indulging in
the lethal practice of duelling.

Some duelling encounters have become famous and others have
become infamous due to the notoriety of the action and nature in which
they were conducted. Duelling has a history which can be traced back
to the earliest of military societies and reached its peak in the form of
the joust and tournament during the medieval period, when sword, lance
and mace were used. These expressions of fighting prowess originated
in France around the eleventh century and developed into the mêlée
which were in effect mini battles fought in front of an audience. These
events evolved into the joust when popularity in the spectacle changed

and the meetings became more organised and very formal affairs. Young men who had just been knighted would frequently travel from one joust meeting to another to gain valuable experience which could stand them in good stead for time of war. The joust was also where a man could win money or valuable prizes and even claim the possessions of the opponents they defeated. Jousts were well organised and it was possible for a knight to participate in a circuit of meetings and, depending on his success, his reputation would be enhanced. William Marshall, first Earl of Pembroke, 1147–1219, amassed a considerable fortune in such tournaments and his reputation was such that he was a favourite at the king's court. However, these meetings were not without their dangers and men were often maimed or killed during the joust. In June 1559 a joust was arranged to celebrate the Treaty of Cateau-Cambrésis which brought to an end the warring between France, Spain and Italy. The meeting was held in Paris at the rue Saint Antoine and scheduled to last for three days. It was attended by royalty and knights from across Europe, some of whom were entered in the tournament as participants.

Among the nobles taking up the lance as part of the celebrations was King Henry II of France. Such contests were not for the faint-hearted and kings had more to prove than anyone else when it came to showing courage. Their opponents in these bouts were not expected to show any leniency just because they were facing the king and were not inclined to pull the weight of the impact of the lance. On the last day of the contest in Paris the French king was faced by a captain of his bodyguard, Count de Montgomery, a young, well-spirited soldier. On the first encounter the king received a powerful blow from Montgomery's lance which almost threw him from his saddle. Henry demanded satisfaction and faced the captain again. As the lances crashed, a splinter from Montgomery's penetrated the visor of Henry's helmet and pierced one of the king's eyes and his temple. The badly injured monarch was taken to Chateau des Tournelles to have his wounds treated. But they were worse than expected. The king hung on to life for ten days until finally he died having endured great pain all that time. Kings believed they had to show they could hold their own in these contests, regardless of the dangers. The death of Henry II was unfortunate but not an isolated event during jousts; the nobility felt it necessary to prove themselves. For example, King Henry VIII of England was an ardent jouster in his youth and in 1524 during one tournament was very nearly killed. Not unnaturally the Church condemned jousting but despite the opposition it was still practised and remained popular. A huge event with over 600 noblemen attending was arranged at Carew Castle in Pembroke in Wales to celebrate Sir Rhys ap Thomas being appointed to the Order of the Garter in 1507.

The imagery of knights on horseback jousting entered public imagination as an age of courtesans and chivalry and there was an air of romanticism concerning two knights fighting for a lady's favour. Duels fought on horseback were among some of the earliest recorded which involved the use of pistols. The historian and author Frederick Wilkinson attributes this to the fact that large numbers of cavalrymen were armed with pistols. This may well have been the case, and certainly cavalrymen were prone to believe they were part of an elitist group. Sometimes this could be their undoing, but encounters with riders charging at one another and firing their pistols was in keeping with this idea of superiority. In truth, the chances of a mounted man hitting a target while moving, even at a gentle trot, is unlikely because the movement of the horse would not permit a steady aim to be taken. Some pistol duels were conducted on horseback in a fashion similar to the traditional joust with the barrier dividing the opponents. Some mounted duellists were known to load their pistols with several small pellets in an attempt to hit their opponent, very similar to the effect of a shotgun. It was during the early stages of the reign of King Charles I of England that one of the most unusual duels came to be fought on horseback.

Not long after his marriage to Henrietta Maria, Charles was being entertained by the Duke of Buckingham and as part of the festivities a dwarf by the name of Jeffery Hudson made his entrance by appearing from a large pie, much to the delight of Charles's young bride. In fact, so taken was she by this man who measured only 18in high that she asked him to join the Royal Court. As protocol of the day demanded, the Duke of Buckingham, not wishing to offend his Royal guests, respected the Queen's wishes and Hudson found himself a favourite of the Royal Court. The Queen nicknamed him 'Lord Minimus' and the king elected him to the rank of captain in the army. He amused his royal masters and was frequently used as a stooge for practical jokes and taunts about his size. Hudson accepted most of these in the course of good humour, but on one occasion a courtier went too far. According to the story, Hudson had been attacked by a large male turkey known as a 'stag' and very badly mauled by the bird. When word of the incident circulated around the court a young but portly officer called Charles Crofts made continual fun of the small man's plight. It was no doubt the endless puns which pressed Hudson to the point of breaking and challenged the officer to a duel. Some records state the officer was called Cross and was a courtier to the queen. The turkey incident involving Hudson should also be examined in a bit more detail. If it was indeed a stag turkey it would have been a wild variety, probably from stock brought back from the New World where the first colonies were being established in America. The bird would have undoubtedly been very aggressive, nowhere near the size of modern hybrid birds which can weigh in excess of 50lb, and would have been very mobile. The turkey would have probably weighed around 20lb, but coupled with its agility, natural aggressiveness and powerful claws, which it would have used to defend itself against predators, it was no wonder that Hudson, given his small stature of only 18in, was badly hurt. Anyone of normal stature who has had the misfortune of being attacked by a large bird such as a goose, which can weigh up to 14lb and use its wings to inflict painful bruises, will readily sympathise with the ordeal the diminutive Hudson must have endured.

Crofts' (or Cross depending on the account) remarks finally made Hudson retort by challenging him to a duel, which was something the officer did not expect. Allegedly he did not take the challenge seriously and turned up at the appointed hour unarmed. But Hudson was incensed and demanded the duel went ahead; to balance out the height difference between the two men the duel was to be fought on horseback. Crofts (or Cross) may have been an officer but Hudson too was an appointed officer by the king and, although lacking in stature, did not want for courage. At a signal the two men rode towards each other. Hudson fired, hitting his opponent in the chest and killing him. It was no mean feat of arms because firing from a moving horse to hit a moving target is very difficult. Nonetheless, his skill at arms failed to impress the king and he was banished from court. His life story in exile is extremely colourful with tales of being captured by pirates, imprisoned in Africa and other adventures along the way before returning to England more than twenty-five years after the duel. It was a much-changed country he came home to in the aftermath of the Civil War, but Jeffery Hudson has not been forgotten in Rutland where he lived in his later years; there they drink a beer named after the doughty dwarf.

Around 1650, less than one hundred years after the tragic death of King Henry II, a formal style of duelling emerged, probably from Italy and later popularised in France, with pistols eventually replacing swords. At this time Europe had just emerged from the bloody period known as the Thirty Years War (1618–48), a conflict which cost the lives of countless soldiers and civilians alike. In England the last stages of the Civil War between Parliament and the Royalist forces of King Charles I was being fought. Roaming the Continent and the British Isles were mercenaries, who were unemployed now the fighting was at an end, and soldiers whose services were no longer required. With no prospects and no pay, such itinerants took to crime and began to squabble among themselves with arguments being settled by impromptu duels.

Duelling as a form of expression may have found supporters and ardent enthusiasts but it was not wholeheartedly accepted. Emerging from the chaos of the Civil War, England was ripe for duelling with young men eager to prove themselves. Oliver Cromwell took a personal interest in the question of duelling and in June 1654 issued an edict condemning the practice. His opinions almost echoed the words of John Despagne's work *Anti-duello* which had appeared in 1632 and, as the title implies, was against all forms of duelling. Cromwell declared duelling to be a 'growing evil' and introduced severe penalties for anyone involved in a duel in any shape or form. For accepting or issuing a challenge to duel the penalty was six months in prison without being granted bail. All challenges to duel were to be informed to the authorities within 24 hours of receiving it, and failure to do so would be seen as tantamount to accepting the challenge. Fatalities arising from a duel would be classed as murder and as such a capital offence. Anyone involved in a duel in any shape or form would forever be banished from England.

What these draconian measures did was to make it clear that it was illegal to have anything whatsoever to do with duelling. In the eyes of the law there would be no mitigating circumstances and ignorance of the law was to be no excuse. Three years earlier in 1651, Members of Parliament had proposed that duellists should have their right hand chopped off, property confiscated and exiled. The penalties of Cromwell's laws which were passed may have been harsh but it is extremely unlikely that they stamped out duelling. The laws may actually have had the opposite effect by driving duelling underground. This is quite probable because several years later with the Restoration of the English monarchy in the form of King Charles II, following the death of Oliver Cromwell, there came a sudden outbreak of duelling. For a short period this state of affairs lingered until some semblance of calm returned as the country once more settled down after so many upheavals.

Duels had not always enjoyed the king's toleration. For example, during the reign of James I, Charles II's grandfather, a leading lawyer of the day, Sir Edward Coke, declared that 'to kill a man in a duel was murder, but there was no bar to sending a challenge or acting as a second.' King James I himself wrote a treatise against duelling and his attorney general, Francis Bacon, stated that he would prosecute should: 'any man appoint the field, though no fight takes place; if any man accept a challenge, or consent to be a second; if any man depart the realm in order to fight; if any man revive a quarrel after the late proclamation.' Again, strong words indeed which left no one in any doubt as to the illegality of the duel.

Royal opposition to duelling in England was made clear when King Charles II declared that any nobleman caught participating in a duel would be pursued with the 'utmost rigours of the court' and threatened with being excluded from the Royal Court, which was probably the worst fate which any courtier could suffer if he were seeking to advance himself.

Being outside the king's circle of favourites left one vulnerable to any plot to seize his position or money.

In Spain laws were passed to prohibit duelling dating back to 1480, almost 200 years before duelling with pistols gained a widespread following. Italy too banned duelling and in France Cardinal Richelieu and his successor Cardinal Mazzarin banned duelling and passed edicts against the practice. As early as 1609 duelling was made a capital crime in France. Richelieu personally ordered the execution of two noblemen caught duelling. Frederick the Great of Prussia joined the ranks of those heads of state determined to stamp out forever the practice. He informed the officers of his army that if any wished to duel they had to obtain permission from him. When two officers met with the intention of conducting a duel, Frederick welcomed them to the appointed place of the duel where a gibbet had been erected. He informed them that he intended to hang the survivor of the affair. But even such stern measures did not prevent duelling and officers continued to meet clandestinely, often with the active knowledge and support of their fellow officers. In view of this there was really very little a monarch could do in the way of stopping duelling, and instead had to tolerate it. Duelling may not have flourished as with other fashionable events, such as boxing or horseracing, but the fact remains it was practised and each incident had to be dealt with as it became known.

It is generally agreed that the formal duel as a means of satisfying honour originated in Italy some time in the first half of the sixteenth century. These affairs would have been conducted with swords, but as firearms spread so the trend to use pistols in duels gained fashion. These early duels with pistols were informal affairs, with the involved parties arming themselves with any pistol that was ready to hand. Over the years a 'Code Duello' was established, followed by a series of compiled codes and specific terms, each of which related to the conduct of a duel. They contained very precise instructions and in almost every case it was stated that a formal handwritten letter was the proper and polite etiquette when issuing a challenge to duel, for whatever reason, including an insult arising out of something even as mundane as the opinion that someone's eating manners at the dinner table were disgusting. The code most favoured was that called the 'cartello', which recommended that the letter to challenge should be formal and list the facts, not contain any rudeness and be signed, dated and witnessed. This was the form of letter and apart from a few changes over the years would otherwise remain the standard communiqué between duellists. Almost 300 years after the 'cartello' was standardised, the appearance of *The Art of Duelling* in 1836 reemphasised the necessity of a formal letter when issuing a challenge. The anonymous author of the treatise points out that: 'A man should conduct himself (however grievous the offence he has received) during the whole affair with the greatest possible politeness.' The guideline goes on to warn that the letter should be written 'carefully and expressed clearly; avoiding all strong language: simply stating, first, the cause of the offence; secondly, the reason why he considers it his duty to notice the affair; thirdly, the name of a friend; and lastly, requesting that a time and place may be appointed.' For the most part such protocol had always existed, such as the letter sent by David Landale to George Morgan on 22 August 1826, ten years before the appearance of *The Art of Duelling*, prior to the two men meeting in their engagement to conduct the last fatal duel fought in Scotland.

As the European Continent of the seventeenth century stabilised and peace was restored, the troops returned back to their homelands, taking with them the Italian legacy of duelling. This practice spread to become established in France, England, Spain, throughout the Prussian states, and eastwards into Russia. Even small islands were not immune from the effects of duelling. On Malta in the eighteenth century it is recorded how a Knight of the Order of St John declined to participate in a duel. For refusing it is recorded how he was punished severely and eventually sentenced to life imprisonment; all for having the courage of his conviction not to duel. Even the islands of Jersey and Guernsey in the Channel Islands were affected. These islands have a long history of being garrisons for English troops and the several instances of duels on these islands invariably involved officers of different regiments. On the other side of the Atlantic, the island of Barbados in the West Indies of the Caribbean became a Crown possession in 1663, and during the American War of Independence and the Anglo-French wars the island took on a new importance as it found itself transformed into a military base. Thousands of miles away from the high society of London or other towns like Bath, the officers and men were frequently left for prolonged periods with nothing to occupy them. Boredom quickly and easily set in and solace was often found in drink. It was only to be expected, then, that trifling matters which would probably be of no consequence in the cooler climes of Europe suddenly became exaggerated points over which challenges to duel were issued. The islands of the Caribbean in the eighteenth and early nineteenth centuries were not the romantic destinations of the twenty-first century we know today. Not for nothing were the West Indies described as the graveyard of the British Army in the 1790s. In a two-year period from 1794–6 it is recorded how the 23rd Regiment of Foot (later to become the Royal Welsh Fusiliers), lost 12 officers and 600 men to the ravages of yellow fever on the island of St Domingo. In the same period the 13th Light Dragoons lost 19 officers and 296 men from a compliment of 452 all ranks, also due to yellow fever.

With few prospects and a high mortality rate it was no wonder that men turned to drinking to while away the long hours. But the combination of alcohol and the hot tropical sun did nothing to dilute tempers in overseas garrisons. On 15 January 1811, when the fighting on the Iberian Peninsular to drive the French out of Spain and Portugal was at its height, two officers from different regiments fought a fatal duel on Barbados. Captain Broadman of the 60th Regiment (later to become the King's Royal Rifle Corps), challenged Ensign de Betton of the Royal West Indian Rangers to a duel, 'in which at first fire, the former was shot through the heart, and instantly expired'. Ensign de Betton fled the island never to be heard of again.

The practice of duelling found its way to India, where it was also taken up by the military who were posted there to protect England's richest prize in the empire. Although thousands of miles from home and away from familiar surroundings, officers in India conducted themselves as though still in England. It was a strange existence and news between the countries took time to travel. In America, with its French and English settlements, the duel would, over time, evolve into a myriad of forms, but the formalised duel was the style usually conducted between antagonists, including such luminaries as the Vice-President of America, Aaron Burr; he shot dead Alexander Hamilton, his opposite number, in July 1804 during a formalised duel which included seconds in a manner worthy of European traditions.

The 'Golden Age' of duelling, if indeed there ever was a period which could be defined as such, has been identified by historians as flourishing in the years between the 1770s and the 1850s. One is inclined to agree with this summary because most of the significant affairs appear to have occurred during this period, and after the closing date there is a trend where duels are shown to be less frequent. To put the time span into context, this period would cover historical events from the Jacobite Rebellion in Scotland and the American War of Independence through the French Revolution and Napoleonic Wars before beginning to peter out around the time of the end of the Crimean War in 1856. Such was duelling then that it existed against a backdrop of warfare which at times enveloped whole continents. The losses of troops in battle during this period were published in newspapers and the public became used to reading such news, but the mention of a duel was something entirely different. This was at home and between two men, which somehow made it more tangible and personal which people were able to relate to. Wars were distant and fought by men trained to perform such deeds; after all, they were soldiers and doing their duty. Duelling on the other hand was a matter of choice and when fought in small towns like Tenby or Haverfordwest in Wales the participants were often known to many local people, making it a much different thing altogether.

Gentlemen of the period in the eighteenth and nineteenth centuries were wise to be extra vigilant in keeping good manners lest they offend someone with even the most seemingly innocent word or gesture. Certainly it was the question of honour which triggered the challenge to a duel. However, some men could become serial duellists simply to prove their point. For example, one Neapolitan nobleman fought no fewer than fourteen duels simply to 'prove' that in his opinion Dante was a finer poet than Ariosto. It was not until he lay on his deathbed that he admitted to the fact of never having read any of the works of either poet.

Duels were frequently sparked by either alcohol or gambling, or a combination of the two. Events which culminated from such affairs did not always begin with animosity between the men who later found themselves adversaries. In October 1824 Captain Gourlay met a certain Mr Westall, whose acquaintance he had made in September that year while visiting the races at Doncaster. On this occasion the men happened to chance upon one another while taking refreshment at a public house in Edinburgh. They joined company and during the course of a few drinks Captain Gourlay reminded Westall that he was still owed the sum of 70 guineas, a not inconsiderable amount, which was outstanding from their meeting at the races the previous month. Rather than pay out the debt from his own pocket Westall suggested that a friend of his who owed him a similar amount pay Captain Gourlay in his stead and settle the matter. It seemed like a reasonable financial arrangement, but the captain would have none of it and demanded that Westall pay off the debt himself and accused him of being a cheat.

In response, the civilian called the captain a liar, whereupon the officer seized a poker and struck out at Westall. His aim was probably impaired by the amount of alcohol he had consumed and, missing Westall's head, the blow landed on the man's shoulder instead. Such was the force that it was several minutes before he could compose himself and repair to a small side room. Raised voices emanated and a duel was convened for the following morning of 31 October. Together with their respective seconds they met at South Queensferry where they were rowed over the river. Joining them in their passage were the doctors who had been summoned to attend the duel, making the deadly gathering complete. The two principals took up their positions and fired. It was the civilian Westall who scored by shooting dead Captain Gourlay, probably to the astonishment of all those present. The words of insult would alone have been enough to provoke a challenge to duel, and even then it may have been possible at that stage for the seconds to settle the affair without recourse to shooting. But when a physical blow was added to the insult it was guaranteed that a duel had to be called. In hindsight, if the two men had been of a sober mind there could have been in all probability an amicable solution. Theirs was not the first such meeting to be caused by alcohol, nor was it the last, but it served as another reminder of how quickly things could change and duels could be fought.

The following year, in 1825, Bernard Blackmantle wrote in *The English Spy*: 'The practice of duelling has become almost a profession and the privacy with which it is of necessity conducted renders it always subject to suspicion.' Duels were often conducted in the early hours of the morning or in the evening when there were very few people about. They were usually held at places which were rarely frequented and in this respect duels resembled some sort of gathering by a secret society. Yet somehow, despite all the secrecy, news of a duel ended up in the pages of the newspapers. The story was often 'leaked' by a witness – usually one of the seconds. John Ker, who had served as the second to Sir Francis Burdett in his duel against James Paull, wrote of the encounter, details of which later appeared in a newspaper:

> I should observe, that while they were waiting for the signal, I observed that Sir Francis held his arm raised, and his pistol pointed towards Mr Paull. Knowing that this was not with the view of taking any unfair advantage, but the effect of accident, I said, 'Burdett, don't take aim; I am sure you are not doing so, drop your arm, as you see Mr Paull has his pistol pointed downwards'. Mr Paull then asked me why I advised Sir Francis not to take aim? I said, anyone might see that I could only mean for him not to take aim, or prepare to do so, before the signal, and from desire to see that they were on equal terms.

Such accounts gripped the reading public in local newspapers and the more widely distributed national newspapers. *The British Code of Duel* advised that newspaper reports, 'should be a simple and unornamented narrative of the facts in few words. No expiation on the conduct of either party is admissible.' John Ker's account met this advice and other similar accounts also passed on the essential facts; the readership of these news sheets eagerly devoured such reports in the same manner as gossip magazines are read today. Some local newspapers, such as the *Carmarthen Journal* in Wales, were weekly publications which meant that any account of a duel they carried was already at least several days old, and any details passed verbally probably circulated more rapidly and were usually more ridden with gossip.

Taking up from where Bernard Blackmantle referred to the fact that duelling has 'become almost a profession', some duellists were feted with almost celebrity status. Fashionable circles buzzed with enquiries about who had shot at whom and for what reason and who had been killed. Duels were the talk of the town in polite gatherings, where their news was met with either nods of approval or the shaking of heads in disapproval. Novels and plays of the day often contained a duel as part of the storyline and poems were even composed on the subject. But this acceptance and readiness to talk about such affairs did not make duelling proper and men with reputations as duellists were just as often to be avoided as they would be found gracing the dinner tables as guests.

In the days before slander and libel were settled by law suits, claiming financial compensation in a court, men were more of a mind to settle the matter between themselves as gentlemen in a duel of honour. The pages of history contain many instances where authors, publishers and printers have been challenged to a duel for their actions. As is widely known, slander is the spoken insult and libel is the written form of insult. Authors and publishers left themselves open to challenges of duels when they undertook to exercise their right to freedom of press. There were limits as to what was acceptable, and when they went beyond these boundaries the insulted party felt obliged to resolve the matter in a duel to establish his honour. Similarly, freedom of speech could be exploited, but the difference and the dangers lay in the fact that such utterances were usually passed on by word of mouth, in which case it was hearsay and therefore no more than gossip. However, when relayed to the person about whom it had been said it was very much different, especially if the person heard the insult for themselves or it was directed at them personally in an exchange of words. Slander could be due to the story being altered to make things more colourful. A simple thing gone wrong and the consequences were too terrible to contemplate. In such cases a straight forward explanation sometimes resolved the problem, but when insults had been traded face to face a duel was inevitably bound to be called, unless the appointed seconds used all their tact to settle the matter. Libel was a different matter altogether and not nearly so easily retracted since so many people would have read it, unlike the spoken word which was limited in circulation, so libel could therefore be viewed as being the more insulting form.

In 1821 a tract appeared in the Glasgow sentinel newspaper, written by an author using the *nom de plume* of 'Ignotus', in which it was implied that James Stuart of Duncarn was a coward. Being named and publicly libelled, he not unnaturally sought to discover the identity of the author to settle the matter. His enquiries revealed that it was in all likelihood Sir Alexander Boswell, who had a talent for composing comedic monologues. Most of these were harmless and passed off with the humorous vein in which they were intended, but here was one which was going to get him into a great deal of trouble. Stuart certainly failed to see anything humorous in the article and through an acquaintance sought to gain confirmation that Boswell was the author. Boswell in turn had a mediator, and through him he let it be known that he would not confirm that it was he who had written the offending item. In view of this, Stuart challenged Boswell to a duel which was arranged for early on 26 March 1822.

Each of the principals made it known that they did not wish to harm each other and would fire into the air. This intention to delope, as firing harmlessly was known, indicated that the meeting was really one of honour to prove a point. At a distance of twelve paces they fired and Stuart's ball hit Boswell in the shoulder, penetrating to smash the bone of the shoulder blade. Whether it was an intentional wounding of his adversary contrary to his earlier statement or an accident of monumental misfortune is not entirely clear, but the consequences were fatal. Such are the erratic ballistic properties of a pistol ball that it can move in any direction on striking the target, and in this case the lead ball slid down the length of Boswell's spine. The man was mortally wounded and would have probably known it, for seventeen years earlier, when Admiral Lord Nelson had had his spine shot through by a musket ball at the Battle of Trafalgar, he was composed enough to realise his wound was fatal. Boswell, like Nelson, was paralysed by the wounding but he could still speak and uttered to his second that he 'had a live head on a dead body'. He was carried to the main house on the Balmuto Estate where the duel had been conducted and there he died the following morning. Stuart fled the country for a short time to avoid prosecution but he eventually returned to face justice. His defence councillors argued that he had not borne any ill-feeling towards Boswell and that he was of an otherwise good character. He was acquitted of the charge of murder, with the fact that he had absconded after causing the death of his adversary being conveniently overlooked.

Women were frequently a prime cause of duels, either directly or indirectly, through their presence at social gatherings. It was not necessarily the lady's fault if she attracted the unwarranted attention of an unattached gentleman, as was the case which led to the duel between Charles Cook Wells and Captain Francis Rivers Freeling in 1842, when the officer was taken with the charms of Mrs Wells during a dance in Tenby. The historian Brian D. Price writes in his short history on the matter, *Two Tenby Duels and Their Associations*: 'Can it be that Freeling made a pass at Wells' wife during the Ball, a pass which was amiably received, and that consequently Wells challenged Freeling to a duel?' The lady in question is known to have been aged 27 years and, while still relatively young, she would have been wise to the ways of social etiquette of the day and should have known to dismiss the young officer's admirations of her. Unfortunately, some women liked to be flirtatious even though they knew their actions to be dangerous, and somehow it was as though the very thought of the illicit nature of their actions dared them to go just that stage further. This may have been the case here, and the two men duelled without any injury being inflicted and honour was restored. *The British Code of Duel* specified that, 'the positive seduction of a female of an honourable family' could only lead to a duel, and as the wife of the Mayor of Tenby the lady would have been beyond reproach.

It was not just physical actions which could be used. Women could be manipulative in the way in which they used words to bring about a duel to exact some kind of perverse revenge, even though to do so would mean she should 'resign the character of lady' according to the pages of *The British Code of Duel*. The most notable example of this was the case involving a lady by the name of Mrs Symonds, who wished to avenge her husband; he had been accused of cheating at cards and had been chastised by Captain Best, the man who had thrashed him. He got off lightly, for such actions could lead to a duel.

The lady began to hatch her plot for revenge by writing to Lord Camelford, who was her former lover, and as it would turn out by coincidence was also an acquaintance of Captain Best. The devious Mrs Symonds claimed that the officer frequently insulted the earl, especially when the worse for drink. Lord Camelford was an experienced duellist and very hot-headed into the bargain; he rather unwisely did not seek to confirm the lady's words. In any case, why should he have cause to doubt her? He issued a challenge to Captain Best to meet him in a duel. The officer must have been perplexed to receive such a summons and wondered what he could possibly have done to warrant such an action, but he had no choice but to accept not only for the honour of his regiment but also to save face in social circles. Attempts by the seconds to resolve the matter, during which the lying machinations of Mrs Symonds were revealed, came to nothing. So it was that the two men who had not argued were brought together to face one another down the length of pistol barrels on 10 March 1804. The tragic episode backfired on the lady when it was Lord Camelford who was killed. The bullet from Best's pistol passed through both Lord Camelford's lungs and the man took three days to die – what must have been in effect drowning in the blood which was collecting in his lungs. Through her actions, the vengeful lady had caused a duel to be fought and the result was the death of a man. Abraham Bosquett, the nineteenth-century author and historian noted in his work, *The Young Man of Honour's Vade-Mecum*:

> There can be no doubt that among the most potent causes of duels were the insinuations of artful, dangerous and vicious females, and inflammatory

mistresses, who prided themselves much in being the object of a duel, and frequently insinuated that dishonourable overtures had been made to them by the nearest connections or intimate friends of their keepers, with a view to enhance the idea of their pretended chastity.

Certainly in the case of Mrs Symonds, never had a female been more 'artful, dangerous and vicious…'

Whether or not Mrs Symonds suffered from remorse is not known but Captain Best, who had foiled her plot by killing Lord Camelford, was haunted by his actions and claimed he often saw his victim standing before him like some tragic character from a Shakespearean play. While most duellists who emerged from their meeting unscathed relished their good fortune, there were some who expressed genuine remorse for their actions, especially when they had killed their opponent.

Captain Best was not alone in being haunted by ghosts. The American Alexander McClung was so stricken with memories of those he had killed in his many duels that he eventually committed suicide. A French diplomat, who while on service in Chile shot and killed his opponent, became filled with such grief that he bordered on the verge of madness for almost a full year. He did not fully recover and carried the guilt of the man's death with him until his dying day. Daniel O'Connor was so remorseful that the Irish politician attended church to swear an oath that never again would he fight another duel after he shot dead John d'Esterre in 1815. Aaron Burr became a social outcast for having killed Alexander Hamilton and his political career was ruined. When Franklin Elliott killed his opponent in 1850, the politician from Kansas withdrew into the wilderness and became a recluse. More than twenty years later some men out hunting found his body in a remote cave. It was a sad and tragic end. These men were not alone in expressing their regret for having killed a man in a duel; many others managed to cope while living with their demons. But for every such one as Captain Best and McClung, there were many more who revelled in the notoriety which their reputations as duellists brought them. While a number of such personalities were civilians, the greater part of those whose reputations were enhanced by having fought a duel could be found among the officer class of the military. Politicians also fought duels and were sometimes castigated for having put personal matters before national importance, particularly when most were fought during time of war. For the military it was more than personal honour which was at stake, it was the honour of the regiment.

Duelling was widespread in all military hierarchical systems across Europe, Russia, America and, of course, Britain and extended from the youngest junior officers to the most senior ranks. It has been argued that without the military influence, it is possible that duelling would not have flourished or lasted half as long as it did. This is probably true, and officers could argue over the slightest matter just as easily as civilians. In some of the tropical postings, the heat may have aggravated situations which in cooler climes would have been resolved.

Duelling was not confined to the army, though that institution could conduct such affairs more readily than others, and meetings between naval officers did on occasion occur. In 1749 Captain Clark killed Captain Innis for which he was sentenced to death, but was reprieved when a Royal pardon was granted. When Captain Macnamara of the Royal Navy was tried for killing Lieutenant Colonel Montgomery in April 1803, he appealed for clemency and based his defence on his character as an officer. The cause of the affair had been a trifling matter over a fight between the men's dogs, but the court saw that a man had been killed. Macnamara called in character witnesses, one of whom was the hero of the age, Admiral Lord Nelson. With such patronage the officer was almost certain to be found innocent because men of the calibre of Lord Nelson did not give evidence unless they knew the true nature of the man they were defending, which only came after years of close acquaintance. The defendant opened his case by stating, 'I am a Captain of the British Navy', a rank which could only be achieved by hard work and diligence to duty as would have been known to those in the court. He continued:

> My character you can only hear from others. But to maintain my character in that situation, I must be respected. When called upon to lead others into honourable danger, I must not [be] supposed to be a man who sought safety by submitting to what custom has taught others to consider as a disgrace.

He had killed a senior officer in the army, but this was a time when the country was at war with France and it was not going entirely in Britain's favour. The sea lanes had to be kept open and officers such as Captain Macnamara were required for that duty. The judge was of a mind to find him guilty but the jury decided otherwise and the case against the Captain was dismissed.

In the British Army, at least, an insult to any officer was an insult against his uniform, which was the king's uniform. Any officer challenged to a duel was obliged to meet his challenger, and it was seen as neglecting one's duty if a man declined to duel. When the honour of the regiment was at stake everything else was of little or no consequence. A case in point involved Ensign Cowell serving with a Guards regiment in the French city of Bordeaux in 1814. While attending the theatre one evening he was insulted by Commissary Hurley, for which the only response would be to 'call out' the gentleman and challenge him to a duel. Ensign Cowell refused to do so and for his dereliction of duty was charged with the offence of 'making a concession' which simply would not do for the honour of the regiment. A court martial was convened and the young officer was found guilty of the charge and cashiered, that is to say thrown out of the regiment in disgrace, for refusing to take up pistols in a duel. It was an expensive mistake for a young man to make because his rank had cost a great deal of money to obtain under the officer purchase scheme. Whether he was right or wrong, his personal opinion counted for nothing when it came to regimental honour. Duelling was illegal but tolerated to varying degrees in civilian society; but in military circles it was being virtually encouraged on an active basis and Cowell paid for his refusal to uphold this tradition. This opinion on duelling applied equally to those European armies from Italy to Spain, even though heads of state frowned on the practice and senior military commanders did not approve either. After all, at the time of the Napoleonic Wars they were already losing officers in battle at a worrying rate, without adding to the casualty list officers who were deliberately shooting at one another over all manner of reasons, such as petty incidents involving dogs fighting in the park.

Dogs may have been rather ephemeral causes for duels, but a man's carriages were a cherished possession and very expensive, much like the high performance cars of today, and viewed with just as much pride. Damage caused to carriages was unforgivable and duels often arose out of incidents whereby collisions occurred. On 22 August 1838 such an incident occurred as two men were driving home from the Epsom races when their carriages collided. An argument ensued and the men exchanged blows, which was the signal to convene a duel. Charles Mirfin and Francis Eliot wasted no further time and settled to conclude the affair that very evening in the company of their seconds on Wimbledon Common. At a distance of twelve paces they fired and Mirfin fell, mortally wounded. The two seconds in attendance were later arrested and charged with murder, but Eliot left the country in haste. The seconds were tried and sentenced to be hanged, but at the last moment they were given a reprieve and instead served one year in prison. The records of the trial state that, 'the affair appeared to have been managed with strict regard to the practice usually followed on such occasions'. But this was not entirely correct; such was the rapidity of the duel there could have been no opportunity for the seconds to try and intercede and no letter of challenge was issued. Judges and juries may have viewed an attempt to follow duelling guidelines in a favourable light and as a result passed a more lenient sentence of a fine or even acquitted those involved. In this case they must have had mixed feelings at passing a guilty sentence and calling for capital punishment.

Certainly the two seconds were most fortunate not to be executed and as for Eliot, no one seems entirely sure of his fate as, like other duellists before him who were fearful of the sentence, he was never heard of again. The duellists in this case were civilians, but similar affairs involving officers did occur as they drove around the many public parks in London or Bath.

Although civilians duelled, it is more than likely to be the military establishment which was the main institution behind the spread of duelling. French troops serving in the Italian Wars during the fifteenth and sixteenth centuries would almost certainly have witnessed the Italian way of settling affairs of honour using swords in duels. When the conflict ended in 1559 the troops, particularly the officer class, are believed to have taken the notion of using swords and then pistols to settle differences back to France, where the practice of duelling was copied as a means of concluding any differences finally and conclusively.

Over the years as pistols replaced swords as the weapon of preference, so the duel was modified and codes drawn up to regulate them, and the practice evolved to keep pace with the change in lifestyles. When hostilities broke out in 1618 in a conflict which has become known as the Thirty Years War, French troops may have instigated the spread of duelling across the Prussian states where they were serving. At this time the flintlock pistol was in widespread use and the ready availability of this weapon could only have added to the introduction of duelling. As wars on a large scale became more commonplace, it had the effect of bringing together foreign armies either as allies or enemies and also brought them into contact with civilians. The military, exposed as it was to all manner of practices, adopted some of these, one of which was duelling. After that, it was not long before officers were resorting to the pistol and the practice of duelling to settle matters between themselves over gambling debts, wives or points of honour.

The practice even crossed boundaries and officers of different nations came to face one another in duels over honour. In 1787, two years before the French Revolution, Chevalier La Brosse of the French army met Captain Scott of the 11th Regiment of Foot (later to become the Devonshire Regiment) in a duel arising from remarks made by the French officer concerning the fighting prowess of the British Army. Incensed by the comments Captain Scott challenged La Brosse to a duel. By all accounts the two men could not have been particularly good shots, because even though they fired at each other at a distance of only five paces, approximately 12ft, they appear to have missed their mark, until finally one of Captain Scott's bullets hit his French counterpart on a tunic button. It did not inflict a penetrating wound but the impact would have been painful nevertheless. The affair was concluded but in other such cases the principals would not always be so fortunate.

Duels were convened between officers from the most junior right up to those holding the highest rank, and also saw army officers facing their naval counterparts – but such meetings did not always end fatally or even with shots being exchanged. The animosity between Rear Admiral Sir Benjamin Hallowell and Major General George Donkin, which led to the challenge of a duel, dated back to an incident during the Siege of Tarragona in Spain during the war in 1811. During the action the senior naval officer accused Donkin of conduct unbecoming an officer. Donkin responded by calling the Rear Admiral a 'damned scoundrel and a damned rascal', following up his outburst two weeks later by sending a letter to meet in a duel. The spat lingered on until 1815 and a duel was only circumvented by intervention from the highest authority, when Hallowell was presented with a letter from Lord Bathurst, Secretary for War, warning him of the consequences should he proceed with the duel. In the end it came to nought and the two senior officers could only fume in frustration, but there was nothing they could do unless they wished to face courts martial and ruin their careers. There had been no shots exchanged between the men but it had been a close call, just as it was in the affair between Major Chapman and Captain de Lancey, both serving in the 18th Regiment of Foot (later to become the Royal Irish Regiment). The young captain is understood to have said that Major Chapman could fire anytime if he so desired, but for his own part he would not shoot until he pressed his pistol against his adversary's chest. Realising there was no alternative to what would almost certainly have been his murder, Chapman discarded his pistol and walked away from the duel without a shot being fired. Although he had refused to duel at the last moment, he had turned up for the affair which showed his intention to duel. Normally a refusal to duel would lead to loss of face, but there could be no such accusation of cowardice and the matter was laid to rest.

Duels between officers of the same regiment were only to be expected, as arguments which began in the mess led to an exchange of shots caused by the consumption of too much alcohol, gambling or even dogs. No one knows what caused the duel between two officers of the 95th Regiment of Foot, who exchanged pistol shots on Jersey in the Channel Islands in 1782, but the practice was endemic in other armies. In Prussia two officers serving in the 27th Infantry Regiment based in Halberstadt met in a duel. Lieutenant von Puttkammer faced his fellow officer Lieutenant von Heeringen at a distance of fifteen paces and shot him dead. The Prussian attitude towards duelling was different to that held in either France or England. Frederick I, King of Prussia, was against duelling and issued laws against the practice because it usually resulted in the death of an officer which could only affect the army. During his reign 1713–86, his son Frederick II 'The Great' of Prussia could on occasion exhibit a more relaxed, indeed tolerant, attitude towards duelling because he felt that the practice could only improve the qualities of his officers. But that is not to say that Prussian officers had carte blanche to blaze away at one another, and if caught following a duel where only wounds had been inflicted the penalty was eight years imprisonment. Frederick II could exhibit an almost daily change in attitude towards duelling and be harsh and magnanimous in equal measure depending on his mood. Duelling spread throughout the military across the world, including America, where Lieutenant Bourne of the US Marines was killed by his opponent who shot him at the rather murderously close range of only two paces in 1826.

The spread of duelling has been blamed on the military, and if one looks at the locations where many of the duels were fought there does appear to be a trend. The British Channel Islands, where so many regiments were based, were the site for several duels between officers. This also applied to the island of Barbados in the Caribbean where the heat and monotony of daily routine produced the ingredients for arguments which led to duels.

In mid-nineteenth century India – the heart of the British Empire and the great military posting for many garrisons – duelling flourished. In 1828 Captain Bull, recently transferred to the 34th Regiment of Foot (later to become the Border Regiment) decided he did not like the attitude of his fellow officers and preferred to make arrangements away from the officers' mess. Lots were drawn as to who would challenge him over the grave insult they perceived his actions to be. Lieutenant Sandys was chosen to resolve the matter and he, along with his second, faced Bull who had insulted them only by their perception and had not actually offended anyone by deed or word. Sandys shot and killed his man and when tried for his murder it was an almost foregone conclusion that he would be acquitted. It was accepted as part of the way of life in the great sprawling country. British regiments serving in South Africa, in the colony of the Cape of Good Hope, took the practice of duelling to that remote expanse of land, and even to the lesser postings as the British Empire expanded to take in islands and regions around the world.

The two great military commanders of the early nineteenth century, the Duke of Wellington and Napoleon Bonaparte, may not have had much in common with one another and only ever faced one another directly in combat across the battlefield at Waterloo on 18 June 1815; but they did share one common belief. Neither man rated highly the wastage of lives in pointless duels, because for them it meant losing one officer to another over usually petty squabbles. Napoleon tried to have a law passed which would prevent officers from duelling and it was actually presented to the Conseil d'État, but with little success. One of the main reasons for rejecting the bill was stated due to the fact that:

> There is a multitude of offences which legal justice does not punish, and amongst these offences there are some so indefinable, or concerned with matters so delicate, that the injured party would blush to bring them out into broad daylight in order to demand public justice. In these circumstances it is impossible for a man to right himself otherwise than by a duel.

In England such matters which could not be settled by the courts were unofficially referred to as being a 'Wogdon's Case', named after the famous gunsmith who made high-quality pistols for the purpose of duelling. Although such affairs were not legal there was a certain amount of toleration attached to them. It is rather poignant that in later life, after retiring from his military career, Wellington would fight a duel while holding political office as Prime Minister of England. Napoleon may not have fought a duel, but his actions could on occasion have led to him being challenged. During the disastrous Egypt Campaign Napoleon took for himself the wife of one of his officers and ensconced her as his mistress in his personal quarters in Cairo. The lady was Pauline Fourès, the wife of a lieutenant in the cavalry who had unofficially accompanied her husband on campaign. Napoleon despatched her husband on a mission to Malta but he was captured by the British who, for some reason, allowed him to return to the French camp. Once back in Egypt the young officer discovered his wife's new position and beat her. Needless to say the couple were not reconciled and Pauline continued to live with Napoleon. Such conduct under other circumstances would almost certainly have provoked a duel, but the young officer, either through inexperience or the thought of such a junior officer trying to shoot his commanding officer, through whatever provocation, did not issue a challenge.

Despite their opinions on their officers duelling, it did not prevent the military from engaging in the act and throughout the long period of the war officers in the French army and the British Army conducted duels. Two of Napoleon's experienced generals, Bonnet and Ornano fell into a dispute and agreed to resolve the matter with a pistol duel. The two men came face to face at the appointed place in Paris and General Bonnet was the first to fire. However, he missed, leaving his opponent General Ornano, who was renowned for his prowess with a pistol, with a clear shot. Taking his time and aiming well Ornano fired and it was evident he had hit his man, but to all present Bonnet appeared unharmed and standing upright. No one was more amazed than Bonnet, who could not believe his good fortune that he had not been killed, but he did know that he had been struck in the chest. Slowly, fearing the worst, he unbuttoned his coat to reveal the extent of the wound he believed had been inflicted. To his relief it transpired that by a freak chance, Ornano's bullet had hit a coin in the officer's breast pocket. His adversary was impressed by his fellow officer's calmness and said: 'You have invested your money most fortunately.' The effect of being struck by a bullet in this manner, while not fatal, would have caused severe bruising and left Bonnet feeling very sore and uncomfortable for a few days.

Other similar incidents happened at various times, but perhaps the most amazing incident was that which occurred in 1837 during a duel in Brownville, Pennsylvania, and described by a witness as 'one of the most extraordinary freaks of firearms'. One of the principals was a man by the name of Banner Anderson, who fired just a fraction before his opponent, hitting him in the chest. His adversary's bullet had by sheer fluke hit the muzzle of Anderson's pistol and entered the barrel. Anderson would have sustained a bruised wrist but his opponent took three hours to die of his wounds. While this was extraordinary, it was not unknown and during a duel in London in 1770 a similar event had been recorded. The duel between Lord George Germain and George Johnstone was conducted under normal conditions but on firing, Johnstone's bullet struck Germain's pistol and shattered it in his hand. Both men walked from the field unharmed, except for Germain who must have been nursing an injured wrist.

General Bonnet's survival due to a coin in his pocket was more by way of fate than design. Duellists were even known to have been saved by the pistol ball striking buttons on their jacket, as in the already mentioned case of Chevalier La Brosse. Any deliberate attempt to protect oneself against bullets was frowned on and considered underhanded. For this reason duellists were sometimes required to open their coats for examination to make sure they were not using padding to protect themselves and some rules actually stated that principals should meet stripped to the waist. One French duellist used newspapers as protection and consequently survived being shot. However, the force of the impact did cause an inflammation which never healed, probably due to contamination from dirty paper. Some duellists believed that a tight shirt made of silk would make the bullet slide off. While not entirely correct, there was some rationale behind this thinking. The troops in the armies of Genghis Khan 500 years earlier sometimes wore loose shirts into battle that were made of raw silk to protect them against arrows. The silk did not prevent the arrows from piercing the flesh but the material was dragged into the wound by the barbed arrowhead without ripping. This made it easier for doctors to remove the arrow from the wound by gently tugging at the surplus silk. It would still have been extremely painful and it is unlikely that the same principle would have applied to a lead ball which travelled at greater velocity and hit with more power than an arrow shot from a fourteenth-century bow.

Spectacles were recommended to be removed prior to a duel in case they acted as protection to the duellist. Looked at from the other point of view, if struck in the face the splintering glass could cause blindness when the duellist may otherwise have only sustained a slight wounding. Positive steps to protect against bullets were not permitted but, as in the case of General Bonnet, some everyday objects such as a coin innocently carried in the pocket could save a man's life. An Irishman on his way to meet his opponent stooped to pick up a horseshoe and put it in his breast pocket for good luck. It proved its worth when his opponent's bullet hit the object and glanced off leaving him with just a bruised chest. Another duellist is recorded as having his life saved when his opponent's pistol shot hit some hard biscuits in his pocket. If they were hard enough to stop a bullet one shudders to think what such delicacies would have done to the man's teeth had he bitten on one.

Animosity could last a long time before the time was considered opportune for the antagonists to convene their duel, especially against the backdrop of war. Affairs between officers could last for years, but none more so than the affair involving two cavalry officers in Napoleon's army. In 1794 a young captain by the name of Dupont was instructed by his commanding officer to locate Captain Fournier, who was serving in a regiment of Hussars, and relay to him instructions that due to his behaviour earlier in the day, when he had shot and killed a civilian in a duel in Strasbourg, he would not be welcome at a ball being held that evening. Fournier did not take too kindly to such instructions and decided to vent his anger on Captain Dupont who was, after all, only passing on the message as ordered. Fournier did not see it that way and drew his sword on Dupont, thereby setting in motion a train of events which would see the two men continuing a protracted dispute for the next ten years. During that time the men fought several duels, but a conclusion was never reached. In 1813, by which time both men were generals, they convened one final duel to settle the matter once and for all. They agreed to meet in woodlands and being armed with two pistols each they would attempt to stalk one another as a hunter would a deer. Dupont laid a decoy by draping his coat over a branch, tricking Fournier into discharging both his pistols and believing he had outsmarted his rival. Dupont then stepped forward with his loaded pistols and had Fournier at his mercy. Instead of firing he spared the man's life but he made it known that there were

conditions to his clemency. If the occasion arose where the two men met
again in a duel, then Dupont reserved the right to fire both pistols at close
range. It was more than a fair exchange for his life and meant that finally
the affair was closed. It was all really a question of misunderstanding for
there had never been any cause, and any insult had only ever been in
Fourier's mind because he wished it to be so. The defeat of Napoleon
at the Battle of Waterloo heralded in a period which would bring many
years of peace to Europe. But in the immediate aftermath, with thousands
of troops from Austria, Prussia, Britain and Russia forming an army of
occupation, it was only to be expected that duels would inevitably arise
from such a situation. For a time the parks around Paris echoed with
pistol shots as affairs were settled. Duels involving French and British
officers were frequent and Prussian officers also added to the numbers.
The outbreak of duelling continued almost unabated and in 1819, four
years after the defeat of Napoleon, shots were still echoing around France,
but by that time not always between former enemies. In that year Captain
Pellew of the Life Guards took himself to Paris with Mrs Welsh, the wife
of a former serving officer in the same regiment. They were pursued by
the lady's husband who challenged Pellew to a duel. At twelve paces they
fired and Pellew fell dead, shot through the head. Officers and gentlemen
they may have been in war but in peacetime a cuckolded husband was a
vengeful man.

Duelling among the military was virtually out of control, not only in
England but also in armies across Europe, and it was clear something had
to be done in order to stop the practice, or at least restrict it. Even though
the military had its own system of laws to cover any situation unique to
the army or navy, they were not beyond the powers of civil law when it
came to matters of killing someone other than on the battlefield.

What was needed was an example to be made of the surviving duellist
where he had killed his opponent. As it would happen, events were about
to unfold which would demonstrate that duelling must not be allowed
to go unpunished. On 23 June 1807 a military parade had taken place at
a barracks in Armagh in the north of Ireland and afterwards the officers
retired to their mess as was normal and began to drink. As the alcohol
flowed some officers began to talk loudly and say things they would not
normally say when sober. Two officers in particular were more affected
by the alcohol and began to argue. This was Major Alexander Campbell
and Captain Alexander Boyd, who held differing opinions as to how an
officer should command his unit and they fell into a heated debate on
the matter.

Shouted words gave way to a challenge to duel and the two officers
convened to fight there and then in the mess. With only seven paces

separating them the men fired in the room and Boyd was fatally hit. It had taken only 20 minutes from the first to the last. Captain Boyd fell to the floor and, alerted by the sound of gunfire, other officers entered the room to survey the scene as their fellow officer lay dying. The duel had been fought hot-headedly, in a drunken argument and without the presence of seconds, who may have otherwise spoken to the men and made them see sense either not to duel there or at least restrain themselves until sober. The duel had broken all accepted codes of conduct and the result was a dying officer.

Campbell spoke to Boyd, who was by now breathing his last, and implored him to say it had been a fair fight. Boyd would not say anything to Campbell other than to gasp: 'You know I wanted you to wait and have friends', which can only be taken to mean he wanted the presence of seconds. Although he called Campbell 'a bad man' he did forgive him as he died. Campbell naturally wanted to be away from the place and took passage to England. He was a fugitive from the law and he went into hiding in London where he lived for several months under an assumed name. Finally, he gave himself up to the authorities, probably due to the strain that such an existence had placed on him and his wife who still resided in Ireland. The officer was tried for murder and at his trial in 1808 he pleaded for clemency on the grounds of his good character, bringing witnesses to testify in his defence that he was a fine officer who had served in action against the French in Egypt. It had a faint echo of the plea used by Captain Macnamara only five years earlier.

The jury was not convinced and decided he had contravened any code of the duel, not that it would have been accepted as mitigating evidence, and he was found guilty of murder. The sentence was to be death by hanging. Such a verdict had not been expected as there were precedents in place for the crime of manslaughter with the charge being dropped. Campbell himself believed that he would be acquitted but his wife, on hearing the dread news that he was to be executed, left Ireland with a view of making an appeal directly to King George III to ask for clemency. The officer's wife arrived at Windsor and received an audience from Queen Sophia Charlotte who promised to pass on the lady's letter to the king. Unlike the case of Captain Clark almost sixty years earlier, no pardon was forthcoming and the Major's fate was sealed.

On 2 October 1808, sixteen months after the affair, Major Campbell was led to the scaffold at Newry. A fellow officer, Major Benjamin Truman, later to become an author and historian, was present to witness the hanging and recorded:

There stood before him nineteen thousand sympathizing men with heads uncovered; and among them Fusiliers, with whom he had intrepidly charged the enemy upon the burning sands of Egypt. The hum of a single bee might have been heard in that respectful crowd, as Campbell addressed it. 'Pray for me' was all the poor soldier said.

The crowd responded by saying 'Amen' in unison. It has been opined that the vast crowd turned out to show their disapproval of the court in imposing such a harsh sentence, but such large gatherings at public executions were to be expected and such attendances were more out of ghoulish, morbid curiosity than a show against the law. During the French Revolution, when the aristocracy of the country were being guillotined in public open spaces, the executions were watched by thousands who wanted to witness their grisly end, and when the highwayman Dick Turpin was hanged in York in 1739 it was watched by a huge gathering. At the time, the military also conducted capital punishment in front of large parades of troops who were ordered to turn out to witness the executions. Only six years before Major Campbell was hanged some 15,000 troops were assembled to witness, by firing squad, the execution of a deserter. The punishment was carried out near Portsmouth and in 1802, during the war against France, was intended to be a severe example of what a soldier could expect if he broke military law. As in Campbell's case, the condemned man had committed his crime due to the excesses of alcohol.

The legal system in any country was not entirely clear on the matter of death caused by duelling and the charge of manslaughter was often applied in the case. In Austria, for example, a death in a duel was always viewed as manslaughter. In 1712 Lieutenant General MacCartney had acted as second to the Duke of Hamilton and witnessed the death of his opponent Lord Mohun in the affair. The officer was tried for murder, even though it was not he who had shot Lord Mohun. In the end he was acquitted and given a token sentence of 'branding with a cold iron', which was nothing more than being touched to give the impression of being branded. In 1786 George Reynolds and Robert Keon were preparing to duel in Ireland but, as they were making ready for the affair, Keon shot Reynolds in the head and killed him. It was murder and Keon was sentenced to be executed by the barbaric method of hanging, drawing and quartering. Within thirty years the courts became more inclined to sentence a man to imprisonment, while in England there was the right reserved to transport a man to one of the colonies such as Australia. But there did remain a tendency to acquit a defendant, and a duellist could never really be certain of the sentence he was to be dealt. If he had influence, however, he was almost sure to be given a lenient sentence or even a token fine. In the American state of

Massachusetts, state legislators believed that duellists should receive the same punishment as a vampire and have a wooden stake hammered into their hearts and buried without a coffin. That was perhaps going to the extreme in punishment.

All countries tried to bring about a halt to the practice of duelling within their military systems. For various reasons their efforts failed and there seemed to be an unexplainable reluctance to stop duelling; in some cases, like Prussia, it was countenanced and almost encouraged. Between 1817 and 1829 some twenty-nine officers in the Prussian army were killed in duels. This was not a huge amount but if left unchecked it could quickly and easily spiral upwards. The King of Prussia tried to enforce laws forbidding his officers to duel, but try as he might figures show there was actually an increase in the number of duels fought in the Prussian military after 1840. What was needed was one country to make the first move towards halting the practice. As one of the most influential nations in the world, England had shown the way in the case of Major Campbell, even though it had been a most tragic example. The anti-duelling movement was gaining support and in 1845 it received what it required in the shape of Royal assent from Queen Victoria. It also received an added bonus from the army which changed the regulations forbidding officers to duel on pain of being cashiered (thrown out of the army) or court-martialled.

The prime moving case which would initiate change was, what has been argued as, probably the last recorded fatal duel to be conducted in England, and took place between two officers. This claim is open to debate as other duels were fought after it, but it would be safe to say that the affair of 1845 was the last fatal military duel to be conducted in the traditional manner in England. In his book *The Face of Battle*, the author Sir John Keegan lists the duel between Colonel Romilly and John Smythe in 1852 as the last duel in England, an opinion which is also held by historian Victor Kiernan. Other duels may have taken place after this date but they are not generally understood to have been fatal.

Like so many other duels, the one which would prove to be the catalyst leading to the undoing of duelling in England was caused by a woman. The lady in question was Mrs Isabella Hawkey, the beautiful high-spirited wife of Lieutenant Henry Hawkey, a serving officer in the Royal Marines and who loved to live life to the full. In the social swirl that was mid-nineteenth-century Portsmouth and Southsea, in 1845 the lady attended many functions in the company of her husband and became acquainted with Captain James Seton, a former serving officer in the 11th Hussars. Seton was unattached and became smitten by the young lady's charms and in return, while she was no doubt flattered, at the age of 24 years and a married woman she would have been well aware of the social etiquette of the day which dictated that such behaviour was not to be tolerated. While not spurning him, Mrs Hawkey did not give herself over to his endearments either, which left it an open-ended affair. That is until one evening when Seton gave her flowers and she proceeded to dance with him throughout the ball rather than stay at her husband's side. Such scandalous displays could only cause people to talk and make remarks about the inappropriate behaviour. It certainly did not escape the notice of her husband who fully observed his wife's flirtations. Trying to assert himself, but at the same time trying to keep it as discreet as possible, Hawkey approached Seton and challenged him to a duel to answer for his outrageous behaviour. Seton refused and brazenly flouted his disregard for his challenger by continuing his dancing with Mrs Hawkey, who showed no sign of refusing his attentions despite the exchange of words with her husband. Hawkey was incensed; he strode across the dance floor and kicked the man, followed up with words spoken in a raised voice: 'Seton, you're a blackguard and a villain. You can either fight me or be horsewhipped down the Portsmouth High Street.'

There was no escape and no retreat, and Seton must have realised that he had gone too far this time. Over the next 24 hours arrangements were made for the duel and seconds were elected. Hawkey would not back down and Seton, who had been verbally challenged and physically struck in front of witnesses, had to accept the challenge or lose whatever remaining standing he had in society and forever be regarded a coward. The appointed place of the meeting was some deserted scrubland close to the water's edge. The principals were placed fifteen paces apart and presented with their loaded pistols by their seconds. The order to fire was given by one of the seconds and the men reacted to the command. Seton's shot missed and Hawkey's pistol failed to fire, but he had showed intention by pulling the trigger in accordance with the duelling codes. It was an unsatisfactory outcome; the pistols were loaded again and the principals prepared themselves once more. On the command both men fired and, with his pistol in proper working order, Hawkey's bullet found its mark hitting Seton in the stomach. Seeing his opponent fall Hawkey made as though to move *towards* the wounded man to help him, but instead turned on his heel and hurriedly walked away from the scene. As he did so he called out: 'I'm off to France.' It would have been relatively simple to catch a boat from the busy port, but it would mean leaving behind everything including his career in the Royal Marines and his unfaithful wife. He was never heard of again and, unlike some of his contemporaries, does not appear to have been moved to return to stand trial. The alternative to fleeing may have been the hangman's noose, for a precedent had been set in such matters thirty-seven years earlier when Major Campbell had been executed for killing his opponent in a duel. Hawkey's name is last recorded when he was dismissed from the service in his absence.

Seton's wound was not immediately fatal and in great agony he was moved by boat to the premises of the Quebec Hotel in Portsmouth. A doctor was summoned to attend the man but there was little he could do. However, he did attempt to remove the pistol ball even though such a wound was inoperable and was invariably fatal. The operation was botched and only succeeded in inflicting more suffering on the man. There was nothing left to be done except make him as comfortable as possible. Seton hung on to life for an incredible ten days before expiring. The building in which he died is still standing in Portsmouth today but is now a private residence called Quebec House. It seems incredible to think that such drama was played out there and that the actual building still exists to bear silent witness, 170 years after the last fatal duel in England. What is equally remarkable is that two years before this fatal encounter the Anti-Duelling Association had been formed in England with the aim of suppressing duelling and members had petitioned Queen Victoria with a view to taking action. Even with such sanctioning, the process to try and suppress something as deeply rooted in society as duelling could take time as opposition tried to overrule the move. As a direct consequence of social and political pressure being brought to bear, in 1844 the House of Commons had been moved to amend Number 98 of the Articles of War, the rule book of the British Army. It was now set out quite clearly that in future any officer who took part in a duel would be cashiered and court-martialled. This firm order had not prevented the duel between Hawkey and Seton but it virtually marked the end of duelling in Britain because it was mainly the military who took part in such affairs, and over the coming years other European armies would follow suit and finally stop duelling.

In an ironic footnote, twenty-two years before the duel between Hawkey and Seton, Lord Brudenell, the future commanding officer of the 11th Hussars, the regiment in which Seton had served as a captain, came close to fighting a duel for exactly the same reason, which is to say over a woman who was the wife of another man. In 1823 the young Lord Brudenell, who would become better known in history as the 7th Lord Cardigan and the man who led the Charge of the Light Brigade during the Crimean War, wooed away the wife of a fellow officer Captain Frederick Johnstone, who then divorced the lady, leaving her to marry her new suitor. Brudenell wrote to Johnstone to apologise for his behaviour and let it be known that he was prepared to meet the captain to settle the matter in an affair of honour, if that was what he wanted. Johnstone was not as upset as Brudenell may have believed and rather than be filled with enmity towards a fellow officer he let it be known that the man had actually done him a favour and he was content to suggest that he had already been given satisfaction by removing from him, 'the most damned bad-tempered and extravagant bitch in the kingdom'. Brudenell, or Lord Cardigan as he was to become, had avoided a duel for the time being at least.

Seventeen years later in 1840, Lord Cardigan (as he was then), the pompous senior officer found himself involved in an altercation with a junior officer concerning a question of manners in the officers' mess. Although the argument was between Lord Cardigan and Captain Reynolds, and a duel was called by Reynolds, Cardigan refused on the ground that duelling etiquette demanded that such an affair should only be conducted between gentlemen of the same standing. Therefore, due to the vast difference in their rank, Cardigan had no choice but to refuse. That should have been the end of the affair but Captain Tuckett published remarks in the newspaper. Cardigan ignored the protocol on duelling between officers of different ranks and met Tuckett on Wimbledon Common on the evening of 12 September 1840.

Standing twelve paces apart the seconds ordered the men to fire, which they did, but both missed. Accuracy could be poor in such matters either due to nerves or lack of experience in shooting, but the noise of the first shots could at times calm the duellist and his accuracy could thereafter be improved. A second exchange of shots was fired and Cardigan hit Tuckett in the ribs, but it was not a serious wound. At that point a constable by the name of Thomas Dann appeared on the scene as if from nowhere. It transpired that he was the miller from the windmill which stood close to the spot where the duel was conducted, and it was in his capacity as a special constable that he hurried to the spot. It may have been that he genuinely attended the scene on hearing the sound of gunfire and went to investigate, or he may have been tipped off and arrived just too late to prevent the affair. Dann arrested Lord Cardigan and his second Mr Douglas on the charge of breach of the peace. When the trial came before the court the men were charged with intent to murder along with other related charges.

Cardigan with his peerage elected to be tried by the House of Lords, where not unnaturally he was acquitted, while the case against Douglas was heard at the Old Bailey. Cardigan was lucky, but even had his case been heard at the Old Bailey, he would probably still have only been fined because of his social standing and because he had not killed Tuckett. Never a greatly popular figure in society before the duel, his standing in society plummeted and he was even heckled in public after the affair. It would not be for another sixteen years that he would regain some popularity following his service in the Crimean War in 1856. What the 1840 court case did was to show up the inequalities in the class structure, for while Major Campbell had been executed for killing his opponent in a duel, here was a peer of the realm being acquitted, as others were, due to connections in society. But what can be seen here is the public's growing intolerance of duelling and, after the decision following the Hawkey and Seton duel, and the military establishment's change in attitude towards duelling, the future of the practice was sealed not only in Britain but also across the world. Duelling was now being seen in a different vein as it was viewed as a threat to society as a whole.

2

TYPE OF DUEL

The most common impression anyone has of how duels were conducted comes from the image of two protagonists standing back to back, pistols held at the ready with the muzzle pointing directly upwards. They then step out ten paces each, turn, aim and fire simultaneously. This is the image of Hollywood feature films and would appear to be an amalgam of different types of duels. That is not to say that such simplistic forms of duels did not take place, and in all likelihood would have been straight-forward to arrange and lacking in any formalities or rituals. The problem with this 'ten paces' impression is the question of timing, because it is unlikely that both men would pace out the distance at the same time without some kind of control being exercised by a third party, probably one of the appointed seconds, who counted out the paces. If this were not so, then the first man to reach his point could turn and fire whether the other man was ready or not and this could lead to someone being shot in the back.

Such incidents did occur on occasion, and it may well have been this kind of misunderstanding which led to Thomas Heslop being shot in the back by his opponent, John Beynon, when they met to resolve their differences in a remote field near Newcastle Emlyn in Carmarthenshire in Wales in September 1814. The event is well known in the area and today, almost 200 years after the duel, several stories abound concerning what led to the affair, even if they have become somewhat clouded and embellished over the years and with the retelling. In the early nineteenth century Wales was far removed from the social whirl of the large cosmopolitan towns and cities in England, but that is not to say that the country was cut off from events. The road infrastructure and newspapers of the day simply meant that news tended to travel at a much slower pace than in places like London or Bath. And so it was with the Heslop and Beynon duel; the news of which was not circulated until days after the affair.

Thomas Heslop was a manservant and, being born in Kingston in Jamaica, he was considered to be an 'outsider' by the townsfolk of Newcastle Emlyn. He was 34 years old when he arrived in the town and with his boasting and poor manners he did not win himself any friends. In fact, these traits probably did more to alienate him from the locals who would, in any case, have been extremely insular due to the close-knit style of their community. John Beynon, on the other hand, was a local solicitor and well-known landowner in the area. One of Heslop's boasts was the claim that his position entitled him to shoot game on any of the large estates in the area, and it is this what is believed to be one of the origins to the argument between the two men which culminated in their duel.

When one strips away at the various local stories, and compares them to the known protocols surrounding duelling, they are simply just that, stories, because the whole scenario does not balance out to be credible, making one think that there was more to this particular duel than outwardly appears. The Heslop and Beynon duel would have been an otherwise minor affair were it conducted in a large town, but in rural Newcastle Emlyn it was outrageous behaviour, because duels in such locations were virtually unheard of, and it was the subject of gossip for many months after.

To begin with, we know that duels would only be fought by men of equal social status, such as officers or landed gentry. We also know that gentlemen could engage in affairs which could be considered a duel. A fight between two men of any lower social position would simply be termed a brawl. In Heslop's case he was a manservant and there is a widely held local belief that he may have been black, simply due to the fact that he is known to have been born on the island of Jamaica. Alternatively, he could quite as easily have been born of a white family resident on the island. His name is nothing to go on because servants were often given the family name as a means of identifying the household in which they worked. If he were indeed white, it may be that he wished to return to the country of his family and found passage on board a vessel sailing directly to one of the ports in Wales.

Beynon's history was much better known, as a landowner with property in the form of a farm called 'Llwyncadfor', position and money, all of which Heslop would have lacked being a servant. It is at this juncture that local stories begin to fall apart, because the two men, not being social equals, would in all probability never have engaged in conversation at any level and certainly would never have hunted together as some tales claim. If, as the local stories claim, Heslop was black it is even more unlikely that

Beynon would have acknowledged him and certainly would never have dined with the man. Even in rural Wales the social etiquette of the day would have been observed and the middle classes, such as Beynon, would almost certainly never condescend to express familiarity to servants, let alone argue to the point where they would duel.

This difference in the status of the two men clearly means that the only possible contact they could have had was if Heslop served at a function that Beynon was attending. But some aspects of the story surrounding the duel do say that Heslop and Beynon met at a shooting party on 8 September, which is when the beginning of the series of events leading up to the duel started. Apparently Beynon invited friends to dine at a local hostelry called the *Old Salutation Inn* at the village of Adpar, and Heslop was one of those invited. It is alleged that for some reason Beynon made improper remarks of an offensive nature concerning the integrity of the barmaid's virtue. Heslop is understood to have taken exception to this behaviour and called Beynon scurrilous names and challenged him to a duel.

As a possible cause of the duel this action can be discredited because Heslop, himself married with at least one son, is unlikely to have involved himself over matters concerning the honour of a barmaid, even if he did feel obliged to save the woman's reputation. It is also unlikely that Beynon, as a landowning gentleman, would have frequented such lowly pot-houses where the working classes congregated when he had his own large house. Furthermore, the fact that Heslop is believed to have verbally challenged Beynon to a duel is against all the codes surrounding such affairs. The standard form was to put one's challenge in the form of a written note delivered by the man's second. This omission seems to discredit this particular aspect of the story, along with the fact that no two men would ever likely fall out over the honour of a barmaid, however fond they may be of her. An alternative story says that Beynon called Heslop a liar over his claims to be permitted to hunt on any land and that Heslop being aggrieved issued a challenge to duel.

The chosen place for the duel was a field known locally as Dan y Werin in Llandyfyriog on the outskirts of the village of Adpar, and the date was set for the morning of Saturday 10 September. In attendance was John Williams, a local doctor, and one of the seconds was David Lewis, understood to be a clothier, also from Adpar. This profession and his residency status would almost certainly make him the second to Beynon, but as for Heslop's second the records fail us. Given the man's poor standing in the community he would have been hard pressed to find anyone to act as his second and may have walked on to the field without any support. The duel is understood to have been the traditionally observed back-to-back, walk out ten paces, turn and fire type. Matters may have reached such a point that any pretence at niceties were forgone and the men just paced out the distance.

As they were walking out, Beynon is understood to have turned on his fifth pace and shot Heslop in the back killing him instantly. It may have happened like that or it may have been that, in his temper, he misunderstood the number of paces; we will never know for sure. A man had been killed and all those present were witnesses to the fact and Beynon stood to be charged with murder. Doctor Williams collected the pistols and, according to tales, threw them into the nearby River Teifi. Beynon was arrested and brought to trial at the Magistrate's Court in Newcastle Emlyn on the charge of manslaughter. The judges hearing the case came from the courts at Blaenplant, Gogerddan and Llysnewydd and would probably have been acquainted with Beynon through various legal affairs. There is some discrepancy surrounding the outcome of the case, with one version saying that he was found not guilty of the charge, while another version claims Beynon was found guilty of manslaughter. In the second version he is fined and imprisoned until the amount was paid in full. His incarceration was not long, because the fine levied was only one shilling, or five pence in today's money. The reason for such leniency is believed to have been due to the relationship between the accused and his judges.

However, there may be more to the affair than an insignificant incident. A more plausible tale of the duel tells how the two men fought over the ownership of a tract of land. What if Heslop had journeyed to Wales to claim an inheritance only to find he had been defrauded by Beynon in his capacity as a solicitor acting as executor to the will? This would seem the more likely cause of the duel because property is always valuable. But whatever the reason, the outcome was the same. Heslop was buried in the churchyard at Llandyfyriog Church where his tombstone bears the fading inscription: 'Sacred, To the Memory of Thomas Heslop, Born 27 June 1780, Died 10 September 1814. Alas Poor Heslop.' As for Beynon, public opinion turned on him, despite enmity shown against Heslop prior to the duel, and the solicitor is believed to have fled to America, never to be heard from again.

In truth, a duel could take many forms. In France, for example, six different types of duel were recognised, while across the Austro-Hungarian Empire seven types of duel were at one time known to be practised. One of the most basic types of duel was the form where the duellists fired from stationary points which had been marked out at a distance of between fifteen and thirty-five paces. The distance from which the men would fire would have been agreed on before the actual duel as part of the preliminaries in arranging the conduct of the duel. *The British Code of Duel* suggested that the minimum distance at which a duel be conducted should not be less than ten paces of 30 inches each, which approximates to around 24 feet. The two positions were to be marked and the principals were to stand a step or two back from the mark. On the agreed signal both men would step forward and the pistols would be presented to the principals in an un-cocked state. If there was nothing else to be said the two men would cock their weapons and fire.

While purposeful aiming with a straight arm in direct line towards one's opponent was frowned on, the duellists adopted a method of aiming using a slightly bent arm. This posture is sometimes seen in illustrations of the day, most notably that depicting the duel between the Duke of Wellington and Lord Winchilsea, which shows the Duke with his right arm bent and his left arm behind his back. Some duellists chose not to fire at all and some fired in the air or deliberately wide of their opponent. This was simply to prove a point, that they had attended the duel when challenged, but such shooting was not considered fair play. There was even a special term for avoiding deliberate shooting and this was called 'deloping'. It was more frequent than one would suppose and the Clonmel Rules from Ireland of 1777 stipulated:

> No dumb shooting or firing in the air is admissible in any case. The challenger ought not have challenged without receiving offence; and the challenged ought, if he gave offence, to have made an apology before he came to the ground; therefore children's play must be dishonourable on one side or the other, and is accordingly prohibited.

If one man or the other thought duelling to be the ultimate in bluffing and counter-bluff, it was indeed a dangerous game and had to be played in deadly earnest, for a man's life depended on the outcome.

In one basic form of the duel, once both principals had taken up their station, the offended man may fire first with the other man firing a fraction afterwards once the agreed signal had been given to exchange shots. It may well be from this and other similar forms of duels which have been altered to present us with the version we see in films. In reality, some duels stipulated a time limit of one minute in which the first man must fire. If he missed his adversary or he was only wounded, then the other man could fire in return within the time frame of one minute.

A variation on this form of duel called for the opponents to face away from one another, holding their pistols in readiness. At the command to fire they would turn, cocking their pistols in one movement and fire without hesitation. It may not sound the ideal way of achieving any accuracy, but there was a high chance of hitting one's opponent at least somewhere on his body.

Those duels fought from fixed positions were relatively easy to arrange and conduct, and once shots had been exchanged those involved simply walked away, providing no injury had been inflicted, with neither man having uttered a word. In the case of superficial wounding, the doctor would tend to the injured man, but where a fatality had occurred there was a great deal of mess to sort out because a death had to be reported. The so-called 'moving duels' were more difficult to arrange because of the rules of engagement and the space required for the duellists to traverse. In the case of such affairs, the final distances at which the opponents actually fired at one another could vary but was never less than fifteen paces and could be up to twenty paces. This was a very formal type of duel with the firing point marked off and each man positioned a further ten paces or more back from the firing point. Facing each other with their pistols held muzzle upwards the men stood in readiness. At the command 'march' the principals would cock their weapons and begin to advance. Either man could fire at any time before reaching the line marking the firing point, beyond which point they were not allowed to advance forward.

These moving duels required an enormous amount of organisation and preparation. Both principals had to be instructed in what was expected of them during the affair, the area set aside and doctors had to be summoned, all of which had to be kept secret. Duels were recommended to be conducted in remote places where people did not normally congregate, which could be something of a problem when moving duels were to be fought. Any activity preparing the ground, which had to be examined by the seconds, would be likely to attract attention if those making the arrangements were seen engaged in conduct out of the norm, such as laying out the markers from where the principals were to fire. For this reason duels were often fought early in the morning when no one was about. Even so, at the earliest hours of the day somebody was often to be found nearby; the lamplighters, deliveries to stores, workmen setting out for a day's labour, particularly in the summer months when the mornings were light very early. This is what happened during the affair between David Landale and George Morgan in 1826. Despite the best efforts in preparing their duel in secrecy a householder, engaged in filling his pails with water, observed Landale making his way through the backstreets of the town causing him to wonder where such a gentleman should be off to at such an early hour.

In France one of the most common forms of duel was that known as the *a la barrière* to mean 'the barrier duel', of which there were several variations and naturally took up great room in a field which had to be laid out like some deadly game of tennis to mark the boundaries. These were the equivalent of the 'moving duels' fought in England, but far more elaborate in their arrangement. The barrier separating the duellists could be a single rope or a piece of wood simply placed on the ground, or it could be a whole 'no go' area some several yards wide defined by markers and posts. In barrier duels the principals stood facing one another from opposite sides of the area marked out, and on the given command walked towards each other. Either man could fire at any time during the walk forward towards the barrier. If a man fired and missed his opponent he was obliged to stand still at the spot from where he had fired. His opponent could continue to walk up to the barrier, thereby closing the range to make it easier to hit his target. There was usually a time limit, agreed on before the duel, in which a man under such circumstances could walk to the barrier. On reaching it the man had to fire.

Another form of barrier duel called for both men to continue advancing towards the barrier, even if one man had fired before his opponent. In 1783 a barrier duel was fought by two senior officers serving in the Guards, following a period of enmity which had been lingering between the two men for a period of three years. The cause of their affair dated back to the Battle of Springfield fought in June 1780 during the American War of Independence. After the action Lieutenant Colonel Thomas accused Colonel Gordon of failing in his duty during the battle and the charge led to courts martial being convened. The investigation concluded that there was no case to answer and the charge against Colonel Gordon was dropped. Angry that his honour should be impeached Gordon challenged Thomas to a duel. After three years of prevarication, the day of reckoning finally came in September 1783. The two men faced one another at a distance of 30 yards in Hyde Park. It was agreed that they could fire at any time as they advanced. The first exchange of shots came after only a few paces, with Gordon missing his man but sustaining a wound to the thigh. The injury was not considered serious enough to halt the encounter and the two men once more set about their mission. They continued to walk forward and fired for the second time, but each missed. The seconds instructed the men to return to their original starting places because they were deemed to be too close. Gordon's accuracy turned out to be much improved on the second walk forward, despite the wound to his leg, and shot Thomas, inflicting a mortal wound on him.

The barrier duel was also the preferred means of conducting such affairs in Prussia. In the method employed there, it was the rule for the principal who had fired first to stand still while his opponent walked forward to fire at his leisure. It could not have been a pleasant prospect awaiting one's fate. In the neighbouring state of Wilhelmine, the method where both principals fired at exactly the same time on a given command was frowned on, because it was not believed the men would fire unless ordered and were therefore not determined enough to duel of their own accord.

It was a barrier duel which was witnessed by Sir Algernon West, who was serving as a private secretary to William Gladstone, at that time a senior British politician. The duel was between a young officer in the British Army and an officer in the French army. It was the version where both men would continue to walk forward even if one man had fired. To arrange a duel where both men were even mildly acquainted was hard enough, but to bring together two officers in the armies of different countries must have been enormously difficult. Relations between England and France at the time the duel was conducted during the 1850s were strained to say the least, even though they were Allies during the Crimean War of 1854–6.

Sir Algernon noted later in his memoirs, *Reminiscences and Recollections*:

> At the given signal, the two combatants started to walk to the rope, with the liberty of firing whenever it suited them … The young officer, with the impetuosity of youth, at once fired his pistol, and having missed his man, continued to walk up to the barrier, when he came face to face with his opponent, who had reserved his fire. The Frenchman put his hand on the young man's heart, and said with a sickening familiarity: 'Brave jeune homme, ton Coeur ne palpate pas', (Brave young man, your heart does not beat) and stepping back, he continued: 'Pauvre jeune homme, je plains ta mere', (Poor young man, I send sympathies to your mother) and shot him through the heart.

It would have been a strange and unforgettable spectacle watching a young man being deliberately shot, in an act of nothing less than murder. The deadly farewell uttered by the French officer echoed the words heard by Captain Gronow more than thirty years earlier, when he witnessed a similar duel between two French officers in Paris. The fact that the duel did not lead to a diplomatic incident says something about the tact exercised in this instance.

In England *The British Code of Duel* allowed for up to three shots in a duel, with the seconds encouraged to try and bring about a settlement between shots. Another version of the barrier duel was termed *a marche interrompue* (interrupted march), during which the principals did not walk forward in a straight line, but rather 'zig-zagged'. Each man took two paces, halted and changed direction, continuing all the way to the barrier. Firing was only permitted during the pauses or halts between paces. Such affairs were not only a trial of skill but also a strain on the nerves. The duel called *à ligne parallèle* (parallel line) was another variation on the barrier duel. In this meeting the principals were kept separated by two parallel lines, from where the duel derives its name, which were laid out about fifteen paces apart. The men were positioned at either end of the lines equal to about thirty-five paces in length. On the given signal they walked along their own line getting closer to each other with every pace. They could fire at any time during the affair, but whoever fired first had to remain standing where he was if he missed his opponent. As with other forms of barrier duel there was a time limit in which the second principal had to fire his pistol. In the case of the parallel line affair the time allocated for completing the duel was set at 30 seconds, during which time the other man had to remain in place. This would have been a terrifying experience as the man with the loaded pistol approached ever closer and the prospect of almost certain death going through the mind. But that was the nature of duels,;one never engaged in such an affair in a flippant manner or lacking the nerve to see it through to its conclusion, because such an engagement was to place one's life at risk.

The form of duel known as *au signal* (to the signal), is credited with being the one type of duel which may have produced the most fatalities. Such was its reputation that it was only reserved for use in cases where the cause of the duel was considered to be of the utmost seriousness. Exactly what it was that defined something as being so serious that it warranted the *au signal* form of duel was open to individual interpretation, from a trivial matter such as kicking someone's dog to cuckolding someone's wife. The most serious offence was to physically strike someone, for which there was no other recourse for satisfaction but to resort to a duel. It was not the kind of duel which could be arranged easily due to all the requirements which all parties involved had to observe. Firstly, the seconds had to draw lots in order to decide who would give the signal for the duel to commence; all subsequent signals would be conveyed by hand claps. Each of the principals had to be made aware of what was required of them, for any mistake would cost a man his life. The duellists were placed at a distance between twenty-five and thirty paces apart, and on the command 'attention', which was the only verbal instruction in the affair, the two men took up their places with pistols cocked and held downwards with a straight arm pointing to the ground.

On the first clap of the hands the two men began to walk forward slowly and deliberately. The second clap was the signal that the men should raise their pistols and level them to take aim. The third clap signalled the men to fire which had to be done in an instant and without hesitation. The rules of this form of duel were very clear on the point of firing, and stipulated: 'If one fires before or after the signal, by so much as half a second, he shall be considered a dishonourable man; and if by the disgraceful manoeuvre he shall have killed his adversary, he is to be looked upon as an assassin.' This left no margin for error and the *au signal* could be equally as dangerous to the seconds as they attempted to adhere to the regulations and control the actions of the principals.

The codes regulating conduct during a duel varied in format, but all were of a similar theme which was to lay out what was expected to happen, including the distances at which the principals would fire. The duel known as *au mouchoir* (to the handkerchief) was a close-range affair with an extremely strange twist to it. The principals were presented with a pair of pistols from which they could make their choice of weapons. Thus armed, each man took hold of the corner of a handkerchief with his free hand. At such close quarters, literally two arms lengths, it was virtually impossible to miss and the wound inflicted would be almost inevitably fatal. However, unknown to the principals, only one pistol had been loaded, and so it was very much 'luck of the draw' as to which of the principals picked up the loaded weapon. It was like some deadly practical joke and the conditions of the mouchoir duel would have caused hesitation in selecting one's weapon. Nevertheless, this form of duel *was* conducted.

Captain Stewart, an officer in the British Army, was to face his opponent in a *mouchoir* duel and exercised a bizarre sense of humour by suggesting the affair be conducted in a grave which had been dug for the occasion. The conditions were agreed on and at the arranged time and place the men stepped into the grave and took up the ends of the handkerchief. It was then that the captain's opponent lost his nerve, broke down and refused to duel. He probably feared the worst knowing that only one pistol was loaded and he was almost certainly going to be killed. Incensed by his opponent's cowardly behaviour Captain Stewart thrashed the man, who certainly got off lightly.

The nineteenth-century author and historian Andrew Steinmetz wrote extensively on duelling and actually records the events of an *au mouchoir* duel. The principals were both French and needless to say the cause was the affections of a woman. Steinmetz wrote:

> The seconds prepared the pistols, enveloping them in a handkerchief, and then presenting them to one of the combatants, he took his weapon, and the other was delivered to the antagonist. The ends of the handkerchief were respectively placed in their hands; they raised their pistols; the word was given; they fired and the slanderer fell back, shot through the breast, a torrent of blood gushing at the instant from his mouth and nostrils.

Not all such close-quarter duels called for the principals to hold the corners of a handkerchief. In early 1796 a certain Captain Sweetman consented to meet his opponent at a distance of only four paces, which is approximately 12 feet if one uses the standard measurement of 30 inches for one pace, due to the fact that he was suffering from myopia. Even with such a handicap the captain probably felt a certain amount of confidence owing to his military background. But it did not always follow that all military men were good shots, even at close range, and the captain missed his man. Unfortunately for the officer, the closeness also benefited his opponent who, we can assume enjoyed good eyesight, and he shot the captain through the heart, killing him instantly. In a similar incident, where the vision of one of the principals was impaired through partial-sightedness, he shot his opponent dead on hearing him exclaim, 'By God, I have missed him!' and aimed in the direction of the voice with deadly effect. In 1808 John Colclough and William Alcock stood only eight paces apart, when they met in their duel over the election in Ireland, due to the fact both of them were extremely short-sighted. Alcock shot his opponent through the heart which was witnessed by a large gathering of people who had assembled to watch the proceedings.

While there are conflicting opinions regarding the period when duelling with pistols was at its height, it is generally taken to have flourished between 1770 and 1870 which was a period during which a number of conflicts were fought between major nations. For example, the War of the American Revolution, which had its origins in 1775, saw local colonial troops fighting regular, well-trained English troops as they sought to gain independence. Even amidst all this duels were still arranged, such as the affair between Button Gwinnett and General Lachlan McIntosh in Georgia in 1777, when the war was reaching its peak. An even earlier pistol duel was fought between Edward Doty and Edward Leicester, two men from the original group of Pilgrim Fathers who had established the colony of Massachusetts in 1621. Apart from the names of the two men concerned not much is known about the duel, such as the cause or what the outcome was. It would not be for another ninety-eight years, in 1719, that Massachusetts would pass a law against duelling.

The cause of the feud between Gwinnett and McIntosh stemmed from a decision about who should command forces of colonial troops against the English. McIntosh publicly announced that he believed Gwennett to be a scoundrel, to which the insulted man responded by challenging the General to a duel with pistols. They met to conduct their duel at the distance of only four paces, and given that both men were familiar with pistols it was unlikely that they would miss at such close quarters. Indeed, both men were hit in the thigh. McIntosh survived but Gwennett died from his wound, which we can surmise was caused either though loss of blood, if the femoral artery was hit, or due to infection. It was a stupid and irresponsible loss at a time when the country needed the services of all able-bodied men.

The period of pistol duelling, then, was conducted against the backdrop of virtually one continuous chapter of warring; not the least of which were those affairs fought during the Napoleonic Wars which dominated the closing years of the eighteenth century and the first fifteen years of the nineteenth century. Much of the fighting was between England and France, but as the conflict spread it involved other countries such as Spain, Prussia, Austria, Russia and America, and these nations also saw duels being conducted.

Despite this fighting on an unprecedented scale, officers in the armies and navies of these belligerent countries still managed to find the time to fight duels, and certainly never lacked the incentive to indulge in duelling. The preparedness by even senior American politicians and statesmen to engage in the practice of duelling reflected the inclination of their European counterparts, and like them, they also fought their duels at close range. One such example was the affair in July 1804 between Alexander Hamilton, a personal friend of George Washington, and Aaron Burr, the Vice-President of the United States. The cause of the meeting between two such distinguished statesmen lay in the contents of a letter allegedly written by Hamilton in which was contained slanderous remarks concerning Burr. The letter had been written some years earlier but the contents had only recently come to Burr's attention. Their duel may have been arranged as though the insult had only just occurred, but in reality the two men had an enmity between them which went back many years. At the time of the duel, Hamilton was a leading figure in the Federalist party, while Burr, who was an equally popular public figure, had only narrowly been defeated in the presidential elections and had to content himself with serving as Vice-President under Thomas Jefferson. At the time, America had been half-heartedly conducting a war against the Pasha in Tripoli since 1801 and had deployed a naval force to the Mediterranean Sea.

The insulting letter may have been written years earlier, but it is understood that while Hamilton denied publishing the letter and making it public, he freely admitted that he had made the remarks concerning Burr. In view of such an admission there was no other possible course of action left and Burr wrote a letter challenging Hamilton to a duel in order to gain satisfaction. Hamilton should have expected such a reaction, but even so, he was caught unaware by the response to such an old document. He was known to hold strict views against duelling on religious grounds and to be challenged placed him in a moral dilemma. Should he go through with it to conclude the matter and put it behind him, or should he ignore it and live with the stigma of being considered a coward who did not have the courage to stand up against his challenger? Only his conscience could guide him, and in the end it was his obligation to meet his opponent that won through and he agreed to meet Burr in the duel. Hamilton spent the evening before the event putting his affairs in order, as did most men in his position, but he went one step further and recorded his thoughts on the matter by committing them to paper in his will. His main concern above all else was, as he wrote, not his political legacy, even though he was retired from politics, or his family as might be expected, but rather: 'First, my religion and moral principles are strangely opposed to the practice of duelling, and it would ever give me pain to shed the blood of a fellow creature in a private combat forbidden by laws.' He was obviously wrestling between what he knew to be right and wrong and certainly trying to avoid contravening the law. Another factor was the memory of his son Philip, who had been shot dead by George Eacker in a duel on 23 November 1801 at the same site where he was to confront his own antagonist.

The following morning, 11 July 1804, the two men made their separate ways to the site chosen for the duel, by rowing across the Hudson River accompanied by their seconds in small wooden boats. The location of the duel was in keeping with recommendations that it should be a remote spot and so the affair was to be conducted close to Weehawken Heights in New Jersey. On their arrival at the scene the distance of ten paces was measured out and the principles drew lots to decide where they would stand for the showdown. It had been agreed that the affair should be conducted in a manner similar to duels fought in Europe at the time, but whereas some rules allowed for the exchange of two or even three shots, only one discharge would be fired at this meeting. The pistols were loaded and the principals in accepting the weapons had consigned themselves to their individual fate. The signal to fire was a verbal command, and what happened next has become a controversial subject of debate. There was really no need for instructions in how to conduct themselves, because both men had been party to duels before, with Hamilton having been principal on at least ten occasions, but no shots had been exchanged.

Aaron Burr appears to have been the quickest to react to the command and fired first, and the ball from his pistol hit Hamilton full in the abdomen and entered his liver. It was a fatal wound. At this point the wounded man fired his pistol, an action which has fuelled the debate. It has been opined that Hamilton may have fired at the same instant but aimed deliberately wide of Burr, or it may have been an involuntary action on being hit which caused Hamilton to fire. Another version is that Hamilton actually fired first but missed Burr who was then able to compose himself and shoot his opponent with deliberate aim, something which went against the grain of what was permitted at a duel. The debate into the Burr–Hamilton duel has also produced another theory that Hamilton was resigned to fire wide or 'delope' because of his anti-duelling convictions. If this was the case he did not make this known to Burr, who would have reacted automatically on seeing the man fire and, unaware of the intent to deliberately miss, would have shot at Hamilton.

The wound inflicted on Hamilton was not immediately fatal and he did not expire until the following day. The damage done to Burr's political reputation was catastrophic and his popularity plummeted as it became known what he had done. He may have conducted himself honourably and abided by the rules of the duel but he had killed a man. On reflection, if Hamilton had felt as strongly against duelling as he stated, he should have disregarded what opinions might have said about him, opting for the cowardly way out by not attending the duel. In his will, a legal document signed and witnessed, he expresses his sentiments concerning his family being 'extremely dear' and how his life was of the 'utmost importance to them', which if indeed this was the case he should have had the courage of his convictions and not attended the duel. He also recorded: 'I am conscious of no ill-will to Colonel Burr distinct from political opposition...' Burr, on the other hand, made it widely known that he intended to shoot his opponent dead. Hamilton should have believed in his own writings and weathered the blustering which would have eventually petered out. Furthermore, what could Burr have done to make him attend if he refused to? He could not abduct him and forcibly make him attend. Sadly, Hamilton never knew what General Charles C. Pinkney, who was a member of the Federalist Party and therefore of the same political faction as Hamilton, had written on the subject of duelling in August 1804 a month after the fateful meeting with Burr; had he known he would almost certainly have been influenced by the words, for they would have added to his convictions against the necessity for duelling. Pinkney himself was no stranger to duelling, having served as a second on two occasions, and been wounded on another occasion when duelling as a principal. His thoughts on the matter came from direct experience when he wrote: 'Duelling is no criterion for bravery. I have seen cowards fight duels, and I am convinced real courage may often be better shown in the refusal than in the acceptance of a challenge.' A solitary duellist would have been left mighty embarrassed if his opponent refused to turn up, but such was the stigma attached to refusing to duel that most men felt obliged to attend out of honour, even if it did mean their death, as in the case of Hamilton.

Despite accusations of murder, Burr appears to have acted with all the honourable intentions of a gentleman concerning the duel, but his position as Vice-President of America should have meant more to him than settling a personal vendetta and challenging a man to a duel. After all, the country was engaged in fighting the Tripolitan War, and here he was putting personal matters before state policy. He was not the first senior politician to do so and he certainly would not be the last. He was facing political ruin as the American public turned against him. Writing in the late nineteenth century, Major Ben C. Truman recorded of the duel: 'The affair had the effect of arousing the public mind of the people in the Northern States to a positive horror of duelling.' Burr could not recover his political standing and he was forced to flee south to the states of Georgia and Virginia and into exile. The popular press then joined in the chorus, calling for him to be brought to trial for murder, so it was unsafe for him to go back. Burr tried to return to practising law, but this was unsuccessful and he died in penury on Staten Island in 1836.

This duel has become one of the most famous affairs of its kind in American history and will long remain the subject of great debate. It is rather ironic, though, that history has been more kind to Hamilton's memory and today his image appears on the ten dollar note.

Politics in America, it seems, was just as likely to provoke a duel between politicians as it was in Europe, but perhaps on a more ruthless scale. For example, a challenge was issued in 1802 which did have a connection to the Burr-Hamilton affair which would come two years later to the month. De Witt Clinton, Senator for New York, was accused of misrepresenting Aaron Burr for his own political gains by Republican John Swartwout, who supported Burr. Clinton rebuked the charge and in his response insulted Swartwout by calling him 'a liar', before adding that the man was also 'a scoundrell and a villain'. A duel was the only way to clear the air and end the matter. So it was that the two men met as principals at a spot in Hoboken in New Jersey. They faced each other at ten paces, but what made the duel different was the number of shots they agreed to exchange from their pistols, which exceeded even the number considered permissible under some English codes governing the conduct of duels. The two men had agreed that they would each fire five shots, an act which would prolong the duel and push their nerves to the very limit. Swartwout was wounded twice in the legs before the duel was concluded. The doctor in attendance must not have considered Swartwout's first leg wound to be so bad that he could not continue, and assumed that his nerves must be calm. But on receiving the second wound all parties concerned agreed to end the affair and Clinton had vindicated himself.

The following month, 23 August 1802, David B. Mitchell faced his former business partner James Hunter in a duel set at ten paces, with the affair being conducted, for some macabre reason, in the Jewish cemetery in Savannah in the state of Georgia. Taking up their positions, the two men had previously agreed that after each shot they would step forward two paces in a manner similar to the moving duel. Mitchell missed but was wounded in turn when Hunter fired. The two men advanced two paces each to close the range to only six paces. Mitchell's second shot found its mark and Hunter fell dead. Mitchell had already held office as Mayor of Savannah and, following the duel, rather than being ruined politically he went on to serve two terms in office as Governor of Georgia and to command the State Militia.

While certain aspects of some duels have led to controversy, the one duel which has become the most controversial of all the American duels is that concerning the affair between General Andrew Jackson and Charles Dickinson in May 1806, barely two years after the infamous meeting between Burr and Hamilton. Both men in this instance were of a fiery temperament, and the duel resulted over the charge by Jackson that his wife Rachel had been insulted in comments made by Dickinson, against whom he issued the challenge. At the time of the duel Jackson was 40 years of age and had already lived a colourful life charged with adventure. He had fought briefly in the American War of Independence, during which he was captured by the British Army. After the war he practised law and served as Senator in Tennessee; he gained a reputation for fighting duels, being principal on at least fourteen occasions during his life. Such was his temper that Thomas Hart Benton, himself a veteran duellist, remarked on his duel with Jackson: 'Yes, I had a fight with Jackson, a fellow was hardly in fashion then who hadn't.' Not for nothing was Jackson nicknamed 'Old Hickory'.

Jackson's opponent on that fateful morning of 30 May 1806 was Charles Dickinson, who was widely considered to be the best shot in Tennessee. He was also a lawyer, and although Jackson had not practised law in more than ten years, both men would have been more than aware that their conduct was against the law. Although duelling was illegal, it was tolerated more in the southern states than in the northern states of America, but even there duelling was still conducted. Knowing they risked prosecution for duelling, the two stalwart Tennesseans arranged that they should meet in Logan County, in the neighbouring state of Kentucky. A landowning southern gentleman such as Jackson may tolerate some things, but an insult against his wife was unforgivable.

Jackson was accompanied by his second, General Overton, to whom he confided his intention of allowing Dickinson to fire first, thereby allowing himself time to aim properly before firing. Knowing Dickinson's reputation as a marksman, Overton replied: 'Hickory, if you hold your fire you'll probably not live to pull the trigger.' Jackson answered the cautionary words of his second: 'I know it, but I must have time to get a line on him. I'll take the chance. My luck's always good.' On arrival at the appointed place the distance of eight paces was marked out. It had been previously agreed that the principals would face one another with their pistol arms held straight down by their sides. On the given signal each man could fire in his own time. It would have been a nervous few moments as each man reflected on the reputation of his opponent. Dickinson fired first and witnesses observed a faint puff of dust coming off Jackson's long, loose-fitting coat in the area of his breast, close to the region of the heart. However, he did not fall and instead remained motionless except for a slight swaying, which could have been attributed to nerves. Dickinson, on seeing his adversary still standing, exclaimed in questioning terms: 'Great God, have I missed him?' He recoiled back from his spot, whereupon General Overton admonished him and called him to return to his place with the order: 'Back on your mark, sir.' There was little else he could do but to obey the command.

What he did not know was that he had actually hit Jackson on the left-hand side of the chest and the ball had broken two ribs. Jackson would have been in immense pain, but he steadied himself and in contravention to European rules, which forbade direct and deliberate aiming, he levelled his pistol at Dickinson, who averted his face, and fired. The man fell dying and Jackson walked from the scene in contempt. Some sources say that Jackson's pistol failed to fire and he had to re-cock the weapon and shoot again. The animosity between the two men before the duel had been such that each had made it widely known it was their singular intention to kill the other. It was only as they were walking away that Overton noticed his friend had been hit, but he was motioned to keep silent about it. It was as though Jackson did not want his opponent to die with the satisfaction of knowing he had shot his man after all. It was only later, when he was more composed, that Jackson said of the affair: 'I should have killed him even had he shot me through the brain.' Other sources claim he remarked that, he 'would have lived long enough to have killed his antagonist even if he had been shot through the heart'. The pistol ball remained in his chest for the rest of his life, which he continued to enjoy to the full for another forty years.

Jackson took up a military command again nine years later to fight and defeat a British Army at the Battle of New Orleans in January 1815, giving him hero status. His plantation made him a wealthy man in his own right and his law practice was also successful. Unlike Aaron Burr, who had been ruined for killing Hamilton, Jackson's career went from strength to strength. In 1828 he was elected President of the United States of America, a position he took up in 1829, the same year that the Duke of Wellington fought his duel while serving as Prime Minister of England.

But this was not the last of the duels between the hot-headed politicians in America, particularly in the southern states. And the story of Andrew Jackson's duel does not end there, for like the Burr-Hamilton duel, debate has waged over the affair for many years. He has been accused of cheating in some fashion, but exactly how has never been fully explained. Some say that it was his loose-fitting coat which afforded him some protection, but if it contravened rules of the duel it was surely up to the seconds to say something and ask him to remove it. No such undertaking was required and he certainly did not wear any protection under the coat; this is evident in the fact that he received such a penetrating wound. It was surely the man's stalwartness and belief in himself which saw him through, as much as anything else.

There were no hard and fast rules when it came to distances and duels could be conducted at any reasonable range decided on by the seconds. The problem with the distance at which duels were conducted was something of an ambiguous point, and had to be resolved from the very beginning of a duel. Should the distance agreed on between the principals be too far apart, it would bring the whole affair into ridicule, because it would be too difficult to hit the target, no matter how proficient a man was with a pistol. The more experienced shot preferred some distance, using their skills to their advantage, but the seconds were there to see things were arranged as equally as possible and did not benefit one man over the other. In 1833 Alexander McClung shot his opponent General Allen dead at a range of 100 feet, quite an achievement with a pistol. Before the duel McClung had boasted he would shoot Allen in the teeth. It was not an idle threat as the officer was shot full in the mouth with the ball hitting his spine, killing him instantly. If the distance was set too close, it was little more than murder because it would be impossible to miss, such as the case with McIntosh and Gwennett. Some rules covering the conduct of duels believed the distance between the principals should be measured in yards, while others suggested paces be used. Twelve paces could be judged as being a good distance between principals, which was the measurement used in the duel between Canning and Castlereagh in 1809 on Putney Heath. The Clonmel Rules did not give a minimum range at which to conduct the duel, and the America duelling code of 1838 suggests that the 'usual distance is from ten to twenty paces, as may be agreed on, and the seconds in measuring the ground usually step three feet'. Death was being measured out on the battlefield to settle matters of state policy, and on the field of honour to settle personal differences. It was a strange time to live in.

Most of the duels that were reported in the newspapers were high-profile affairs between men of public note, such as politicians, doctors, lawyers or officers in the army. It is rare to come across details of a duel between two ordinary men but such accounts do exist, such as the affair between two long-standing friends in an otherwise close-knit community.

Such duels rarely warranted recording unless the duel resulted in a death, in which case it would certainly be published in the newspapers.

Wales at the end of the eighteenth century was a rural, indeed remote place, with a sparse population. In 1770 it is estimated that 500,000 people lived in the country, mainly in large towns. At the time of a duel in 1799 Haverfordwest was a thriving market town in Pembrokeshire, but still far removed from the hustle and bustle of large metropolitan towns, as could be imagined. Men folk had gone off to join the army to fight in the wars against France, and the population of Wales as a whole would hardly have increased since the calculation of almost thirty years earlier. Many young men stayed at home to help on the farms in this largely agricultural society which stabilised the community; so the events which unfolded between two young men of Haverfordwest, Samuel Simmons Fortune and John James, would become the talk of the district.

In early September 1799 the two men undertook to ride to the town of Tenby, a journey using today's roads of more than 20 miles, but over 200 years ago such a journey on horseback would have been along muddy lanes and taken more than a full day. The two men were more than just friends; they were soon to become brothers-in-law because Samuel Fortune was engaged to the sister of John James. Their journey began well enough but at the town of Templeton, about 15 miles outside of Haverfordwest, Fortune's horse lost a shoe forcing him to halt at a blacksmith's forge to have it replaced. According to an account John James said he would ride on at a steady pace, thereby allowing his companion to catch up with him and continue their journey together. The friends did not reunite until they met in the courtyard of a hotel in Tenby. There Samuel Fortune accused his friend of riding on without him. It was a trifling matter, probably caused by the blacksmith taking longer to replace the horseshoe than expected. The men began to exchange words and finally Fortune lashed out with his riding whip and struck John James a blow on the shoulder. It was unpardonable and the one action which almost always led to the challenge of a duel between gentlemen in any social class. Research reveals that the location where the two men argued could have been the Red Lion Hotel in White Street in Tenby. It is certainly of the right age and a courtyard with stables used to exist at the rear of the property. Some accounts say the hotel was called the White Lion, but it is quite possible that at one time the establishment may have been partly referred to by its location in White Street and the name above the door, or more probably arose out of confusion over the years.

The men made their separate ways home to Haverfordwest and, after almost a week had elapsed since the altercation, with no word between the two, it would have appeared that the events had been forgotten. Then one evening, as Fortune was settling down to his meal, a note was delivered to inform him that he had been challenged to a duel by John James. The appointed place for the meeting was the Croft, a quiet field which today lies just off a path called, rather poignantly, 'Fortune's Frolic Walk', near to Cartlett in Haverfordwest. The date of the duel was set for 14 September and, even though he was caught unprepared, Fortune must have been sufficiently composed to make preparations for his part in the duel. He met his challenger John James at the site, who was accompanied by his second, a man by the name of Duvan. It is believed that Duvan may have been French, but this is unlikely as Britain at the time was at war with France and French nationals would have been viewed with deep suspicion. Furthermore, it was only two years earlier that a French raiding party had landed near Fishguard, only 15 miles north of Haverfordwest, and caused an invasion scare. Duvan may possibly have been of French descent, whose family had fled to England to escape the Revolution, a fact which would later prove beneficial to James.

For all its remoteness, in rural Wales, the two men observed all the etiquette involved in duelling. The note to challenge, the location in a remote field and the accompanying by a second were all in accordance with the rules, had the duel been arranged in either Bath or London. Even so, evidence points to the fact that Fortune could not have taken the affair all that seriously, although he would have been wise to do so, and he fired harmlessly into the air, deloping his shot. James, on the other hand, was in more of a mind to see it through properly and fired at his former friend, hitting him in the side of the chest and causing him to fall to the ground. Fearing for the consequences of their actions, James and Duvan left Fortune where he fell and fled the scene.

It appears that Fortune summoned enough strength to stagger to a nearby cottage, lived in by a man called Crunn. He arranged to have the wounded man carried to his mother's house in Quay Street on an extemporised stretcher using a door. This would suggest that a doctor had not been present at the duel; either that or he joined James and Duvan in their flight from the scene. On arrival at Crunn's mother's house a doctor was called who he declared the wound to be fatal. Samuel Fortune died the following day aged only 23 years old. Today his grave can be visited in the grounds of St Thomas' Church in Haverfordwest with the date of his death, 16 September 1799, inscribed on the headstone.

The duel had been conducted as clandestinely as possible but in such a small town it would have been virtually impossible to keep it secret beforehand, and after the event it was public gossip. In such circumstances it would have been widely known that John James had been the other principal in the affair, when the identity of the shot man was revealed, and he would have been sought after for murder. James, accompanied by Duvan, wasted no time in fleeing to England before absconding to France, where he remained for ten years. No doubt with the aid of Duvan's French connections James was able to live in the country, which would have been extremely difficult due to the war. Then suddenly, and for no apparent reason, he returned to Wales where he faced the charge of murder. The Fortune family, their animosity tempered by time, did not prosecute James. The coroner's jury, however, had other thoughts on the matter and brought in a charge of wilful murder against John James. But it would appear that he was not prosecuted and avoided the penalty of hanging, because it is known that on the death of his uncle, Colonel James of Pontsayson, he inherited the estate and became a colonel himself, serving in the Pembrokeshire Militia.

The Haverfordwest duel had shocked the town, and it was a sad affair indeed because it was simply a case of hot-headed young men overreacting in a misunderstanding. Had they been less impetuous and exercised more self-restraint, which comes with the experience of years, the affair need not have ended so tragically. The town of Tenby, where the argument had started, would be rocked to its foundations forty years later, when the Mayor engaged in a duel in 1839. But, as if that was not scandal enough, his successor fought a duel three years later, while also in office as Mayor of the town, thereby shocking the seaside resort even further.

The first of Tenby's mayoral duels took place in March 1839 between Henry Mannix and the Mayor William Richards who was in his fourth year of office. The duel was fought over the ownership of a strip of land and was conducted at a place near Howlers Lane, close to Gumfreston Church. Archives of the *Carmarthen Journal* newspaper from the period reveal that there was a considerable amount of gun crime at the time, including highway robbery, for which John Owen received fifteen years Transportation. Firearms were freely available and, considering the seriousness of his crime, John Owen was fortunate not to be hung for the offence. William Richards is understood to have fired in the air, or deliberately deloped, but Mannix took aim and shot his adversary, hitting him in the groin causing a deep penetrating wound. Despite the seriousness of his injury, the Mayor survived his encounter and went on to live for another sixteen years after the pistol ball was removed.

The other mayoral duel in the town, three years later, was between Mayor Charles Cook Wells and Captain Francis Rivers Freeling, as has already been recounted in chapter 1. What was unusual about this affair was the fact that almost nothing was reported on the duel in the local papers given that it was the Mayor who took part. This would seem to indicate that by 1842 public opinion against duelling was growing and people were beginning to lose interest. The fascination with duelling was fading, even in the coastal resorts where nothing so outrageous ever occurred. Had the encounter been fatal, the newspaper coverage would have been different, for that was murder. But in Britain at least, the writing was on the wall for the duel and over the next several years it gradually faded away.

Replacing the public interest in duelling was gossip, which the local and national newspapers published to satiate the growing readership's delectation for scandals. News of court cases involving libel and slander were far more juicy stories to gossip over with a drink in a bar. The lengths to which the aggrieved were prepared to sue for damages as recompense for verbal or written abuse was far more interesting, and the amount of money being sought as compensation would be the talk of the town. It was easier and infinitely safer to sue someone than to face him in a pistol duel, where the odds of surviving were not always good. Better to hurt somebody by taking money from their pocket and benefiting from their comments. Money had become the new way of claiming honour without the attendant dangers, and giving some luxuries at the same time. By the second half of the nineteenth century duellists themselves were becoming more reluctant to engage in such affairs and began to seek financial redress if pressed to engage in a duel.

One man, whose name has been lost over time, sought financial comfort for his family should he be killed in his duel. He was from Prussia, where duelling was viewed as an honourable institution. The letter he sent his challenger would certainly have pricked the conscience of even the most hardened of duellists. The un-named principal wrote:

> I have, as you know, a wife and five children, for whom I am bound to care in the event of my death. My present yearly income is forty-five hundred marks. I require you to pay over to a bank a capital sum, the interest of which will correspond to my present income, so that it may yield a livelihood to my widow and fatherless children.

The reply was not without sentiment as the challenger responded with his own letter:

> In that case, I fear our duel can never take place. A man who has nothing to lose except his own life will scarcely expect me to allow him to shoot me and to beggar my widow and children without any sort of equivalent.

It was a chance to bluff out the challenge and avoid the duel without losing face, and one which paid off. If a challenger thought he had to pay for the privilege of shooting someone in a duel he would think twice, especially as he stood to be shot equally in the exchange of fire. It was too costly an enterprise to contemplate.

Another ploy used by those parties reluctant to take up the pistol to duel, was an unscrupulous move and tore at all the sentiments. On being challenged to a duel, some men managed to avoid the affair by inviting their challenger to partake in a meal with them, using the opportunity to introduce them to their family. It was guaranteed to make a difference and the duel would be cancelled. It was a callous act to put one's family in the way of the affair, but it worked. One such incident is recorded in the writings of someone who called himself 'A Christian Patriot' and recounts how:

> After breakfast, the challenger reminded his host of the engagement. [This elicited the reply:] 'That amiable woman, and the six little innocents who you saw at breakfast, depend on my energies for their support, and until you can stake something of equal value, I think we shall be badly matched in mortal combat.'

It would have been a heartless man who could argue against such a presentation, and in this case the two men put aside their differences and cancelled the duel. But, while such a ploy had its risks, it made men begin to see common sense and be more mindful of their actions so as to avoid being challenged to a duel in the first place. It was not just in Britain that the move against duelling was taking place, it was happening across Europe and America, where admittedly it took longer for the practice to die out.

Not all duels were conducted in conditions which could be considered 'normal' by any stretch. For example, the aerial duel between de Grandprè and le Pique in 1808 was quite extraordinary. Some affairs, if it were not for the seriousness of the situation, could be considered with a modicum of levity. In 1882, rather late in the history of duelling with pistols, Benjamin Constant faced Forbin des Issarts in a duel which they conducted while seated in chairs. The reason for such an arrangement was due to the fact that Constant suffered from rheumatism which prevented him from taking up his position while standing and so elected to sit for the affair.

Also, not all duels were conducted outside, although the very nature of the affair dictated that duels were better conducted in an open space. In Prussia a strange, indeed unique, form of indoor duelling developed which does not appear to have captured the imagination of other countries. Referred to as 'Kukuk', the two principals were shut in a darkened room with only one man armed with a pistol. The second man was unarmed and bereft of footwear. In the darkness he had to utter the 'Kukuk' sound, which upon hearing the armed duellist would react and fire in the general direction of the sound. If he hit his opponent the duel was concluded, but if he failed to hit his barefooted opponent the roles were reversed. The whole affair, if real and not some fanciful early form of urban myth, fabricated for the delectation of story-telling at the dinner table, was like committing some form of prolonged suicide. No wonder, then, that this form of duel never gained the same popularity attached to standard duelling practices. Nevertheless, of the several notable instances where duels were fought indoors, the account of an anonymous Englishman travelling through Europe stands out as perhaps the most extraordinary. (*See* chapter 9.)

The island of Guernsey is the second largest of the Channel Islands and officers of the military garrison posted there would almost certainly have engaged in duels at one time or another. One duel between civilians took place in 1790 between Thomas Sausmarez of a leading local family who faced his cousin, Robert Le Marchant, son of the island's bailiff. Such was the stir it caused that news of the affair reached London, where it became the talk of society. Archives on the nearby island of Jersey reveal that duels were conducted between civilians and also by the military garrison, one of which was investigated by the local authorities in 1782.

On 18 June 1782 the body of an officer in the 95th Regiment of Foot was discovered on land close to the house of Philippe d'Auvergne in the parish of St Ouen, on the west coast of Jersey. It was discovered that the dead man was Lieutenant Alexandre Hamilton and that he had been shot earlier in the day during a duel with Charles Rowan, an officer in the same regiment. The western end of the island was remote in those days and would have made an ideal spot to conduct the affair. Investigations by the authorities, both civil and military, identified a number of officers from the regiment who had been witness to the duel, and the matter was soon concluded by Phillipe De Carteret, who held the position of Greffe at the Royal Court. The account of the affair, written in French, says how each person made a statement before going on to make a number of recommendations. The report names several officers who were either present at the duel or were at least privy to the information that a meeting was to take place between the two officers. In the same document the Greffe of the Royal Court, '… favours their transportation out of this island'. The removal of these men from the island would have brought an end to the affair; it would have been up to their regiment whether or not to prosecute them.

Only eighteen months before the duel, in January 1781, Jersey had been attacked and invaded by French troops. During the fighting, Ensign Charles Rowan had acquitted himself admirably, and had been present during the height of the battle which raged in the Royal Square in the town centre of St Helier. Such was Rowan's involvement in the action that he is depicted in the famous painting by John Singleton Copely, called *The Death of Major Pierson*, and shows Rowan at the moment his commanding officer is mortally wounded. It was an ignominious end to be sent from the island in disgrace for the death of a fellow officer in a duel, especially after such an illustrious action. The expulsion of the officers proved that even though Jersey was a small island, it would not tolerate such behaviour.

Gossip of the duel between the two officers had not long subsided when the island was again shocked by news of another duel, this time between two civilians. Details of the affair are rather sketchy at best, but those which do exist allow one to piece together something of what happened. For example, the cause is not entirely known and the date puts it somewhere in the 1780s. The location of the duel is referred to as Grenville, which has to be assumed is the correct spelling because there are several place names on the island spelled Granville. If it *is* Grenville, it would put the location of the duel in the vicinity of La Rocque in the parish of St Clement on the south-east coast of the island.

The principals were named Barrow and Hogan and it is known that the men would each fire six shots which, in itself, is extremely unusual. After the men had each fired three times Barrow's second attempted to intervene and bring the affair to an end. He did not succeed and in frustration left the scene, thereby abandoning his principal to face his trial alone. The duel continued with the men stepping ever closer to one another with each shot they fired. On the sixth shot Hogan was struck dead through the heart, at a distance believed to be no more than four paces. It was a dereliction of duty by Barrow's second to leave, and a lack of control by Hogan's second to bring about a semblance of order to the affair. The exchange of six shots by each man prolonged the duel and could have led to them being discovered by the authorities. Duels where a single shot was fired by each principal would be over within minutes, but the time taken to reload the pistols in this case meant it would have gone on for some time. The fact that no one interrupted the duel is a testimony to how sparse the population was on the island of Jersey at that time.

An interesting document surviving in the Jersey Archives is an account of a duel entitled *Confutation of a Brief Statement of Facts*, written in April 1803 by Charles Le Maistre, who had served as second to John Pipon, one of the principals in the affair. The fact that the duel was fought at the height of the wars between France and England is not such an unusual case in itself, because many duels were fought in that period. However, what does make it strange is the fact that the affair took place on the Isle de Chausey (sometimes written as Chauzè). This location is a rocky reef lying just off the western side of the Cherbourg peninsular, and only by a stretch of the imagination can they be referred to as islets. In fact, apart from pirates and smugglers they were virtually uninhabited. Historically, Chausey belongs to Jersey, but due to the remote geography of the islets they were abandoned around 1499 and seized upon by France, which then administered them from the town of Granville. In 1803 it was to these rocks that a group sailed in order to conduct a duel far away from interference. The fact that Chausey lies some 25 miles sailing distance in a straight line from Jersey says much about the tenacity of the principals in their determination to see their affair through. It would have taken several hours' sailing to reach the islets, and to maintain a hostile nature towards one's opponent throughout such a voyage would point to a deep hatred indeed. Unfortunately, the document mentioned does not say anything about the cause of the affair, but does mention how startled the French troops posted to the spot were on discovering a small group of armed civilians coming ashore. To sail such a distance in order to conduct a duel without interference by the authorities does seem somewhat extreme, but duellists from England would at times sail to the Continent where the view on duelling was rather more liberal. In America it was not uncommon for the principals to cross over the state boundary or county lines in order to fight a duel without interference.

The place where the duel was to take place would have been almost unnaturally quiet because little or no talking was entered into, and the principals were not allowed to exchange words. However, they did shout comments such as 'no apologies' on being asked by a second if they wished to end the affair before taking the final step and actually shooting. The seconds did all of the talking and passed on any comments made by one of the principals. The location of the duel on the Isle de Chausey, for example, would have been eerily quiet except for the sound of the sea and gulls.

Mostly the principals left the field without uttering a word, even where death occurred, but on rare occasions after exchanging shots the principals actually became friends. Today local history societies or individuals researching duelling have set out to try and locate the spots where duels were fought. Some areas such as Hyde Park, Wimbledon Common or Battersea Park in London, or the Bois de Boulogne near Paris, had so many duels conducted within the vast expanses of their grounds that it is almost impossible to pinpoint exact locations. In Haverfordwest the site of the duel between Samuel Fortune and John James in 1799 has been identified, and in nearby Tenby the sites of the 1839 and 1842 duels have been tentatively located. The site of the fatal duel between Rice and du Barry just outside Bath has been built over but is well known to local historians. For anyone wishing to track down the spot where local duels were fought, it is best to begin a search in the town museum followed by more detective work searching through newspapers of the time and examining maps to compare them to what is known of events. The results can be most rewarding.

3

GIVING FIRE
AND DUELLING CODES

As is only to be expected, there is a slight difference of opinion as to when duelling with pistols became the preferred form of settling affairs of honour. Some place it as early as 1650, rising to a peak between 1770 and 1810. There are incidents to support this earlier date, but these affairs appear to have been an exception rather than the rule and such conduct was rare. Other sources state that pistol duels were common in Europe and America for a period between 1770 and 1870. Certainly some countries saw the practice of duelling continuing long after it had fallen out of fashion or, in countries such as England, after stringent law enforcement tried to prevent duels from being arranged. In some countries such as France, where it has been suggested that as many as 100 duels were being fought annually between 1815 and 1848, and America, for example, pistol duels were still being fought at the end of the nineteenth century and there are even instances of duels being fought well into the twentieth century.

If one takes the commonly shared date stated by sources, then it is with some confidence that we can claim the second half of the eighteenth century to be the period when duelling with pistols was in the ascendancy. This is confirmed by the fact that in 1777 a group of distinguished gentlemen at the Clonmel Summer Assizes in Ireland drew up one of the earliest sets of guidelines which governed the act of duelling with pistols, seen as an attempt to set out a 'Code Duello' to instruct duellists. At the time Ireland was being left to its own devices and considered by many as a backwater society. Even so, the country had to be governed and among the landowning gentry those squabbles which led to duels had to be covered by a set of conventions or guidelines. Duelling was never legal and so any such set of rules had no standing in a court of law should a trial result from someone killing his adversary in a duel. Duels had been fought in Ireland before 1759, the year when Colonel Barrington and Mr Gilbert faced one another. But what was unusual in their particular duel was the fact that they started first on horseback, and then went on foot, using swords and pistols. Between 1751 and 1760 it is believed that some 36 duels were fought in Ireland, and this figure rose to 47 in the decade up to 1770. While not perhaps significant, the practice does increase even further to 159 affairs thereafter, but between 1781, four years after the Clonmel Rules were drawn up, and 1791 there is a slight drop, with 147 duels being conducted, with pistols being the preferred weapon of choice from the 1770s onward.

The gathering at Clonmel may have been self-appointed in their task, but they laid out in print precisely what was considered likely to lead to a duel and the conduct expected of those participating in the affair. This document is known as the 'Clonmel Rules' and was intended to settle any matter concerning duels. For example: 'All imputations of cheating at play, races, etc., to be considered equivalent to a blow, but may be reconciled after one shot, on admitting their falsehood and begging pardon publicly…' This point of conduct was widely recognised and cheating at cards had led to many duels being fought. The Irish set of regulations continued by stating that:

> No dumb firing or firing in the air is admissible in any case. The challenger ought not to have challenged without receiving offence, and the challenged ought, if he gave offence, to have made an apology before he came on the ground; therefore children's play must be dishonourable and is accordingly prohibited.

In other words, all parties will act like mature, responsible adults at all times and have the courage to see the duel through to its climax.

On the subject of seconds, the title given to the principal's friend or accomplice in the affair, the regulations cover not only his conduct before, during and after the duel but also what he ought to do in order to try and bring about a satisfactory conclusion to the difference of opinion. The rules point out that: 'Seconds [are] to be of equal rank in society with the principals they attend.' This sets out immediately the fact that the duel should be kept within the circle of either landowning gentry or officers in the military. It continues on the role of seconds in supporting the principal:

> The challenged has the right to choose his own weapons unless the challenger gives his honour he is no swordsman [that is, providing swords are chosen] after which, however, he cannot decline any second species of

weapon proposed by the challenged. The challenged chooses the ground, the challenger chooses the distance, the seconds fix the time and terms of firing....

This last point was generally accepted and actually used on occasion when setting out arrangements for the duel, such as the affair between the Honourable William Wellesley and Count Hummell from Belgium, in 1843. Count Hummell chose swords but Wellesley was obliged to decline saying he could not use a sword because of an injury to his right elbow and produced a note from a doctor to that effect. In view of this the two men then decided to fight with pistols. Such a list of 'do's' and 'don'ts' is actually all very formal and in keeping with the rules and regulations of any normal gentlemen's social club or association. The importance of the seconds continues to be mentioned throughout the lines of regulations by making such statements as:

> The seconds load in presence of each other, unless they give their mutual honours that they have charged smooth and single ... Firing may be regulated first by signal; secondly by word of command; or thirdly at pleasure, as may be agreeable to the parties.

This showed trust between the seconds when it came to loading the pistols which, in keeping with English custom, were smooth bore without rifling in the barrel and only loaded with a measured amount of powder.

Since the very beginning of formal duelling swords had been the preferred weapon of choice for duellists, but as has already been seen they were gradually replaced by pistols. The use of swords required skill, strength and stamina, and yet there were still those in the mid-nineteenth century who opted for swords. From the above account between Wellesley and Hummell it will be noted that swords had not been entirely dismissed and more than a few duellists still favoured them as a weapon. In Italy, between 1879 and 1889, some 2,759 duels were recorded of which only 165 were conducted with pistols, leaving the remainder fought with swords. Women also duelled with swords and the famous French opera singer Maupin was taught fencing skills by her lover Serana who was a renowned fencing master. She was able to put her abilities to the test one evening when she challenged several men to meet her outside during a ball. She killed or wounded each of them and in the process gained a new-found respect.

A study of duels fought in France from 1880 shows that of 31 duels fought, 24 were conducted using swords. Five years later in 1885, of some 50 case studies of duels investigated, 36 were fought with swords. In 1889 swords were used in a further 32 duels, indicating that the misplaced notion of chivalry and romantic ideals of duelling died hard. But the impression which has become synonymous with duelling is the sight of two solitary figures armed with pistols standing apart in the middle of an otherwise deserted field. Such a sight would have been unusual and as each of the principals stood in his firing spot his head must have been filled with hundreds of thoughts as the final seconds ticked away to the moment when the signal to fire was given.

All points of a duel are specific and appear to take into account any eventuality, including the possibility of a pistol not firing properly, which was seen as being equal to an intended shot. The responsibility of a weapon misfiring could not be blamed on any one person because flintlock pistols were prone to not firing properly even though they were loaded and primed. However, to recognise a misfire as a true shot was to say that the shooter had every intention of giving fire. Even with the principals in position to fire, some guidelines advise the seconds to 'attempt a reconciliation before the meeting takes place, or after sufficient firing or hits as specified. Any wound sufficient to agitate the nerves and necessarily make the hand shake must end the business of the day.' This suggestion would become recognised practice, but in some instances the principals, if the affair had not proved fatal, would leave the field of honour without so much as glancing at one another. In the case of the duel between Colonel Barrington and Mr Richards, they became firm friends.

In 1836, almost sixty years after the Clonmel Rules were drawn up, no fewer than seventy-six gentlemen of 'notable personages' gave their support to a similar set of rules in France, which recognised six different types of duel. In the same year, *The Art of Duelling* had appeared in England which listed a range of suggestions for would-be duellists including both experienced and novice principles; *The British Code of Duel* had already been written in 1824. Even in the Austro-Hungarian Empire such rules were also recognised, but they had several different forms of duel as opposed to the six in France. Across the Atlantic the *American Code of Duel* appeared in 1838.

Although such sets of rules were published, they were not as widely read, or likely to adorn the bookshelves of libraries across the country, to the same extent as works of popular fiction by such authors of the time as Charles Dickens, Jane Austen or Sir Walter Scott. Nevertheless, the printed guidelines were there to be consulted and sometimes inwardly digested by those with a fascination in the matter of duelling. In the event of duellists being brought to trial there would be nothing in such works which could affect the outcome of a trial because they had no legal bearing as evidence. The Clonmel Rules, for example, were witnessed by gentlemen from Tipperary, Galway, Mayo, Sligo and Roscommon with the intention of being used across Ireland. The document can be interpreted in a number of ways but the main aim of the Clonmel Rules was to be used as a guideline to prevent arguments which would in turn lead to a duel. Even so, arguments still arose and duels continued to be fought.

During the period when duelling with pistols was at its height, a whole series of pamphlets joined the weighty tomes on the subject of duelling, all of which were written with the intention of outlining the conduct to be observed by all persons during a duel. For the most part they were general thoughts and opinions, but some were very precise. The authors in some cases were really no more than parties interested in duels and what they penned was only a series of personal ideas. The more heavyweight tomes, some of which were written anonymously, had more structure to them, but even so, the authors of such works often made statements which on close examination reveal that they almost certainly were never present when a shot was fired in anger.

Included in the remarks was the statement that a gentleman should send a formal letter challenging his opponent and this would be delivered by his second. This was considered polite etiquette when inviting someone to face what could be his death sentence. It seems strange today that the challenge to a duel had to be done politely and not while fuming with temper or under the influence of alcohol.

The first step in convening a duel was to issue a formal challenge, which is sometimes referred to as being 'called out'. There was a range of specific terms used in duelling and a man on being challenged for whatever reason became a principal along with his challenger. A man may appoint a close friend to act as an intermediary, to pass letters and make arrangements and this friend was known as the second. There were strict conditions in duelling such as the rule which forbade gentlemen of unequal rank or social standing from engaging in duels. *The British Code of Duel* covers this by stating:

> If a gentleman detracted from another, the combat should be allowed. But if a clown, he was to take the remedy of legal action. A clown might not challenge a gentleman to combat because of the inequality of their station.

Although class meant everything this was a point which on occasion could be ignored, and indeed was disregarded in a number of affairs. The historian John Atkinson points out:

> No matter how angry an offended party might be, he would issue a challenge only if the offender were a man of his own social standing. An insult offered by a person of inferior status was punishable there and then

by horsewhipping the rascal, but never by inviting him to meet you on the duelling ground.

This is what should have happened in the case of the duel between Thomas Heslop, believed to have been a servant, and John Beynon, a local landowner near Newcastle Emlyn in Wales in September 1814 (*see* chapter 2). Several accounts say Heslop challenged Beynon to a duel, but if they were from such different backgrounds then Beynon would have been in his right to dismiss the challenge; Heslop would have been chased out of the town and sent packing, but the duel did go ahead and ended with Heslop being killed. Even when in the act of killing someone there had to be standards.

The challenge to duel was to make clear the intention that a man was seeking restitution for some act to which he had been subjected and for which he believed required settlement. It was not advisable to challenge someone while in the heat of an argument, and the various books with their guidelines advised against sending such notes at night. It was recommended that there be a short interlude between issuing a challenge and the actual duel, so that when the time came to exchange fire the principals would conduct the affair in a calm manner. Suggestions are one thing but when put into practice are another thing entirely and many a duel was fought within hours of a challenge and would have seen both principals agitated.

The note to inform the intention to duel was advised to be brief and to the point, such as the short message written as a form of question by an Italian duellist, who despatched his letter saying: 'Sir, if your courage is equal to your impudence, will you meet me tonight in the wood?'

But brevity does not mean politeness and the guidelines all emphasis that rudeness should be avoided when composing the note to challenge. *The Art of Duelling* states that a duellist should 'conduct himself during the whole affair with the greatest politeness'. The work goes on to suggest that letters should be composed 'carefully and expressed clearly; avoiding all strong language: simply stating, – first the cause of the offence; secondly, the reason why he considers it his duty to notice the affair; thirdly, the name of his friend; and lastly, requesting a time and place be appointed.' This format would certainly go some way to answering the question of why a man should want to shoot someone in the first place.

The more sober and level-headed duellists laid down their intentions in writing, and this was certainly the action of David Landale when he corresponded with his adversary George Morgan, who had struck him with a cane in the street. Several notes could pass between the antagonists before the duel was convened, during which passage the seconds could try to bring about a solution. But should all avenues fail then the duel would be fought.

With the intention to duel made known, and the challenged party made aware of the reason why, then the location of the affair had to be settled on. The various rules and guidelines did not agree on who had the choice of the spot, with some specifying the challenged party had the right to choose the place. But nearly all agree on one thing, that the affair should be conducted 'away from the haunts of men, and also from any quarter that has been recently often used as a resort for that purpose'. Large open spaces such as the parks around London, including Battersea, Wimbledon Common and Hounslow Heath were sprawling enough to avoid duels being held in the same spot. Likewise, the Bois de Boulogne near Paris could accommodate duellists.

With stringent laws against duelling, some duellists went to extraordinary lengths to avoid being detected in their mission, and having the affair halted by the authorities. In their duel, Pipon and Janvrin sailed to the rocky islet of Chausey where they were nearly arrested by French troops in 1803, but for the most part those involved in duels travelled to the appointed spot either on horseback or in a carriage. Edward Sackville and Lord Bruce were accompanied to the Netherlands with their seconds to conduct a duel. In America duellists could cross from one country or state to another to avoid interference, and in 1839 Lord George Loftus and Lord Harley sailed to Boulogne in France, exchanged shots and returned to Dover within a day. Lord Valentia and Henry Gawlor sailed to Hamburg in 1796 to fight their duel in a remote spot just outside the confines of the city. Lord Valentia was hit in the chest but remained calm enough for the doctor in attendance to remove the bullet at the scene of the duel. He survived the experience and returned back to England.

The reason for conducting duels in remote places was to avoid being disturbed or discovered by passers by, but there was no guarantee that someone would not just happen to stumble across the meeting. When duellists were discovered in the course of their affair they were either forced to postpone the event, or one of the seconds could be sent out to find another location.

Duels by their very nature were complicated affairs to arrange, for men's lives were in the balance, and there were many points of conduct to be arranged in addition to the time and place of the meeting. For example, at what distance would the principals stand apart and how many shots would they exchange? The seconds were responsible for pacing out the agreed distance and placing their man in the right spot. Pistols would be prepared and handed to the principals and the command to fire given. The practice would be repeated until the number of shots had been fired or someone was wounded. One recommended position for a duellist was:

> [to] stand with his right and left shoulder in a line with the object he wishes to hit; his head bent to the right, and his eyes fixed on the object. His feet should be almost close together; his left arm hanging down, and his right holding the pistol, with the muzzle pointing to the ground close to his feet. He should keep his shoulders well back, and his stomach rather drawn in: then stamping his feet twice or thrice on the ground to feel that he stands firmly, let him raise his right arm steadily, bending it at the elbow, and, drawing the pistol into a line with the object, bring that part of the arm between the shoulder and elbow close to the side, throw out the muscles strongly and let it cover the breast as much as possible.

The suggestion that the firing arm should be bent at the elbow and the upper part of the arm pushed firmly against the body to give a steady aim is a difficult stance to assume, and one made all the more difficult when someone is shooting in return. Modern pistol shooters have tried this stance and report that it is very uncomfortable and that a straight arm is much better. But duellists were expected to raise their arm to fire as soon as they were level with their opponent and not to take deliberate aim. The shot would be taken in a fraction of a second and never intended to be held for any time. Thus, an arm bent at the elbow was never going to make a great deal of difference over that of a straight arm, apart from when controlling the weapon after firing, when the force of the recoil would jerk the arm.

Positive aiming was generally frowned on in Britain and principals were admonished for such conduct, but in Prussian states it was permitted and in America, Andrew Jackson took a calculated aim which killed his opponent Charles Dickinson in 1806.

The signal to fire could be verbal by either second or by a signalled action, or, the principals might fire at their leisure. These alternatives were covered by the 1777 Clonmel Rules but another way was to flip a coin. In America principals could draw lots to see who fired first.

When the word of command was given both principals had to fire in unison or at least as close together as possible. It was all very democratic and unbiased. Once the principals had arrived at the appointed spot where the duel was to take place, the most difficult part of the meeting still lay ahead for those involved. It would have required extraordinary effort for each man to make the journey to their date with destiny, but the events being played out were of the individual's own choosing. Had words or actions been conducted with more prudence the challenge to duel would not have been issued. Discretion is the better part of valour, but there was nothing discreet in a heated atmosphere as the argumentative exchange of words becomes a challenge to exchange shot from a pistol.

We will never know how many walked out to the duelling field wondering how they came to be there. For the most part the contestants were resolved to complete the duel, while for others, the prospect of ordeal by gunfire would have been terrifying. How does one stop hands and legs shaking uncontrollably and suppress nerves to even speak coherently and understand events as they unfold?

Fear can also paralyse and, just as rabbits caught in the headlights of a car are too frightened to move out of harm's way, so too did some duellists find themselves unable to move through fear. This fact had been observed on a number of occasions, enough for it to be covered in the pages of *The Art of Duelling*, in which 'A Traveller' wrote:

> It requires some nerve to elevate the hand, and keep the pistol perfectly steady, when the muzzle of an adversary's weapon is directed upon you, and when aware that a very few moments will bring its contents much closer than is agreeable.

Despite the note of levity in this remark, standing before a man with a loaded pistol took enormous human effort. Men were known to faint when the order to fire was uttered and there is at least one instance of a duellist being literally scared to death. In France, in January 1812, one of the antagonists died from a heart attack, no doubt brought on by fear at the prospect of being killed.

In most instances, however, any fear would have been repressed in order to avoid showing any outward emotion, and duellists coolly took their stance and conducted themselves as gentlemen. In effect, there was no way of knowing or predicting how someone would react when the time came to conduct the duel. Would the duellist see it through or would he cry off at the last moment regardless of what his peers may think of him for such a cowardly act?

Fear could cause other problems, and in his terror the duellist could misunderstand certain parts of commands. Just as with athletes 'jumping the gun', causing a false start to a race, so too could duellists fail to hear certain orders, and misinterpret 'Ready, aim, fire' to just hear the word 'fire' and shoot at the opponent. In such cases the mistake was often deadly.

It would appear that it was a series of misunderstandings which led to the fateful encounter between Captain Smith of the 32nd Regiment of Foot (later to become The Duke of Cornwall's Light Infantry) and Standish Staner O'Grady, a barrister in the city of Dublin in Ireland.

The incident which led to the duel occurred one day in March 1830, as O'Grady was riding his horse down Nassau Street in the city when Captain Smith and his fellow officer Captain Markham drove past in a carriage. They passed so close to O'Grady that his horse was forced onto the pavement, causing it to lose its footing. As the animal slipped, O'Grady tried to retain his balance in the saddle and in so doing his hand holding the riding whip slapped Captain Smith's carriage. The movement was probably a natural instinct; it is unlikely that O'Grady meant to cause offence and his action may have been without malice and certainly was not premeditated. The carriage containing the two officers continued its journey for a short distance before coming to a halt. Captain Smith then alighted and retraced his passage to confront O'Grady. Until that point neither man had exchanged a word and, as far as is known, had never before met. What happened next was conduct unbecoming an officer and gentleman. Captain Smith using a whip began to lash out at O'Grady, who must have been bewildered by this assault upon his person. It was only at this point that Captain Smith identified himself as a serving officer in the 32nd Regiment, before returning to his carriage and continuing his journey. Gathering his composure O'Grady rode to his father's house where he met with an acquaintance, Lieutenant MacNamara, whom he asked to act his second; he intended to challenge Captain Smith to a duel as a consequence of his actions.

Of all the insults likely to cause a duel it was the physical striking of a person that was considered the most serious and there could be no settlement of the affair until honour had been satisfied. No amount of protestations or the proffering of apologies could assuage the assault upon the person. In his role as second Lieutenant MacNamara duly undertook the task of delivering to Captain Smith the formal challenge to meet O'Grady in a duel the next morning. Events had unfolded probably faster than anyone could have realised. The time taken between the alleged striking of the carriage by O'Grady and Captain Smith's assault could only have been minutes. After being assaulted, a couple of hours more would have passed and feelings would have still been very inflamed.

At this time, it should be remembered, that officers in the British Army purchased their commissions, a custom that would not be rescinded until 1871. The cost of purchasing commissions depended on the rank desired and the regiment in which one was seeking service. For example, the rank of Lieutenant Colonel in a regiment of the Foot Guards would cost £6,000, while the same rank in a Dragoons regiment was £3,200. James Brudenall, 7th Lord Cardigan, is understood to have paid more than £20,000 for the command of the 11th Light Dragoons which he would lead at the famous Charge of the Light Brigade in October 1854 during the Crimean War.

Yet, even he was prepared to risk all this investment when he fought a duel against Harvey Tuckett in September 1840.

Captain Smith's commission had probably cost him at least £1,000 while Lieutenant MacNamara would have purchased his rank for about £300. Military protocol called for all officers to accept challenges to duel, especially if the honour of the regiment was to be upheld, and to refuse any challenge was tantamount to cowardice. The affair between Captain Smith and Mr O'Grady was convened for 6 a.m., and the fatal misunderstanding happened as follows:

> Captain Markham [Captain Smith's second] then gave the first signal to fire; but from whatever cause, he did not give it in the terms fixed upon. He said, 'Gentlemen, are you ready?' or 'Are you ready, gentlemen?' Mr O'Grady conceived the word was to be 'Ready! Fire!' and that this was a preliminary inquirey [*sic*]. Captain Smith, however, did not labour under this mistake; he levelled his pistol, and covered Mr O'Grady for a few seconds. Mr O'Grady perceiving his antagonist prepared, raised his pistol; but, before he had levelled it, Captain Markham, whose eye was upon him, gave the signal. Captain Smith fired, and Mr O'Grady fell.

The civilian died the following day, and for their part in the affair, Captains Smith and Markham where charged with manslaughter and sentenced to one year in prison.

Sometimes fear struck a duellist to such a degree that he pleaded for his life. This is what happened during a duel fought in Salisbury in December 1784. The details are rather vague and neither duellist is named and the cause is not entirely clear either. Apparently an argument broke out between a gentleman and a clergyman, with the result that a challenge to duel was made by the clergyman. It appears that his unnamed opponent had a wife and young family and was reluctant to take part in the duel. Dismissing his opponent's reticence to fight, the clergyman insisted on the duel. It is known that arrangements were made and the two men did meet.

The duel began in the time-honoured tradition of standing back-to-back and pacing out the distance before turning and firing. The challenging cleric fired first and missed his man. Left totally vulnerable, he should have behaved like a gentleman and stood steady to receive his opponent's shot. Instead, his courage left him and the clergyman slumped to the ground and pleaded for clemency. In view of the belligerency of the cleric at the start of the duel, to now witness him grovelling prostrate before him, the unknown duellist would have looked at his challenger with disdain. He took pity on the man and spared his life. We do not know if either principal in this case had ever fought a duel before. In the case of the clergyman we can safely assume he had not, and in view of his conduct in this instance it is unlikely he was ever again rash enough to challenge anyone to a duel.

Six years earlier in November 1778 in the town of Bath, some 40 miles north-west of Salisbury, the Viscount Du Barrè and Count Rice met in a hastily arranged duel following a dispute over a game of cards. At the time, Bath was a city revelling in its reputation as a place of elegance, an epithet it had been enjoying since 1702 during the reign of Queen Anne. During the 1750s Bath was popular with aristocracy, including foreign nationals, and this popularity was due in large part to one of the city's leading figures, Richard 'Beau' Nash, who instigated a series of public works.

Nash had risen to prominence when the city's Master of Ceremonies, Captain Webster, was killed in a duel over a game of cards. With his air of sophistication Nash was the natural successor, and it was he who banned the wearing of swords within the city and oversaw the ejection of thieves to make the population feel safer. However, Bath gained notoriety as a centre for gambling and card houses flourished. Indeed, it was in one such card house in the Royal Crescent, operated by the Irish-born Count Rice, that Rice fell into an argument with the French Viscount Du Barrè. Gambling in those days involved very high stakes and fortunes could be won or lost at the turn of a card. One such gambler of the day was Charles James Fox who is believed to have lost £140,000 – a vast sum – in a period of three years. Fox was a Member of Parliament and a wealthy man, who would later take his stand in a duel against William Adam in November 1779 and live to tell the tale.

The argument between Rice and Du Barrè, who was the husband of 'Madame Du Barry', the mistress of King Louis XIV of France, led to a challenge to a duel being issued, and a coach was summoned to take the two men and their seconds to Claverton Down just outside the city. The coach arrived from the Three Tuns public house in Stall Street at 1 a.m. on 18 November, to transport the party to the appointed place where the duel was to be conducted. There was some discrepancy concerning the date of this fateful meeting, with some accounts placing the duel in 1773. However, according to a report held on file at the *Bath Chronicle* newspaper the duel was fought in 1778. This confusion is cleared by visiting the cemetery at St Nicholas's Church in the village of Bathampton, where the body of Du Barrè lies, and the date of the duel is inscribed on the tomb which gives us incontrovertible proof.

Each of the duellists went well-armed, bearing a brace of pistols and a sword, ready to engage in a form of duel sometimes referred to as 'hybrid', to denote that both forms of weapons were used. The seconds paced out the distance at which the men were to fire, and as the first rays of the winter sun brought enough light to the proceedings Rice and Du Barrè took their appointed places. The Viscount was first to fire and hit Rice in the thigh with his opening shot. Rice remained composed and returned fire, hitting the Viscount in the chest. The men then fired a second time, but one pistol misfired and the other shot missed the target. The men then drew their swords and began to advance, ready to cross blades. As they drew near Du Barrè threw himself on the ground and asked to be spared, but it was already too late; the wound to his chest was fatal. Realising his opponent's weakened state Rice acquiesced and gave him the quarter he asked. Du Barrè succumbed to his wound and died within moments of being spared. How much of the Viscount's prostrations were caused through loss of blood due to his wound or a genuine plea to be spared further pain is a question which can never be answered. He had certainly remained in control of his actions until the very last and it could have been the point of passing out, due to loss of blood, which allowed his fear of dying to come to the surface.

The body of the Viscount remained on Claverton Down until the following day and was later interred in the church in Bathampton. Rice recovered from his wound and was arrested on the charge of murder. He was tried at Taunton in Somerset and was acquitted after the coroner returned the verdict of manslaughter. His title, position and reputation in the town meant he had good influential contacts, which almost certainly added to his acquittal. As for the late Viscount's widow, Jeanne 'Madame du Barry', she returned to France, and fifteen years later in 1793 was executed during France's 'Reign of Terror', when the Revolutionary mob sent her and other aristocrats to the guillotine.

Firearms of the period could inflict terrible wounds and none more so than the 'blunderbuss'. It had a flared muzzle which spread the shot of a number of small projectiles and at close quarters it was lethal. In the seventeenth century, just when pistol duels were becoming more common, there was also a rise in the crime rate involving firearms.

One such victim of firearms was Thomas Thynne, who is believed to have been killed on the orders of John Philip, Count of Konigsmark, who is understood to have arranged the murder to look like a robbery gone wrong. Thynne was shot at close quarters by one of the perpetrators using a blunderbuss. His body was examined by Mr Hobbs, a surgeon, who recorded how he 'found in Thynne's body four bullets which had torn into his Guts, wounded his Liver, and Stomach, and Gall, broke one Rib, and wounded the great Bone below'. He concluded his observations by adding: 'Of which Wounds he dyed.' The weight and calibre of a pistol ball varied but even one of average size could inflict terrible wounds by smashing bones and rupturing vital organs. While pistols were the preferred weapon of choice for duellists, there is only one occasion where the 'blunderbuss' has been selected by the principals, and that was under extraordinary circumstances (*see* chapter 6).

Some guidelines advocated that duellists should wear dark clothes with cloth buttons, so that a shining button could not be used as a point of aim. Dark clothing not only prevented a man taking precise aim, it also reflected the solemnity of the occasion. Illustrations of the day show duels being conducted by men dressed in long frock coats and wearing top hats. The Duke of Wellington, duelling against Lord Winchilsea, is shown dressed in such a manner, as are the French politicians Deroulède and Clemenceau. In the Germany which came about after the unification of the Prussian States, the attire of the duellist was almost always black frock coats and top hats. In Italy a set of guidelines advised wearing tip (top) hat and frock coat and recommended that the principals should agree prior to the duel whether trousers should be secured by belt or braces.

In County Sligo in Ireland a duel was fought between Thomas Fenton and Major Hillas in 1816, which showed how sometimes this form of thinking could be proved wrong. Fenton being a civilian was dressed in normal clothes, but Major Hillas broke from tradition and divested himself of his top coat to show that he was wearing a bespoke waistcoat made with long black sleeves. This display of fashion was among the last things the Major ever did because Fenton shot him dead.

It was also advised that a man should turn up the collar of his coat so that the white material of his shirt did not attract the eye and allow an aim to be drawn on the spot. But no matter what one did to try and avoid being hit, if one's opponent was steady and had a good eye for shooting, he was going to hit his target.

Dark may have been advised for the dueller's attire, but some duellists took to the field of honour with a considerable flair. In 1827 the Irish judge Sir Jonah Barrington published his memoirs, *Personal Sketches of His Own Times*, in which he describes his first duel. His adversary was a young man from Galway by the name of Richard Daly and Barrington wrote of the affair:

> At 7am with a cold wind and sleet, I set out with my second, the brother of Sir Edward Crosby, for the field of Donnybrooke Fair, having taken some chocolate and a plentiful draught of cherry brandy to keep out the cold. On arriving we saw my antagonist [Daly] and his second, Jack Patterson, nephew of the Chief Justice, already on the ground.

Daly has been described as a 'macaroni', a term for someone who had taken the 'Grand Tour' of Italy in search of culture, and sometimes affected the habit of dying one's hair yellow as a mark of fashion of the day. On the occasion of his duel he is described as wearing a pea-green coat, a large tucker (a form of large flamboyant lace collar) pinned with a diamond brooch, a three-cocked hat with a gold button loop and tassels and silk stockings. His appearance must have caused something of a stir and Barrington's second whispered: 'Never aim at the head or heels. Hip the macaroni! The hip forever my boy!' Here the second was advocating that the principal aim deliberately, in order to permanently cripple his opponent by shooting him in the hip. Perhaps not entirely ethical, but it may reflect the level of contempt in which Daly was held. The future judge continued his description of the encounter:

> Daly presented his pistol but gave me most gallantly a full front. I let fly without a moment's delay. Daly staggered back two or three steps, put his hand to his breast and cried: 'I'm, hit, Sir!' He did not fire. We opened his waistcoat and a black spot, the size of a crown piece with a little blood, appeared directly over his breast bone. The ball had not penetrated, but his brooch had been broken and a piece of the setting was sticking fast in the bone. Daly put his cambric handkerchief to his breast and bowed. I returned his salute and we parted without conversation or ceremony.

This meeting has a number of interesting aspects about it, not the least of which is why Daly should present himself facing his opponent 'full front', when all guidelines suggested standing side on so as to present a narrow target. One observer on duelling wrote: 'The risk in duelling may be considerably lessened by care in the matter of turning the body towards the adversary.' It was good advice and he continues: 'I have often seen a raw, inexperienced fellow expose his person most unnecessarily, standing with full front towards his antagonist…' Daly was certainly lucky that the bullet hit his brooch, otherwise the projectile would certainly have penetrated his chest and possibly killed him. Despite his foppish appearance Daly was no whimpering 'Dandy' and like Barrington showed every determination to see the duel through. Certainly neither man could be accused of lacking courage. Daly probably only held his fire because he thought himself to be more seriously injured than was actually the case. This was quite understandable, because to be hit in the chest by a pistol ball would have stunned him and the pain of the impact would be indistinguishable from a more serious wound. When both men departed in silence, apart from a courteous salute, they were continuing a practice which was quite common in the aftermath of a duel. Even when the meeting was fatal, the surviving duellist in some cases rarely even glanced back at his adversary, as though showing him every disdain even in death.

Daly's dress code for the occasion may have been ostentatious when all conventions suggested that dark colours be worn; a gentleman's clothes were well tailored to show his wealth, that he could afford a good tailor and his coat would contour to his body. Even so, adversaries were obliged to unbutton their coats to show they were not wearing any form of padding which could limit any wounding in the event of being hit by a bullet. General Andrew Jackson, in his meeting against Charles Dickson in May 1806, wore a rather baggy coat even though he not yet 40 years of age and still in his prime. Jackson's attire was later commented on by an authority, who noted the fact and came to the conclusion that it was a ruse on Jackson's part to fool his opponent:

> There is one feature about this duel that seems a little peculiar, and that is that General Jackson, who was a very spare man in his person, should have been dressed in a loose-fitting gown or coat, so that his antagonist could not readily tell the location of his body. Dickinson aimed right; and if Jackson's body had been where Dickinson supposed it was, and where the code duello would say it ought to have been, there is no reason to doubt that Jackson would at that time have 'passed in his checks' [that is to say that Dickinson would have shot him dead] … Having dressed in a manner to deceive Dickinson as to the precise location of his body, and having received Dickinson's bullet without serious injury, it was not a just, fair thing in Jackson afterwards to take deliberate aim at Dickinson and kill him.

Jackson had not contravened any aspect of the Code Duello but had merely taken advantage of the suggested dress code for the affair. Whether it was his intention to do so remains unanswered and to assume otherwise is purely speculation. Dickinson stood as good a chance as any man, given that he had only a fraction of a second in which to fire and would have been unable to take precise aim. Accuracy only comes with practice and two men firing at the same target will always produce different results.

It has been calculated that the chances of a duellist being killed during a meeting stood at about fourteen to one. The chance of being shot has been calculated at around six to one. Indeed, 'Traveller', in his work *The Art of Duelling*, claims that a man stood a three-to-one chance against being killed, a figure he reaches after examining the results of some 200 duels.

In the case of Andrew Jackson it could be argued that he was within his rights, as far as the duel was concerned, to return fire despite his injury – for Dickinson had hit him in the ribs – issuing a steady shot which killed Dickinson. On the matter of aiming and accuracy Traveller wrote:

> A person can never fire with accuracy unless he aims at some small object. Were he to endeavour to hit a man, he would probably miss him: but

if he aimed at one of the buttons of his coat, the ball is almost certain, providing he is a passable shot, to strike within a circle of two or three inches around it.

But if all duellists followed the guidelines and wore black with no embellishments, to prevent their opponent aiming with any accuracy, the Traveller's suggestion would be pointless, as was the case with Andrew Jackson.

For the most part duels were conducted on as even a basis as could be determined. It was of no great consequence to, say, an army officer if his opponent had never fired in anger or even fired at all. For when it came down to it even a novice stood as good a chance as hitting, and probably even killing, his opponent as even the most experienced shot. There were rare occasions when a duel became little more than murder. In the aftermath of Napoleon's defeat at Waterloo in June 1815, the Allies occupied Paris and the French monarchy was reinstated; but even so hardly a day went by without a duel being fought.

However, duelling was not confined to the English and French, the Prussians could on occasion also become involved. In 1816, during the course of a ball being held at Faubourg St Honore, the French Admiral de la Susse argued with a Prussian and the two agreed to meet in the Bois de Bolougne to resolve their differences in a duel. The Prussian fired first but missed. The Admiral took aim and fired, hitting his opponent, who amazingly appeared unharmed. Closer inspection revealed the Prussian had been wearing a breastplate which had stopped the bullet.

Eventually, such meetings grew less frequent and, as tempers cooled, the post-Waterloo duels ran their course. But this was France and duels continued to be conducted for other reasons.

The regulations concerning duels even had suggestions on how a man should stand during a duel. The side-on stance was considered best as it presented a narrow target, but a man could always do more to reduce the possibility of being hit during the exchange of fire. Traveller wrote on this point and questioned why a man would want to stand in any other position than side on, when he would offer 'the other party a much larger surface to fire at than the laws of duelling require, rendering, of course, the danger to himself greater'.

In 1887 William Douglas wrote about George Robert Fitzgerald, a well-known duellist, in his work *Duelling Days in the Army*. He did not know Fitzgerald personally, because the hot-headed Irishman had been hanged 100 years earlier. However, by using contemporary accounts Douglas was able to piece together the technique used by the man called

'Fighting Fitzgerald', who had fought twenty-seven duels by the age of 48. At the time of his execution aged 59 in 1786 it has been estimated that he may have fought at least twelve further duels, bringing his total to thirty-nine duels by the age of 59 years. Douglas describes Fitzgerald taking his stance:

> ... to bend his head over his body until the upper portion of him resembled a bow ... His right hand and arm were held in front of his head in such a manner that a ball should pan all the way up his arm before it touched a vulnerable part.

In this way he could apparently reduce his slim build by a height of some 6in, a considerable feat, and greatly reduced his chances of being hit. Fitzgerald's techniques may have appeared strange but were perfectly acceptable under the regulations of duelling codes. But that is not to say his style prevented him from being wounded.

Born in 1748 to a wealthy Irish family with titles he was a polite, studious man having been educated at Eton and Trinity College in Dublin. All that changed when he was badly wounded in the head during his first duel. The wound affected him mentally and there were notable changes in his mood. His temper became quick and ferocious, leading to many challenges to duel. He married a wealthy Irish lady and they travelled to France in 1772. They returned to Ireland three years later heavily in debt.

Not all of his challenges to duel were conducted in accordance with rules of the day, and some of his encounters could be interpreted as murder, after having bullied his opponent into meeting him to settle affairs of honour. In 1786 his luck ran out, and he was arrested for the murder of Patrick McDonnell who Fitzgerald had shot during a meeting which did not resemble a duel in any shape or custom. He was sentenced to hang and after the execution, which aroused great interest, a local newspaper published an account of Fitzgerald's battered body. It described it as being:

> ... scarred with wounds, which he had received in the various duels he had been engaged in. There was a large hole where a ball had lodged in one of his hips, another in the small of one of his legs; his head had been trepanned...

The account mentions many scars due to swords wounds, and the reference to his head being trepanned no doubt dated back to the time of his first duel when part of his skull was shot away. Why anyone would want to put himself through the ordeal of fighting a duel more than once is a difficult question to answer. There were those who thrilled at the prospect of danger, and there were those who could not help it and found themselves the victim of circumstances at they were thrust into fighting a duel against their will. There was no profile to define a would-be duellist and any man could find himself involved in a duel if he was unfortunate enough to be in the wrong place at the wrong time. In which case there was usually only one way out and that was to fight the duel.

But time would tell and opinions were beginning to change, and aggrieved parties were discovering that it was profitable to take someone to court over libellous or slanderous actions rather than take the deadly course of engaging in a duel. At least in a court of law there would be a settlement, but on the field of honour fate could decide otherwise and the aggrieved person end up dead.

The laws forbidding duelling could have been enforced more rigorously, but duellists were resourceful at finding remote locations to conduct their affairs; plus, the fact that a duel was about to be fought was not something to be bandied about like idle gossip. Over the years duellists had been threatened with a range of punitive punishments, including from having one's hands cut off, banishment or even hanging. Other measures included a term in prison, a fine or one's estate being confiscated. None of these measures worked as a deterrent and duelling continued. The authorities knew duels were being convened and details were carried in the newspapers. The duellists knew their activities were tolerated, but they had to be careful not to go beyond the limits; examples had been set, with executions taking place such as those carried out on George Fitzgerald and Major Campbell.

But duelling still flourished.

On the day of the duel a principal was in the care of his second, but in the hours before the affair he was alone with his thoughts and many men spent the time putting their affairs in order. In most instances their wives or families did not know of the ordeal which lay ahead of them and if they did, there would have been little they could have done to prevent it. Like a man awaiting his execution, the night before a duel would have been a long, almost endless time.

There were a number of published observations on the hours before a duel, which suggested that a man may wish to spend the time in the company of friends, playing cards and having a few drinks. Not that many duellists would have felt jolly, or unconcerned about their impending fate, even those who had fought several duels. Some authorities suggested reading a book, such as a romantic novel, or perhaps trying to relax quietly.

Nervous tension would have increased as the hour approached when one was summoned to depart, and a man could reflect on his life. Businessmen and landowners would become absorbed by the last minute details of setting right their affairs and the time would have flown by. Composing one's last will and testament was common as though anticipating almost certain doom. One man who had such a sense of his own death was Lieutenant General Thomas, who in 1783 wrote his farewell note almost like a prayer:

Almighty God, I commit to you my soul in hopes of mercy and pardon for the irreligious step I now (in compliance with the unwarranted customs of this wicked world) put myself under the necessity of taking life.

He was killed the next day when he faced his adversary. Forty-four years later, an American by the name of W.G. Graham wrote his farewell note in a manner which was full of resignation to his fate: 'It is needless for me to say I heartily protest and despise this absurd mode of settling disputes. But what can a poor devil do except bow to the supremacy of custom?' He too was killed when he stepped onto the duelling field in 1827.

The anonymous 'Traveller' countenanced that a duellist should be:

… cool, collected and firm, and think of nothing but placing the ball on the proper spot. When the word is given, pull the trigger carefully and endeavour to avoid moving a muscle in the arm or hand – move only the forefinger and that with just sufficient force to discharge the pistol.

It all sounds so very simple and straightforward when written like that. An author, Joseph Conrad had fought a duel against Captain J.K. Blunt, an American, while living in Marseilles in France in 1878. Conrad had been wounded in the chest and was lucky to survive the ordeal, so his words on the subject hold more relevance than those of someone reluctant to give their name. Conrad wrote:

A duel, whether regarded as a ceremony in the cult of honour, or even when reduced in its moral essence to a form of manly sport, demands a perfect singleness of intention, a homicidal austerity of mood.

He knew that duelling could be a case of kill or be killed and that a duellist had to be focused on the task which lay ahead.

★★★

The question of whether to eat and drink anything prior to a duel was rather vexed. Some authorities suggested a man should, while other sources advised against it. If a man did eat a meal before his meeting and then was shot in the stomach, he would almost certainly die of peritonitis. In 1852 an American newspaper editor by the name of Henry De Courcy was shot in the stomach during his duel, but he survived the wounding. The reason for his good fortune was due to the fact that his second had kept him confined in a room for 48 hours prior to the duel and allowed him only drinks of tea. The result was that when the bullet hit him, it passed through the soft tissue and missed the vital organs and intestines.

Some advocated a drink of tea or coffee and a biscuit be taken to settle the nerves. A man was permitted to smoke if he thought it might have a calming effect, but apart from that it was unlikely that any duellist would have been in a frame of mind to eat a hearty meal before his meeting, regardless of the time of day. On the subject of the use of alcohol as an aid to steadying a man's nerves it was suggested that no more than a small measure be taken. If more was taken it could act as a suppressant due to the numbing effects alcohol could have on someone's responses. One did not want to be killed for having over-indulged; therefore, moderation was recommended until the affair was over. With all these factors taken into consideration, all that remained was for the principals to conduct themselves properly as true gentlemen and obey the rules of the duel as agreed on at the outset. Should a man choose to delope or fire wide, that was down to the individual and did happen on occasion to simply prove a point. It was to convey that the intention was there and the duel was going to be seen through to the very end.

Once the agreed number of shots had been taken or someone was either killed or wounded then the affair was deemed to be concluded. The principals and their attendants would depart the ground without passing comment lest something be said to renew the feud. News would then be circulated in the newspapers and the actions would become the talk of taverns, coffee rooms and dinner parlours.

The alternative to duelling was to be ever-mindful and avoid offending anyone through action or word; it was far better not to get into the situation in the first place where one had to stand with pistol in hand and shoot at a man.

1 Aaron Burr shooting dead Alexander Hamilton during their duel in 1804. It was to be the end of Burr's political career.

2 The Duke of Wellington meets with Lord Winchilsea in their duel. It was a question of honour, and satisfaction was achieved without injury.

3 Heslop's grave at Llandyfriog Church near Newcastle Emlyn. He was killed in his duel on 10 September 1814 when he was shot in the back by John Beynon.

4 The Llandyfriog Church near Newcastle Emlyn where Thomas Heslop was killed in his duel on 10 September 1814.

5 The sad and rather untidy grave of Viscount Du Barrè who was shot in a duel by Count Rice on 18 November 1778.

6 The church at Bathampton, just outside Bath, where Viscount Du Barrè is buried following his duel on Claverton Down in 1778.

7 Samuel Fortune's grave in St Thomas' Church, Haverfordwest, Wales. He was killed in a duel on 22 September 1799 by his friend John James following an argument. This shows that men killed in duels were still buried in consecrated ground despite calls forbidding such an act.

8 Recreated scene showing a principal, an officer in the British army, with his second who is loading his pistol in readiness for the duel.

9 Recreated impression of an army officer preparing to fire in a duel using a replica
flintlock pistol.

10 Recreated scene showing how a duellist might shoot his pistol during a duel.

11 Recreated scene showing how a gentleman of the period *c.*1812 might prepare for a duel using an ordinary flintlock pistol.

12 Recreated scene showing a gentleman *c.*1812 presenting his flintlock pistol, ready to fire in a duel.

13 Close-up detail showing the loading of a replica duelling pistol with the octagonal-shaped barrel.

14 Once loaded, the pistol is presented to the principal in this recreated scene showing the preparations for a duel.

15 The duellists meet on the field in this recreated scene, which shows how close the principals usually were in their meeting.

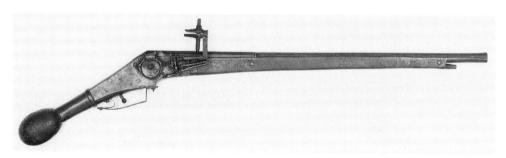

16 Example of a wheel-lock pistol, the type used by Hudson in his duel and also similar to that with which Laux Pfister shot the lady.

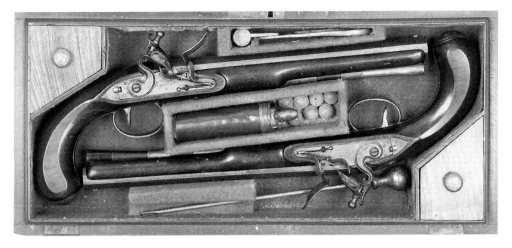

17 A cased pair of flintlock pistols showing powder flask and other items. These types of pistol were often used for duelling purposes.

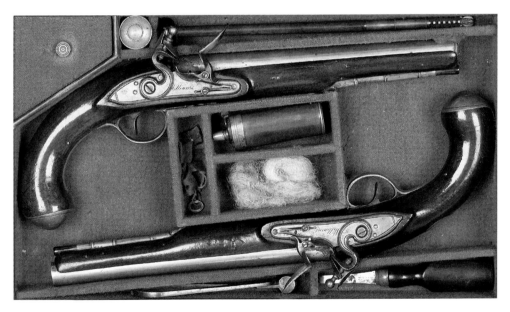

18 A cased pair of naval officers' flintlock pistols which could be used for the purposes of duelling.

19 A pair of flintlock pistols made in Ireland; before purpose-made duelling pistols, such weapons would have been used for the duel.

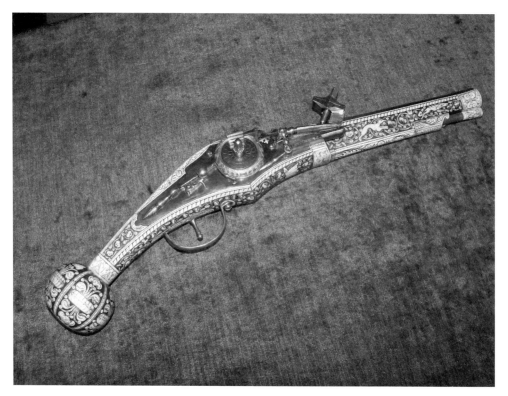

20 Wheel-lock pistol of the style used in early pistol duels, but which was replaced by the more reliable flintlock type.

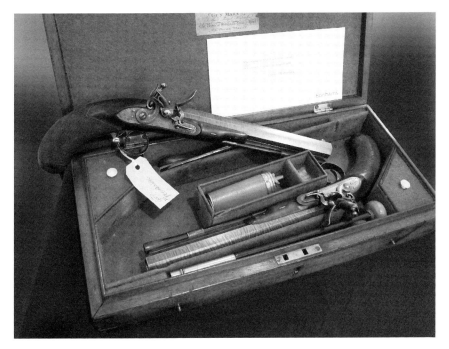

21 A cased set of duelling pistols produced by John Manton. They have the octagonal barrel which marked out duelling pistols. The case contains the ramrod and powder flask.

22 A cased pair of hexagonal-barrelled percussion pistols of a style which replaced flintlock weapons and may have been used for the purposes of duelling.

23 A cased pair of hexagonal-barrelled percussion pistols of the type which marks them out as being purpose-made duelling pistols. Notice the front 'bead' sight and the cross hatching on the handle to ensure a secure grip.

24 A cased pair of flintlock pistols with 'hockey-stick' type handles. This image shows the powder flask and ramrod used for loading. Twigg was a leading gunsmith who specialised in duelling pistols such as these.

4

PISTOLS AND POLITICS

From the accounts on file it would seem as though duelling was dominated primarily by military men, in those countries where affairs of honour were conducted. The records of duels where officers were involved provide us with the names of specific individuals, along with their ranks, regiment and the outcome. However, it would be remiss to think that officers in the army or navy held the monopoly when it came to defending one's honour at the point of pistol. Landed gentry and merchants resolved matters through duels and politicians displayed an equal willingness to settle matters with pistols. But while officers in the British Army would come to have their duelling activities curtailed by an amendment in the Articles of War in 1844, politicians, it seems, avoided being restrained by any similar legislation. Duelling was obviously illegal as it was tantamount to murder, but the practice was countenanced in a number of countries. Emperor Leopold of Austria issued an order in 1682 which forbade duelling and anyone caught in the act would be prosecuted, have their property confiscated and be banished from the country. The Austrian edict – like so many other such promulgations in other countries aimed at specifically stamping out duelling – had little or no effect.

Military men eventually saw the folly of engaging in duelling and it began to fall out of practice. Perhaps they considered that they already faced enough certain danger across the battlefield without exposing themselves unnecessarily to further jeopardy. Politicians, on the other hand, not facing the same hazards as officers, continued to engage in duels long after military men had ceased shooting at one another. Even into the early twentieth century duels between politicians, while not an everyday occurrence, were not unheard of and got reported in national newspapers. In 1904 the French politician Jean Juares faced fellow politician Paul

Deroulède in a duel. They fired two shots at each other, missing on all occasions. Deroulède had fought a duel against Georges Clemenceau twelve years earlier and so was experienced, but Juares was a man of peace and by the law of averages should have been at a disadvantage. The affair had settled the point of honour without fatal consequences and showed that each man in turn had the courage to stand up for his beliefs.

Politicians and government officials of many countries, from the lowliest to the most senior, appear to have participated in duels. Benjamin Roberts, while serving in the British Indian Department (native affairs) in Canada, was confronted by a gruff-looking person whom he had never seen before and from whom he gathered was called Rogers. The stranger suddenly challenged Roberts to a duel for no apparent reason and the official noticed the man was armed with pistols. To placate him Roberts agreed to meet him and decided on a place and time. He turned up at the appointed place and waited; the time for the duel came and went, but his adversary remained absent. He continued to wait but the man never showed, no doubt sober by now and the confrontation long forgotten. Roberts remained concerned, however, and forever after went about his business armed with a pistol in case his adversary turned up unexpectedly.

This was not an isolated incident in Canada and in 1800 John White was shot dead in a duel against John Small, who was serving as a government official. In the April of 1819 Dr William Caldwell and Michael O'Sullivan, a member of the Legislative Assembly of Lower Canada, met in a duel. Each fired five shots during which exchange of fire O'Sullivan was hit twice and Caldwell's arm was shattered. Canada may have been an untamed frontier country but it was not as entirely lawless as one might imagine.

Politicians have been accused of putting personal matters before the affairs of state when engaging in duels. But when challenged they were in a most invidious position. If they elected *not* to take up pistols they would be seen as cowardly and lose face in public opinion. However, if they *took up* pistols to defend themselves and their honour they were equally vilified for being reckless. Even in Russia politicians engaged in duels, such as Pavel Kiselyov, who was shot and killed by his adversary General Ivan Mordvinov in 1823. The Russian author Mikhail Lermentov was killed in a duel in 1841, and five years earlier the Tsar of Russia Nicholas I had been challenged to a duel.

It is difficult to say with any great certainty when the first duel was fought using pistols, but among one of the earliest political casualties was Sir Chlomey Dering, MP for Kent, who was shot dead by his adversary Mr Thornhill in 1711. Following that incident a great number of political figures engaged in duels, some of which ended in either tragedy or disgrace.

In November the following year James, 4th Duke of Hamilton and Charles, 4th Baron Mohun, fatally stabbed each other with swords during their duel, which also saw their respective seconds wounded in the fight. For some men their political career was ruined because of their rashness to engage in a duel. Swords were still used on occasion, such as the fight which broke out between Horace Walpole and William Chatwynd, both Members of Parliament, following an exchange of words in the House of Commons in 1743. Blades had been crossed but such displays were becoming rarer as swords were gradually discarded as a fashion accessory for gentlemen.

Twenty years after his own encounter Horace Walpole would pass comment on another politically motivated duel. In 1763 John Wilkes published a journal called the *North Briton* and through its pages he made political criticisms which not unnaturally caused him to make enemies. One of his targets was Samuel Martin, MP for Camelford and secretary to the Treasury, who he accused of corruption. This was a grave charge and on learning that Wilkes was the author of this tract Martin issued a challenge to a duel. They agreed to meet at the somewhat unusual time of 1 p.m. on 16 November 1763 in Hyde Park and exchange two shots each, for which purpose four pistols would be used. The affair appears to have been also unusual because both principals moved as though trying to avoid being hit in the exchange of fire. Wilkes fired first and missed but caught Martin off guard by suddenly producing his second pistol without warning. Martin, who had not fired until this point, fired at the same instant that Wilkes fired his second shot. Wilkes dropped his expended pistol claiming he had been wounded. Unbuttoning his coat a red stain could be seen spreading across his abdomen. Martin believed he had killed his opponent, but the wound in reality was not so bad and Wilkes hurriedly made away from the scene.

On hearing of the affair Horace Walpole commented about Wilkes's conduct:

> Don't be frightened, the wound was not mortal – at least it was not yesterday. Being corporally delirious today, as he has been mentally for some time, I cannot tell what to say to it. However, the breed will not be lost, if he should die. You still have countrymen enough left; we need not despair of amusement.

It was caustic and rather put the man in his place, but investigations soon revealed there was a sinister move afoot concerning the duel. It emerged that Martin was in all probability urged to issue the challenge to duel by the government in an effort to silence Wilkes. The publisher discovered that the year before the duel Martin had covertly been paid the vast sum of £40,000 by the government for unspecified services. It would appear that Wilkes was right to have his suspicions but for the wrong reasons and was, in part at least, vindicated in his attack through the pages of the *North Briton*; but had learned his lesson the hard way. Horace Walpole would also make comment on Charles Fox's duel in 1779, but on that occasion the government had nothing to do with its arrangements.

On 25 May 1798 the English Prime Minister William Pitt – known as 'The Younger' to distinguish him from his father, also William Pitt, an elder statesman who was created Earl of Chatham – entered the House of Commons in London and braced himself for a tough political debate. The frail man plagued with ill health, which belied his 39 years, was to present an Emergency Bill to the Commons calling for an increase in the manpower for the Royal Navy to deal with the war against France. The country had been at war with France for several years and was anticipating a full-scale invasion mounted by Napoleon's armies.

Only the year before, a French force of some 1,500 men had landed near Fishguard in Pembrokeshire in Wales and for a few days had caused great fear across the region. This enemy landing was actually in the process of collapsing by the time the local militia forces, led by Lord Cawdor, who were of a better calibre than the rabble which had scrambled ashore at Carregwastad Point, arrived to round them up.

The main French Army was a different matter altogether and armed to a higher quality. Furthermore, the French navy was still to be reckoned with and the Royal Navy had been wracked by mutinies in 1797, which, when considered with the attack at Fishguard, highlighted the country's vulnerability to enemy naval action. Pitt wanted the country to be ready and he realised that a strong naval force would best serve the purpose for the defence of the country, regardless of the price to be paid. With seventeen years experience as a leading politician, and serving as Prime Minister since 1783, Pitt must have known that he was going to meet with opposition, but nothing could have prepared him for the events which would unfold over the next 48 hours.

Having been elected as a Member of Parliament in 1781, the same year that the British surrendered Yorktown which ended the American War of Independence, Pitt had grown up in an age when England was almost constantly at war. He was born in 1759, the year General James Wolfe captured Quebec and secured Canada for England, but it was not just war which shaped his life. He was a reformist, supporting William Wilberforce with his motion to abolish slavery, and he also repealed a number of penal laws against Roman Catholics. The other side of his character could be ruthless and he introduced the Traitorous Correspondence Act and suspended Habeas Corpus in 1794. Pitt had his loyal supporters, but he also had political enemies, so on the fateful day of his appeal to increase naval manpower he was severely barracked by George Tierney, a Foxite MP in the Whig party, who delighted in making things difficult for the Prime Minister. Tierney called for further time for the Bill to be considered, which would have effectively delayed or even stalled Pitt's proposals.

Confronted by such resistance Pitt reiterated his proposal. Tierney responded by appealing to Henry Addington (later to become Lord Sidmouth) as the speaker of the House of Commons to make a ruling on the matter. Addington prevaricated, which did nothing to ease matters and led Pitt to accuse Tierney's blocking motions as 'obstructing the defence of the country'. In effect, Tierney was being called defeatist without the term actually being used. His honour had been sullied but he showed no emotion to gave away the response he had in mind to exact his revenge. The Commons meeting was adjourned with all parties withdrawing.

Pitt did not appear to give another thought to the exchange of words and probably believed that was the end of the affair. The following day, 26 May, a letter was delivered to him from Tierney in which he was challenged to a duel on Sunday 27 May, to settle the argument. True to his character Pitt accepted and finally settled on appointing his friend Dudley Ryder to act as his second. As a matter of protocol he sent a letter to Addington, in which he made known the challenge he had received and his acceptance to meet Tierney in a duel. It can be assumed from Pitt's readiness to accept the challenge that he was almost expecting such a course of action from Tierney. Naturally he had to accept the challenge as a matter of honour if he were to retain his dignity in the House of Commons. After he had despatched the letter to Addington, Pitt set about putting his affairs in order and composing his will.

Addington, on receiving the letter outlining the duel, was taken aback with the news that the Prime Minister was even contemplating taking up pistols. He recorded the moment he received Pitt's letter:

> I was dining with Lord Grosvenor, when a note was brought me from Mr. Pitt, stating that he had received a hostile message from Mr. Tierney, and wished me to go to him, which I did as soon as the party at Lord Grosvenor's broke up. Mr. Pitt had just made his will when I arrived. He had sent in the first instance to Mr. Steele to be his second; but finding that he was absent, he sent next to Mr. Ryder. On the following day I went with Pitt and Ryder down the Birdcage Walk, up the steps into Queen Street, where their chaise waited to take them to Wimbledon Common.

As those involved in the affair gathered in the early hours on Putney Heath, the final preparations were being made as the principals and their elected seconds arrived. Pitt certainly had knowledge of firearms having been invited to attend sporting shooting parties. The firing distance of twelve paces was measured out. It had been decided that each man would fire two shots in the match after which, whatever the outcome, the matter would be declared to be ended. Tierney and Pitt both fired and each missed. Pitt then deliberately fired his second shot into the air as an almost symbolic gesture, bringing the duel to a conclusion. With both pistols now discharged and safe, Pitt then presented them to Ryder as a memento of the day's affair.

The two protagonists may have believed the matter to be over but the news was too sensational for the newspapers to ignore; they even turned on Addington who, in his position as Speaker in the Commons, they accused of not intervening stridently enough during the exchange of words between the two men which led to the duel. Tierney received severe criticism for issuing a challenge which he knew no self-respecting gentleman would back away from. As for Pitt, his Right Honourable colleague William Wilberforce joined in with the newspapers in criticising the Prime Minister for taking part in the duel and putting himself in jeopardy when the country was at war. Three days after the duel, King George III added his ire to the barrage of words on the matter when he sent a letter to Pitt in which he stated:

I trust what has happened will never be repeated. Perhaps it could not have been avoided, but it is a sufficient reason to prevent its ever being again necessary. Public characters have no right to weigh alone what they owe to themselves; they must consider what is due to their country.

The letter was a severe reprimand, but the words veil a thinly disguised semi-approval of the duel, especially the part where the king writes, 'Perhaps it could not be avoided'. Taken as a whole, the letter is really no more than a slap on the wrist. Had the affair been taken more seriously, there is no doubt the king would have summoned Pitt to give a full and personal account of his actions.

Pitt did not enjoy robust health and the duel placed a heavy strain on him physically, to the extent that he took to his sickbed and was absent from the House of Commons for a number of weeks. The gossip circulating about the duel was soon being diluted by events in Ireland, where in June that year a rebel uprising burned Enniscorthy in County Wexford and military intervention was required to restore order. More significantly, when news of Nelson's defeat of the French at the Battle of the Nile on 1 August 1798 finally reached England three months after the engagement, it overshadowed the duel and further unrest in Ireland filled the newspapers giving the public something else to talk about. The duel between Pitt and

Tierney was not to be the first or the last high-profile affair of its kind, nor was it the only occasion when a British Prime Minister exchanged fire with a Member of Parliament as a result of differences of opinion. The fact that Pitt could conduct himself in such a manner, when the country was at war, says something about his character. Did he see his meeting with Tierney as the chance of a diversion from the pressures of seeing his country through the crisis of war, or did he really believe he had to vindicate himself to prevent political humiliation? The conclusions to be drawn are numerous and no more surmountable than the accounts of duels involving the political leaders of other countries. On reflection, Pitt probably believed he had no other choice but to put aside national problems to resolve the matter which otherwise would no doubt have come back to haunt him for the remainder of his political career.

Meanwhile, on the other side of the world in India, which was at the heart of England's growing Empire, duels were being fought by army officers. On 23 December, only several months after Pitt's duel, Major Allen of the 12th Regiment of Foot (later to become the Suffolk Regiment) fatally wounded his commanding officer Colonel Henry Hervey Aston. Aston was an experienced duellist, having fought at least three duels, but here he was shot by one of his serving officers. The wound to his stomach was not immediately fatal and the colonel took a week to die. In the same year, the British Minister to Florence, William Wyndham, faced his challenger Count Carletti in an affair resulting from an incident while riding in their carriages in a park. Duelling was showing its capability of being practised from the most remote outpost of an Empire to one of the cultural centres of Europe, where it has to be said was perhaps the birthplace of the duel.

The historian Andrew Steinmetz studied a list of 172 duels fought during the reign of King George III (1760–1820) – one of which would have been the affair involving the king's son Prince Frederick, Duke of York, against Colonel Lenox – and found that 91 had resulted in death. This was quite a remarkable figure and yet only eighteen cases went to trial, of which two men were sentenced to death. Another nineteenth-century historian, Humphrey Woolich, studied a similar list of duels fought over a thirty-year period from 1803 to 1832, a time span which included the Duke of Wellington's duel, the Canning and Castlereagh affair and the duel between Lord Paget and Colonel Cadogan. He found great disparity in cases coming to court and revealed that eleven people were convicted of duelling, of which six were sentenced to death. Certainly none of the cases just mentioned came to trial which says much for having good connections, and a man could be acquitted or have the charge reduced to manslaughter should he kill his opponent in a duel if he just happened to be a politician or public figure, such as a high-ranking officer. The same could not be said for the ordinary man should he kill someone in an affair involving pistols. In such cases the accused had to take his chances.

Another leading politician of the day to find himself 'called out' to face an accuser in a duel was William Wilberforce, who was the foremost and somewhat vociferous figure calling for the abolition of slavery. The trafficking in human cargo had a history going back many centuries and by the eighteenth century the trade was still flourishing and was as well organised as the trade of any other commodity. Slaves were shipped from the continent of Africa to America, with goods such as spices and sugar brought to Britain, and ships then sailed back to Africa to collect more unfortunates destined for the plantations in the Caribbean islands and North America. This maritime route was referred to as the 'slave triangle' and the suffering was enormous. This was beginning to be recognised in the late eighteenth century and calls to abolish slavery were being voiced. Denmark abolished slavery in 1792, and in the same year the British politician William Wilberforce committed himself to the cause of ending the trade, speaking out against it on many occasions in the House of Commons. It won him some friends but it also won him a number of enemies.

In April 1792, while participating in a debate, Wilberforce highlighted the case of Captain John Kimber who had, it was alleged, flogged to death a young pregnant slave girl being transported on his ship. The case was brought to trial and Kimber accused of murder. He was acquitted of the charge which should have been an end to the sordid matter, but Kimber became filled with revenge directed against Wilberforce, who he saw as being responsible for bringing the case to court. He threatened Wilberforce with violence and demanded 'a public apology, £5,000 in money, and such a place in government as would make me comfortable'. Such demands were of course outrageous and went far beyond what he could reasonably expect to be recompense. These demands were ignored, leading to Kimber calling at the home of Wilberforce and even intercepting him in the street. The sea captain cried short of actually challenging the politician to a duel. But the affair could have ended with the men resolving the matter with pistols, had Lord Sheffield not intervened. He warned Kimber to stop harassing Wilberforce, who had taken to travelling with an armed bodyguard in his entourage, and the matter quietly faded. However, several weeks later Wilberforce found himself being berated by another sea captain, who did not prevaricate and challenged him to a duel. Although a politician, Wilberforce was not afraid to stand up to his responsibilities, but the challenge to a duel caught even him off guard. Duelling was another act which went against the politician's nature and he had no problem in dismissing the challenge.

Under normal circumstances, any man refusing to meet a challenger in a duel over an affair of honour was automatically accused of cowardice. But luckily for Wilberforce he was more thick-skinned than that and realised that any such judgement would soon become boring to those engaged in name-calling and the matter would be forgotten. He recorded his decision to refuse the duel in his journal and wrote a 'proper and easy explanation of my determination and view in respect to duelling'. In effect, he had called the man's bluff and by ignoring the challenge there was nothing anyone could do. If two men wanted to fight they could do so, likewise if a man declined then no one could force him to engage in a duel. Wilberforce received many threats against his life but he always appeared to deal with them in a casual, almost dismissive manner.

Six years later, in May 1798, he was 'more shocked than almost ever' when the Prime Minister William Pitt, who was also his colleague and friend, engaged in a duel. Even though they had been friends for many years he could not bring himself to condone it on whatever grounds it was fought, and he argued that such actions were 'the disgrace of a Christian society'. He believed duelling to be a crime and he wrote as such by recording: 'Indeed perhaps there is No Other, which mankind habitually and deliberately resolve to practise whenever the temptation shall occur.' William Pitt fought his duel on Sunday 27 May, which outraged churchgoers and religious bodies for he had contravened the sanctity of the Sabbath. When Wilberforce learned of the duel the following day, he immediately added his voice to the condemnation and resolved to 'do something if possible'. On Wednesday, only three days after the duel, he put down a motion in the House of Commons in which he condemned duelling and called for it to be outlawed. Pitt took this as a personal affront to his actions and believed it to be a call for him to stand down from his office as Prime Minister. This was not what Wilberforce had in mind and for three days he deliberated his statement before deciding he 'could not push the point'. Besides which, the country was facing the more pressing point of war with France. His outspokenness against duelling was one of the earliest examples with any weight behind the words, but it was not thought through properly. He may be viewed as being ahead of his time and indeed, there would be others who would take up the mantle calling for the abolition of duelling once and for all; Wilberforce, however, remained firm in his personal conviction that duelling should be outlawed.

By 1829 Europe had been at peace for fourteen years due to the Allied victory in June 1815, which had finally crushed Napoleon Bonaparte's designs on conquering the Continent. This period of peace had been achieved through the victory gained by the Duke of Wellington at the Battle of Waterloo. On leaving the army, Wellington entered British politics in January 1819 and took up the appointment of Master-General of the Ordnance in Lord Liverpool's Cabinet. It was a role to which he was ideally suited with his military background and for eight years he served in government. In April 1827 he temporarily left the Cabinet before agreeing to return in January 1828 to form a government and serve as Prime Minister.

Wellington was a disciplinarian and although he had strict ideals he knew when it was prudent to give ground. So it was in 1828 he conceded Catholic emancipation which gave them the right to sit in Parliament. The British voter could vote for a Catholic and elect him, but in a Protestant country that Catholic was barred from taking his seat. Wellington's decision overturned that stance and in the process won him a number of outspoken opponents who made it clear they did not agree with him. For example, Lord Eldon the Lord Chancellor, declared that 'the sun of Great Britain would be set' when a Roman Catholic sat in Parliament. Others opposed to his decision included the Duke of Newcastle and, in particular, George Finch-Hatton the Earl of Winchilsea (sometimes written as Winchelsea), who wrote a series of defamatory letters to the *Standard* newspaper in which he expressed offensive opinions about Wellington. In those days of liberalism it seems strange that such a move should create such a furore, but early nineteenth-century British politics was a fickle topic and could stir up enmity among even the most tolerant elements in society.

The question of Catholics in Parliament was one which would not go away and Wellington would not be allowed to forget. Matters finally came to a climax when Lord Winchilsea declared that in allowing Catholics to take their elected seats in Parliament Wellington must have some ulterior motive, and stated that 'under the cloak of some coloured show of zeal for the Protestant religion [he was planning] an insidious design for the infringement of our liberties and the introduction of Popery into every department of the State'. Such a tirade could not be ignored and Wellington wrote to Winchilsea requesting an apology. What was about to unfold has become one of the best recorded confrontations in British history.

Letters were exchanged between the two men, throughout the course of which correspondence Winchilsea remained unrepentant. Wellington wrote to his accuser and demanded 'that satisfaction for conduct which a gentleman has a right to require, and which a gentleman never refuses to give.' The letter to demand satisfaction in a *duel* must have been difficult for Wellington to compose, because he was known to be opposed to duelling, but it showed how far he had been provoked to issue the challenge. The appointed place for the two men to meet was Battersea Fields on Sunday 21 March 1829.

The Duke believed himself to be a creditable shot and like Pitt had participated in hunting trips and would often shoot a fair amount of game. In 1820 he told Lady Shelly: 'I have been shooting pretty well lately.' But his prowess with firearms did cause consternation on more than one occasion, such as the time he began firing wildly in all directions and terrified Lady Shelly's young daughter. On another occasion the Duke shot Lady Shelly's laundry woman to whom he made a token reparation payment of one guinea for the wound. Lady Shelly remarked to her servant, '… this ought to be the proudest moment of your life. You have had the distinction of being shot by the great Duke of Wellington.' Another victim of the Duke's poor aim was Lord Granville who received facial wounds, and gamekeepers frequently found themselves targets in Wellington's sights. Captain Thomas Browne, who had known Wellington since the Spanish Campaign, considered his commanding officer 'a very indifferent shot'.

Wellington had grown up at a time when England was invariably at war with some country around the globe. Wellington was born in 1769 and at the age of 18 his family had purchased for him the junior commissioned rank of ensign in the 73rd Regiment of Foot (later to become the Black Watch). He had fought on two continents and in 1815 faced the arch-nemesis of the European continent Napoleon Bonaparte across the battlefield at Waterloo. With this victory Wellington became the hero of the age and with so much service he was no stranger to the sound of gunfire; the acrid reek of gunpowder had filled his nostrils more times than many men. So, when he arrived at Battersea Fields he was far from nervous, having witnessed more killing in one day than many men would see in an entire lifetime. In fact, if anything, he was anxious that the whole affair be conducted with as much expediency as possible in order that he could return to the normal proceedings of his daily activities running the country.

The adversaries had elected their seconds, which in the case of Wellington was Sir Henry Hardinge, while Winchilsea nominated Lord Falmouth. The attendant doctor was John Hume, who was Wellington's physician and would play a more prominent part in the proceedings than most other doctors at a duel. To pick Hardinge as his second was a natural choice for Wellington because the two men had served together at the Battle of Waterloo, where Hardinge had lost his left hand. Now, fourteen years later he was serving in the post of Secretary at War in Wellington's Cabinet, and together the two men were facing the ultimate test in friendship. Wellington did not own his own duelling pistols and neither did Hardinge and it was he who requested that Dr Hume report to his house at 7.45 on the morning of 21 March, bringing with him a set of pistols for a meeting between 'persons of consequence'. Even without being told the background of this request, Hume would have been able to work out for himself that he was being asked to attend a duel, but he was not at this point privy to the names of the principals. This point is really all the more remarkable that, despite all his wartime trophies, Wellington should not own a set of duelling pistols, when many men of standing had a set, even if they had no intention of using them. It probably came down to the fact that he saw no need of owning such weapons because people simply did not question his decisions.

At Battersea Fields there was a calm atmosphere and Hume noted the approach of a rider who he recognised as Wellington, and noted that he was only anxious to begin the affair. He greeted his doctor with friendly familiarity: 'Well, I daresay you little expected it was I who wanted you here.' Hume spoke in a conversational tone and replied: 'Indeed, my Lord. You are the last person I should have expected here.' While waiting for the arrival of Lord Winchilsea, Wellington leaped over a small ditch and gave instructions to his second, 'Now then, Hardinge, look sharp and step out the ground ... I have no time to waste.' A distance of twelve paces was measured out at which point Wellington called out his objection to where Winchilsea was to be placed. 'Damn it, don't stick him up so near the ditch. If I hit him, he will tumble in.'

Hardinge's other duty was to prepare and load the pistols, but he was having great difficulty with only one good hand. Winchilsea's second, Lord Falmouth, was shivering severely with the cold and perhaps more than just a hint of anxiety, and was incapable of loading the pistols also. It fell to Dr Hume to complete the task, a role which went above and beyond the normal duties of a doctor attending a duel. A man of his position would normally be inconspicuous and avoid direct involvement. But here was a medical practitioner openly aiding in the preparation of a duel.

Finally all was ready and both parties satisfied with the preparations. Hardinge gave the command for the men to fire. Winchilsea's pistol arm remained lowered, suspended by his side. Noticing this, Wellington deliberately aimed wide and fired. It was a calculated gamble in the hope that his opponent lacked either the will or moral fibre to return fire with a deliberately aimed shot. He had guessed correctly and in reply Winchilsea fired in the air. After the duel the Duke declined to receive a written explanation from his opponent unless the word 'apology' was inserted. With this amendment made to the correspondence the Duke of Wellington touched his hat and said, 'Good morning, my Lords', and the two men departed with the same 'cold civility' as they had met.

An acquaintance of Wellington, George Gleig, wrote of the encounter:

> It is a curious feature in this somewhat unfortunate occurrence, that when the moment for action arrived it was found that the Duke did not possess a pair of duelling-pistols. Considering the length of time he had spent in the army, and the habits of the military society towards the close of the last century, that fact bore incontestable evidence to the conciliatory temper and great discretion of the Duke. Sir Henry Hardinge, therefore, who acted as his friend, was forced to look for pistols elsewhere, and borrowed them at last – he himself being unprovided as his principal – from Dr. Hume, the medical man who accompanied them to the ground. The combatants met in Battersea Fields, now Battersea Park. Lord Winchilsea, attended by Lord Falmouth, having received the Duke's fire, discharged his pistol in the air. A written explanation was then produced, which the Duke declined to receive unless the word 'apology' was inserted; and this point being yielded they separated.

Wellington later expressed that it was his intention to aim at his opponent's legs. He may have been a fair shot with a shotgun or musket, but with a pistol he was known to be a poor shot, in which case he may have missed had he taken aim at Lord Winchilsea. What does become evident from the conduct of the two men is that they appear to have shown themselves to be reluctant duellists, and their meeting can be viewed as a deadly charade being acted out to save face and honour. As the Duke of Wellington later confided to the Duke of Buckingham: 'The truth is that the duel with Lord Winchilsea was as much part of the Roman Catholick [*sic*] question, and it was necessary to undertake it … as it was to do with everything else that I could do to attain the object which I had in view.'

The duels fought by William Pitt and the Duke of Wellington had been convened for very different reasons, but in each case the men had shown the courage of their convictions and seen the affair through to its final conclusion. Each of the men as public figures holding the highest political office in England, should have known better than to engage in an act which could have resulted in dire consequences had either been killed by their opponent, as they held office. Each of the scenarios led to both men being held up to public ridicule in the popular press and in pamphlets, which in Pitt's case showed him as a lank, skinny figure against the more robust frame of Tierney. The *Morning Herald* proclaimed that Wellington's actions had thrown London into 'great ferment' and cartoons depicted him in the form of a lobster's claw, the colour red being an allegorical reference to his military career. The same caricature showed him garbed in a monk's robe with a rosary suspended from his waist. Rather than being incensed by this portrayal, Wellington found it most amusing. The physique between Wellington and Pitt differed greatly. After his encounter Pitt confined himself to his sickbed. Wellington, at the ripe age of 61, repaired to the home of his mistress Mrs Arbuthnot to regale her with the events of the morning, with the opening question: 'Well, what do you think of a gentleman who has been fighting a duel?' The Duke's popularity had actually been waning before his duel, but in the aftermath he received a boost and he was viewed as the hero of the day.

It seems strangely ironic in a way that although Pitt had fought his duel over a question of national defence, he promised in a statement in 1800 that Catholic emancipation would be granted. But it was not to be in his lifetime due to Protestant domination in Parliament. It would be a further twenty-nine years before Catholic emancipation actually was granted and it was the Duke of Wellington who brought it about, but, quite literally at the point of a gun across the field of honour in a duel. *The Times* of London chided in by stating:

> [the] Duke of Wellington is the last man on earth who should be called upon to defend himself by duel against any attack on his public character. We must also add, that of all men existing, Lord Winchilsea is precisely the one from whom nobody need think of demanding satisfaction for offences arising out of the Catholic question.

The final word on the matter was left to King George IV, with whom Wellington had an audience at Windsor Castle some hours after the duel. The King upbraided Wellington saying that despite 'being a soldier his Grace might be perhaps more sensitive on such points than an individual of a different class of society'. Another account of the meeting claims the king is understood to have said he was delighted with the duel and that he would have done the same. However, the fact remains that duelling was not legal, even though the King of England might approve in a taciturn way, and the two men had broken the law. The fact that neither man was charged, shows how the practice of duelling was unofficially tolerated. But if Wellington had killed Winchilsea it would have been problematical to try the Prime Minister for murder, something which had probably never even occurred to the great man himself.

Duels involving politicians always became high profile in any country; particularly so when conducted against the backdrop of war. This was never more evident than in England when William Pitt, the then Prime Minster, in 1798 fought a duel when the country was at war against France. This action was seen as putting personal matters before state affairs and led to him being reprimanded. Nine years later, and with the war against France still being fought, Lord Portland formed his government in

1807 and the conduct of the war obviously took up much of his attention. Among his ministers he appointed George Canning as Foreign Secretary and Viscount Robert Stewart Castlereagh as Secretary for War. The two men may have been serving in the same government but that is not to say they got along as political colleagues, and over the next two years they bickered and argued before their differences finally reached the stage where a duel was inevitable.

The year of 1809 was to be a busy period for duelling by eminent persons engaging in affairs of honour, beginning with Mr Powell, who shot and killed the 9th Viscount Falkland in February following a drunken argument. Just as the scandal was dying down the amorous actions of Lord Paget were uncovered, which would lead to him being challenged to a duel. He had begun an affair with Lady Charlotte Wellesley, sister-in-law to the Duke of Wellington, and when their illicit assignations were discovered by the lady's brother Colonel Cadogan he became incensed and challenged Paget to a duel. The two men met on Wimbledon Common in May and exchanged shots, as a course of honour. There was irony in the aftermath of the affair when Lady Wellesley absconded with Lord Paget, which meant her brother had put himself in the face of danger only to receive what would amount to a metaphorical slap in the face for his efforts. Around the same time the newspapers were carrying news of the first reversal for French troops who had been halted by the Austrian army at the Battle of Aspern 21–22 May 1809. Further good news in the war against France came in July that year with a stand-off for Napoleon at the Battle of Wagram on 6 July, followed by news of a French defeat in Spain by British troops at the Battle of Talavera on 28 July. Such good news showed that France could be beaten and this overshadowed any mention of duelling in the newspapers.

That was until September 1809, when the duel came which some people had been expecting, indeed predicting, for some time. Castlereagh and Canning had been at loggerheads for months, and when the 38-year-old Viscount learned of Canning's machinations to have him removed from office, that was as much as any man could take and he issued a challenge to duel with pistols. The appointed place of their meeting was Putney Heath and as his second Canning was accompanied by Charles Ellis; Viscount Castlereagh had Lord Yarmouth as his second. On the evening of 20 September Canning, who had no experience of shooting, spent the time composing his last letters and putting his affairs in order. This was a standard practice as men, fearing the worst, wrote their wills and testaments and put into writing any legacies or requests. One of his letters was addressed to his wife, to whom he wrote: 'If anything happens to me, dearest love, be comforted with the assurance that I could do no otherwise than I have done.' It was the usual, fatalistic statement to be found in hundreds of similar letters, along with his expressions of love and being resigned to his fate. Canning continued: 'I am conscious of having acted for what I thought best for my country; with no more mixture of selfish motives than the impatience of misconduct in others and of discredit to myself....' However, unlike many politicians before them, the men had the magnanimity of resigning from their official government posts before conducting the duel. That way there could be no accusations levelled against them that they put personal enmity before affairs of state.

On 21 September at 6 a.m. the two men walked out onto the field to settle their matters once and for all. They stood twelve paces apart. Canning's unfamiliarity with pistols was explained by his second Charles Ellis, to his opponent's second, stating: 'I must cock it for him for I cannot trust him to do it himself. He has never fired a pistol in his life.' In deference to this fact, Lord Yarmouth agreed as it was the gentlemanly thing to do and gave each man an equal chance. The two men fired and each missed. That should have been the signal to end the affair but it was decided that a second shot should be fired by the antagonists. On the second command to fire the shots rang out and Canning again missed, but Castlereagh's shot hit his man in the thigh. It was not fatal but it would have been painful and caused the man to walk with limp for some time after while the wound healed.

Over the next two weeks the affair was debated, and news of the duel was published in the newspapers leading the public and professional colleagues to criticise both men for their actions. Only eleven days after the Canning and Castlereagh duel, the unfortunate Major Campbell was hanged for killing Captain Boyd in his duel two years earlier. It was a stark reminder that, but for good grace, either one of the men could have met a similar fate had their affair ended fatally. Five years later, and with Napoleon Bonaparte in his first exile in 1814, Viscount Castlereagh was one of the leading figures in the Congress of Vienna to restore stability to Europe after many years of war. Sadly, his health deteriorated and in 1822 he committed suicide by cutting his throat. Canning's political career was almost ruined by the duel and he remained out of government office for several years following the affair. Serving in various positions he became Prime Minister in 1827 and died later that year aged 57 years.

Politicians continued to duel for many years after the practice had fallen out of widespread usage in the military. In some countries army officers did resort to the use of pistols, but politicians seemed to enjoy the way in which they flouted the law almost as though they wanted to excite the public with their activities. This extended up to the most senior of politicians such as the 60-year-old Charles Floquet who, in 1888, was serving as the 55th Prime Minister of France when he fought his duel.

There had been heated debates in the Chamber and exchanges led to an argument between Floquet and General Georges Ernest Boulanger, a soldier and politician who had served during the Franco-Prussian war of 1870–1, and had been involved in the defence of Paris. Floquet was a career politician but he showed no sign of wavering when he met Boulanger. In fact so resolved was he that he managed to shoot the general in the throat, but it was not a fatal wound despite the vulnerability of the area, and Boulanger could count himself lucky not to have been killed.

On the other side of the Atlantic, and four years earlier, the attitudes to duelling were changing in America as demonstrated by the reaction of Congressman John Wise on being challenged to duel by Page McCarty. Wise wrote of his refusal to give the man satisfaction: 'With a sweet home, filled with merry children, with enough to live comfortably, with a paying profession, I am happy to want to live.' He was not so much as making a plea but stating the obvious, and pointing out that duelling was coming to an end as men found better, less violent ways of settling their differences. He continued:

> In God's name, what would a man like Page McCarty put in stake against this when we stood at ten paces with pistols? His abuse of me has no more effect than a dog barking at the moon. His invitation comes too late. Time has been when I might have been fool enough to indulge in such folly, but with age, and a broader view of life and its responsibilities and duties, I have bidden farewell forever to the McCarty type of manhood.

If John Wise recognised duelling was becoming a thing of the past, others recognised it also and while some might delay it, the time when the last duel would be fought was approaching, but it was dragging its heels. In Russia at the close of the nineteenth century there was a sudden resurgence of duelling on a scale which outnumbered European countries and the United States of America. Between 1876 and 1890 there were perhaps only fifteen duels fought in Russia, but from 1894 until 1914, and at the outbreak of the First World War, a further 186 affairs were conducted. A separate list compiled of duels fought in Russia looks at the period between 1894 and 1910 and reveals that 320 duels were conducted, which is some 20 per year over the 16-year period. This is almost one duel every other week, which points to the fact that the practice of duelling in Russia died out very hard. In fact, one of the last duels between Russian politicians involved Guchkoff, President of the Dumas (the Russian Parliament), who wounded his opponent Count Uvarov, when they met to settle their differences in 1909. Russia had caught the duelling bug rather late, but seemed reluctant to let it go when the time came.

5

THE AFFAIR OF THE PRINCE AND THE PISTOL

The attitude against duelling was not universal and in some quarters it was held in the same regard as fox hunting, enjoyed by landed gentry and officers in the military, the very classes who gambled on cards and boxing matches. Indeed, during his reign, King George III exhibited a somewhat ambivalent attitude towards duelling which may have been caused by recurring bouts of illness. He is understood to have been interested in duelling, particularly among his officers of the army, but mainly for the reason of trying to prevent them. However, from correspondence it would appear that the king may have occasionally condoned duelling. He is known to have been asked to personally intervene on at least two cases where army officers fought duels, and he sought reconciliation between the officers which bought about a satisfactory solution in both instances. In the case where Captain de Lancy killed Major Chapman, the king called for the captain's removal from the army list. This officer was extremely fortunate that he was only thrown out of the army, because he could just as easily have been tried for murder and could have faced the possibility of being hanged.

The king's attitude remained unaltered, even in late June 1789, when the actions of his second son Frederick, Duke of York, were made public. King George III had ruled since 1760, and with his wife Sophia Charlotte had had nine sons, of which, by tradition, the eldest son George held the title of Prince of Wales, with the second son Frederick having the title Duke of York bestowed on him. Being the eldest, Prince George was destined to inherit the throne, thus assuring his role in society. But the problem remained what to do with his younger brother Prince Frederick? This quandary was resolved by appointing him Commander-in-Chief of the army. It is understood that the children's rhyme, *The Grand Old Duke of York*, with his 10,000 men is a reference to his military career, which at times was less than inspired. However, Frederick was not a complete buffoon and although some of his military decisions were ill thought out, he was not without personal courage and took a keen interest in the affairs of the army. In fact, he would later establish the famous Military College at Sandhurst. In 1789 it was the practice of wealthy families to purchase commissions in the army for their sons, and the person to whom such applications were made for consideration was the Duke of York.

In his position as Commander-in-Chief, the young Duke came into close association with officers of all ranks from the most junior lieutenants to senior generals. One of the favoured meeting places where officers gathered to gossip and engage in polite conversation was a club called 'Daubigny' in London. One visitor to this establishment was Lieutenant Colonel Charles Lenox of the Regiment of Coldstream Guards, who as the nephew of the Duke of Richmond was in line to succeed to the title of fourth duke. During one of his visits to the club the Duke of York was informed of 'observations' concerning Lieutenant Colonel Lenox, who was accused of making insulting remarks about his brother, the Prince of Wales, and engaging in conduct unbecoming a gentleman. Lenox, in turn, was later informed of 'words spoken to him … to which no gentleman ought to have submitted'. What then transpired could have had grave implications for the Royal family.

On 15 May, having learned of the accusations concerning his conduct, which alleged that Lenox had made 'certain expressions unworthy of a gentleman', the officer approached the Duke of York during his inspection of a parade and asked for an explanation. By way of reply he was ordered to return to his post, and after the troops had been dismissed the Duke of York repaired to the Orderly Room. He summoned Lenox and the two conversed with a view to try and bring some understanding to what had caused the confrontation. Lenox had asked the Duke of York during the inspection earlier in the day, to make known to him who had told him of the insulting remarks he was alleged to have made. At this second encounter, witnessed by officers, the two men exchanged words and the Duke said in no uncertain tones that he did not hide behind his rank as Commander-in-Chief or his royal title as prince. Lenox denied making any disparaging remarks concerning the Prince of Wales and had never made any 'expressions unworthy of a gentleman'. The Duke continued by saying that when not on duty he wore a 'brown coat', to mean civilian attire as a private gentleman and that, furthermore, he was quite prepared to give his inquisitor 'satisfaction'. In other words Lenox was being informed in terms, which could only be interpreted, that the

Duke was prepared to meet the officer in a duel, if such a challenge should be issued.

Lenox then composed a letter and sent a copy to every member of Daubigny's Club asking if anyone knew anything about an exchange of words. He stated in the letter that if he did not receive any correspondence to the contrary he would take it to mean that no one could recall anything. When he did not hear anything, Lenox then wrote to the Duke of York reporting:

> That not being able to recollect any occasion on which words had been spoken to him at Daubigny's to which a gentleman ought not to submit, he had taken the step which appeared to him the most likely to gain information of the words to which his royal highness had alluded, and of the person who had used them; that none of the members of the Club had given him information of any such insult being in their knowledge; and therefore he expected, in justice to his character, that his royal highness should contradict the report as publicly as he had asserted it.

The missive was delivered to the Duke of York by the Earl of Winchelsea (the spelling as it appears in the accounts of the day). The reply despatched by the Duke of York was not satisfactory to Lenox. He then sent another note to the Duke in which he was informed that the officer desired to meet him at Wimbledon Common. In accordance with protocol the two men met at the appointed place on the 26 May, with the 22-year-old Duke of York being accompanied by Lord Rawdon as his second, and the 21-year-old Lieutenant Colonel Lenox with the Earl of Winchelsea as his second. The ground was set at twelve paces and the men agreed to fire at a given signal. According to some sources neither man fired, but an account of the affair which appeared in the Annual Register for 1789 and other documents furnished by the Royal Archives at Windsor Castle, tells us otherwise. Lenox fired first and the ball came so close to the Duke's head that it clipped one of his curls. The Duke of York, for whatever reason, refused to fire. The affair appeared to have reached an impasse and had to be concluded with the Duke returning fire in order to satisfy honour.

Lord Rawdon then intervened between the two young men by saying that 'enough had been done'. Lenox said that 'his Royal Highness had not fired'. Rawdon continued by pointing out that: 'It was not the Duke's intention to fire; His Royal Highness had come out upon Lieutenant Colonel Lenox's desire, to give him satisfaction, and had no animosity against him.' The officer pressed that the Duke should fire, and again he received a curt refusal as an answer. Lord Winchelsea, Lenox's second, then approached the Duke and asked whether 'His Royal Highness could have no objection to say, he considered Lieutenant Colonel Lenox as a man of honour and courage'. This was tantamount to putting words in the Duke's mouth and the response he elicited was no less than he should have expected. The Duke of York said that 'he should say nothing; he had come out to give Lieutenant Colonel Lenox satisfaction, and he did not mean to fire at him; if Lieutenant Colonel Lenox was not satisfied, he might fire again.' The officer replied that 'he could not possibly fire again at the Duke, as his Royal Highness did not mean to fire him'. There was no more to be said or done and with that the affair was deemed to be concluded and both parties left the field.

The affair, though, was far from finished as over the next few days a flurry of letters flew about. Rumours circulated, newspapers carried accounts and the story of the duel became the gossip of taverns and coffee shops alike. One of the first tracts on the matter came from the Member of Parliament Charles Fox, who had himself fought a duel ten years earlier. Fox wrote an account of the Duke's duel even though he had not been present, and addressed it to his mistress Mrs Armistead. The contents, because of his absence, are little more than gossip but still hold quite personal opinions, as he tells her:

> the Duke of York had one of his curls shot off, & when the King and Queen heard of it, the first showed little & the second no emotion at all, and both said coldly that they believed it was more Frederick's fault than Lennox's. As to the poor man he is mad, but the mother seems to me to go beyond the worst woman we ever read of. Lord Winchilsea, a Lord of the Bedchamber, was Lennox's second and no notice taken of it by the King or Queen. Friend & enemy, excepting only his father & mother, agree in praising the Duke of York to the greatest degree.

This correspondence makes reference to the king's mental health, but even more telling is the fact that many were in favour of the Duke's conduct in fighting the duel.

On the evening of Sunday 30/31 May the Prince of Wales, over whose reputation the Duke had taken up a pistol, wrote to his younger brother from Carlton House:

> I have just heard that Lord Sidney is going about saying yt. you need not exult much at getting rid of Lenox out of the Coldstream, as you are to have one yt. will be fully as obnoxious to you to replace him. This you may make what use you please of when you see the King, or none at all if you think it best not to do so; however I thought it right at all events that you shd. be acquainted with this matchless piece of impertinence.

This note was written four days after the duel and the Prince was probably only reacting to gossip he had heard. The question of Lenox's future as an officer in the regiment of the Coldstream Guards was now becoming a subject for consideration, because it was unheard of for one of His Majesty's officers to shoot at a prince of the Royal family, and could lead to all manner of problems if left unresolved. But the Prince of Wales in his letter is not taking any responsibility, leaving that decision up to his brother.

Earlier in the same day as this note was written, Lieutenant General Sir William Fawcett, Adjutant General to His Majesty's Forces, summoned Generals Lord Dover and Amherst to a meeting at midday to discuss the affair of the duel. The men met and Sir William Fawcett conveyed to the two officers, who were also serving colonels in the Regiments of Lifeguards, the concerns of the king regarding the Duke's duel. King George III believed it might be necessary for him to intervene due to the gossip being circulated, which could lead to 'further improper consequences'. He wished to have a full account of the affair and the opinion from general officers, which was the reason behind the summoning of Lords Dover and Amherst. This meeting instigated by the king contradicts the opinion of the king's state of mind held by Charles Fox in his letter to Mrs Armistead. It was obviously now too late for the king to prevent the duel, and the only thing he could do was to play down the matter in order to limit further gossip, allow time to take its course, and for the whole affair to become a wearisome topic for conversation. If this was the case, then it would seem that Charles Fox had not fully understood the king's attitude to the affair, believing him to be uninterested, when in reality the king was trying to prevent more harmful gossip circulating.

The two general officers were informed by Sir William that he had learned, in an 'authentick manner', that no consequences of a serious nature were likely to happen for the present in the Coldstream Guards, but the officers of the regiment were to convene a meeting to bring about a resolution. Indeed, the officers of the Coldstream Regiment had already conducted their meeting and reached their decision. Among their considerations was the question submitted to them by Colonel Lenox himself as to 'whether he had behaved in the late dispute as became a gentleman and an officer?' After 'considerable discussion' the officers adjourned and on being reconvened issued their statement:

It is the opinion of the Coldstream Regiment, that subsequent to the 15th of May, the day of meeting in the Orderly Room, Lieutenant Colonel Lenox has behaved with courage; but, from the peculiar difficulty of his situation, not with judgement.

In other words they understood why he had fought the duel but they knew he had acted rashly, and had he thought his actions through, the encounter with the Duke of York need never have taken place.

The Duke of York wrote a letter to his father on the 12 June, seventeen days after his encounter with Lenox, who during the intervening period had fought another duel. This second duel by Lenox came only two weeks after his meeting with the Duke of York, but the event was overshadowed by the affair with a member of the Royal family. This second duel did not alter the decision of his brother officers and he remained with the Coldstream Regiment. The Duke's letter only gives passing references to the events and takes the assumptive form that the king knew what had transpired over the previous seventeen days.

Sir,

Having informed Your Majesty When I had the honour to pay my duty to you at Kew The day before yesterday of what the officers of The regiment intended to do upon being acquainted With Lieutenant Colonel Lennox's intention of not leaving the Regiment, I think it right to take the earliest opportunity to report to Your Majesty that just as we arrived upon the ground upon Sidenham Common yesterday morning, I received an express from Lieutenant Colonel Lennox desiring me to sign his requisition To exchange with Lord Strathaven which I accordingly did and sent it back directly so that should Your Majesty be graciously pleased to approve of this exchange the whole of this disagreeable affair will be over.

The officers who were present at the review of the Coldstream yesterday were so good as to approve very much of the appearance of the Regiment. It would have given me the highest delight had I had the honour and the happiness of exercising them before Your Majesty.

I am Sir,
Your Majesty's Most dutiful son and subject.
Frederick

From these lines it appears that the young Duke accepted the decision of the officers of the Coldstream Regiment and was keen to put the whole affair behind him. Lenox went on to enjoy a successful career being promoted to full Colonel in 1795, followed by Lieutenant General in 1805 and General in 1814. He succeeded to the title of 4th Duke of Richmond on the death of his uncle in 1806, the same year as he stood down as the MP for Sussex, a post he had held since 1790. He also served as Lord Lieutenant of Ireland between 1807 and 1813 and died six years later in

1819. His duel with the Duke of York was soon forgotten as news of events from France became the talking point in July 1789.

For many weeks there had been great unrest among the French populace which finally erupted into full-scale revolution with the monarchy being overthrown, and the Royal family seized and thrown into prison. In light of this, and news of the mass executions of French nobility, the Duke of York's duel was forgotten. The Duke's military career continued and by 1793 was leading an expeditionary force into the Low Countries in support of the Austrians and Prussians against France which had invaded the Austrian Netherlands.

The last word on the affair belongs to Lords Dover and Amherst, who decided to compose a series of recommendations for Royal approval with a view to stopping, or at least curtailing, the practice of duelling within the army establishment. They highlighted a number of points and cited precedents, such as the duel between Lieutenant Colonel Roper, Commander-in-Chief at St Vincent and Ensign Thomas Purefoy of the 66th Regiment of Foot (later to become the 2nd Battalion The Royal Berkshire Regiment) in 1788. These two officers, despite the disparity in their ranks, fought a duel on 21 December that year and Roper was shot dead by Purefoy who was subsequently arrested and stood trial at the Maidstone Assizes in Kent in 1794. The young officer was acquitted at his trial and could consider himself extremely fortunate that he was not found guilty and hanged. Lords Dover and Amherst went on to write:

> We cannot therefore but deem it highly expedient that your Majesty should be graciously pleased to exert your Royal authority to check these alarming and increasing evils by manifesting in the strongest manner your displeasure with them, enjoining all officers, under pain of incurring that displeasure, to conform to the Rules and Articles of War, peremptorily forbidding every act which may be contrary to the letter or spirit of them, and declaring in the most explicit terms that any officer who should hereafter presume to transgress the orders laid down for their conduct, should be immediately dismist [*sic*] your Majesty's Service.

They were trying to prevent further duelling and in seeking dismissal from the ranks they brought about a precedent in the case of Captain de Lancy, who was removed from the army list for killing a fellow officer in a duel. Despite their best efforts and those of others who would follow them, such as the Duke of Wellington, duels were still conducted and a good number of officers fell either wounded or killed in encounters which were contravening all military codes and civil laws.

The incident involving the Duke of York and Lenox could have so very easily ended in disaster if either man had been killed in the affair. The consequences, had such an eventuality occurred with the Duke being shot, would almost certainly have polarised the military in the eyes of the public. Had the Duke shot and killed *his* opponent, the very thought of a member of the Royal family standing trial on the charge of murder or manslaughter would have been reprehensible to even consider. The fact that revolution erupted in France when it did certainly helped to play down events and draw a veil over the affair. The great British public now had something else to concern itself with, as the horrors in France became known.

Note: There is some question over the spelling of Lenox – as it is written here – which is sometimes written as Lennox. In this instance, the spelling of Lenox, with a single 'n', is used as it is the most common form of the spelling used in reports dating from the period. Indeed, Lenox is the form used by Lord Rawdon, the Duke of York's second, in correspondence relating to the affair. Correspondence written by Lords Dover and Amherst also uses the spelling of Lenox. However, the Duke of York in a letter to his father King George III, on 12 June 1789, uses the spelling of Lennox, as is evident in the transcription of his letter which is reproduced above in full with kind permission of Her Majesty Queen Elizabeth II.

6

FEMALE DUELS

Wicked Women

Women have a very different set of ideals to men and if this were not so there would have been far more recorded accounts of female duellists. But those accounts of which we know show them to be just as equal to the task as any man. Among the lower classes in the 'Gin Houses' of Hogarth's London, women probably fought as much as the men, but these would in all likelihood have been classed as brawls. Some affairs were recognised as duels, however, such as that concerning the Comtesse de Polignac and the Marquise de Nesle, who fought for the right to be the mistress of the Duc de Richelieu in 1721.

Women are quite rightly seen as the fairer and gentler sex, but they can also exhibit a darker side which, when pushed beyond a certain limit, can be just as ruthless as men. Not for nothing is the phrase coined: 'the female of the species is more deadly than the male'. When it came to duelling women certainly proved how they were as equal to the task as any man. The number of incidents with women as the principals meeting in duels may have been few, but from those fragmented accounts it would appear that such affairs were not always conducted in the same way as men's duels, and some affairs actually contravened all the regulations proscribed when facing off in a duel.

Duelling is considered as being dominated by men due to their naturally more pugnacious nature and their inclination to imbibe alcohol in greater quantities, which was the root cause to many challenges of duels. Everyone has limitations and when pushed beyond that point it was not unknown for women to take to the 'field of honour' and face down an adversary with a loaded pistol, exhibiting a side of their nature which belied the term 'weaker sex'. The adversaries in these unusual cases did not always necessarily face another woman and there are recorded instances of women facing men. When these meetings took place the female protagonists showed they were equally up to the task, and on occasion proved themselves to be more ruthless than their male counterparts.

The pages of history are replete with the deeds of women who have taken up arms, often against overwhelming odds. From the time of the Roman Empire to the wars of the Middle Ages, the actions of women proving how strong they can be in time of adversity has been used as a stimulus. For example, Joan of Arc became a turning point for France just when the country was facing its nadir against England during the Hundred Years War. The belligerent nature of Joan of Arc and her heroic conduct in battle injected renewed vigour into the French forces, leading to the eventual triumph over the English. More than 300 years later and women still found themselves very much a part of male-dominated institutions, even among pirates, who were probably the most chauvinistic of all male criminal leagues. Outstanding among women pirates was Mary Read (sometimes written as Reade) and Anne Bonney (sometimes written as Bonny). These are but two examples of female pirates, whose deeds can be used to show how women could handle themselves in a fight using firearms and swords.

Ladies of the eighteenth and nineteenth centuries are considered refined and genteel, but they could display another more cavalier side, participating in gambling and enjoying the spectacle of horse racing and boxing during the course of which they could win or lose huge sums of money. Georgiana, Duchess of Devonshire, for example, amassed gambling debts of over £3,000 in 1776 while still only the tender age of 19 years old. She was not the only one; there were others, but they were usually of the titled, landowning gentry with money.

Not all had the finances to pay off their debts, however, and some were forced to sell off lands, possessions or committed suicide rather than face the final ignominy of debtor's prison or bankruptcy. When female duels did take place it was like some lethal exhibition of female equality. Women at the time may not have had the right to vote but when pushed beyond the limit they could, and often did, display their capability of being equal to men when it came to duelling.

Women are more often seen as being the cause of duels, either as wives or lovers, such as the affair caused by Mademoiselle Tirevit, a leading performer with the Imperial Opera in Paris, who shared her favours between two lovers. The love triangle could not last indefinitely and the matter had to be resolved. The lady's suitors agreed that they should fight a duel in order to settle once and for all who would claim her affection. The two principals M. de Grandprè and M. le Pique agreed that the affair should be conducted in a manner which would test their resolve to duel, and the outcome of which would leave no margin of doubt. In other words, they were resigned to duel to the death and would not be content by mere wounding. Plans were put in place which would make the duel one of the most elaborately organised affairs of its kind and probably the most expensive. The arrangements included the construction of two identical hot air balloons, which involved a not inconsiderable amount of money, and it would be from these aerial platforms that the men would fight their duel while flying over Paris.

The two men met for their unique duel at around 9 a.m. on the morning of 3 May 1808, again in the middle of wars between France and Britain. Whereas most duels were normally conducted in a clandestine manner, the elaborate arrangements for the duel between de Grandprè and le Pique, as their balloons were inflated, meant that a large crowd of curious onlookers were drawn to witness the spectacle. The weapons the men had chosen for the affair were not the usual pistol but a form of firearm commonly known as a blunderbuss. This was a single-barrelled weapon with a pronounced bell-shaped flare of the muzzle, and was loaded with a number of small pellets or shot. The flare was believed to spread the shot, but in actual fact the width of the shot was governed by the diameter of the barrel itself. Nevertheless, it was an intimidating weapon, much favoured by coachmen to fend off highway robbers against whom the effects at close range were devastatingly deadly. The term blunderbuss is believed to originate from the Dutch 'donrebusse' or alternatively 'donderbus' to mean 'thundergun'. The fact that de Grandprè and le Pique were armed with these fearsome-looking weapons made their meeting all the more unusual.

On the signal the two men stepped into the baskets of their balloons, accompanied by their seconds, and as the tethering ropes were cut they began to ascend over the gardens of the Tuilleries. It had been agreed that they should not aim at one another, but rather direct their fire at each other's balloon. Accounts of the event tell how the wind was moderate, and the balloons remained about 80yd apart. As they approached an altitude of about half-a-mile above the earth, the signal to fire was given. Le Pique fired first but somehow managed to miss his opponent's balloon completely. When de Grandprè fired he scored a direct hit, which punctured the fabric of the balloon, causing it to collapse and rapidly lose its qualities of suspension. It hurtled to the ground taking le Pique and his second to their deaths. As for de Grandprè, he continued his flight and landed without mishap a distance of some seven leagues from Paris, which is approximately 21 miles. Not only was it unarguably the most unusual duel ever conducted, it was also the ultimate expression in determination to win a lady's affections so conclusively. One can only assume that Mlle Tirevit was worth all the danger and goes to prove how female charms can make men undertake the most outrageous challenges.

Some female duellists proved themselves extremely adept with swords; some even took on male adversaries and, on occasion, bested them in skill and strength. One of the earliest recorded female duels in the proper sense, with the principals using pistols, was the affair between the Comtesse de Polignac and the Marquise de Nesle. It would appear that both these titled ladies were attending a ball as guests at the grand Palace of Versailles just outside Paris, when they began to argue over the right to be the lover of Louis-Francois-Armand, the Duc de Richelieu. The argument turned physical as blows were exchanged; the women began to tear at each other's dresses, pulled hair and scratched each other in a very nasty cat fight. They were separated and the women agreed to reconvene at the Bois de Boulogne to continue their confrontation. After they had composed themselves they met at the appointed place dressed as though prepared for a ride in the park, but very much ready to continue their differences in a duel. Taking up their positions the ladies curtsied to one another, took aim and fired. Some accounts say that the Marquise de Nesle received a superficial wound to her shoulder. Another account of the affair points to the fact that there may have been more than one exchange of shots because neither woman was hit when they fired. This account claims when the second shot was fired, the Comtesse de Polignac was hit in the ear while her adversary was wounded in the shoulder. Nevertheless, it would have been all for nothing because the Duc de Richelieu was an ardent lover and had a string of female admirers, and the duel over his favours would have only added to his reputation. The Duc himself was not a stranger to duels and in 1734 he shot and killed the Prince de Lixen. Two years later he shot and killed the irate Comte de Pentiriender in a duel for having taken his mistress.

Another expression applied to women is, 'Hell hath no fury like a woman scorned', for such a woman was liable to resort to any means in order to exact revenge, an example being a young lady by the name of Leverrier who found herself shunned by her lover, a naval officer called Duprez, who had taken up with another woman. Incensed by his actions she followed him through the streets of Paris to confront him with infidelity. She handed him a pistol and in her rage ordered him to stand and face her to restore honour. Duprez would have done well to take her seriously for while he fired harmlessly into the air in an act of contempt, young Leverrier was more earnest in her desire for revenge and she shot him full in the face. It was not so much a duel but a deadly lover's spat conducted in full daylight in a city teeming with people.

Equally villainous was the affair involving Lady Almeria Braddock, who had invited Mrs Elphinstone to her home for a social gathering, along with other guests. It was during the round of polite conversational exchanges when, for no apparent reason, Mrs Elphinstone venomously turned on her hostess and made a number of rather disparaging remarks of a very personal nature concerning Lady Braddock's fading youth and beauty. The remarks could only be interpreted as insulting to say the least due to the tone of sarcasm with which they were delivered. It was all too much and Mrs Elphinstone found herself being challenged to a duel. The event became the talk of 1792 London as the two women prepared to meet in Hyde Park for their confrontation. They took up their positions some 10yd apart and fired, which left Lady Braddock with a bullet through her hat. Not satisfied, the two women then set about continuing their duel with swords in a manner similar to the affair between Colonel Barrington and Mr Gilbert, who had fought with pistols and then swords in Ireland thirty-three years earlier in 1759. The ladies parried and thrust until finally Lady Braddock inflicted a wound on her opponent and declared her honour to be satisfied. The two women then curtsied and left the spot as though nothing had happened.

It is generally accepted that such affairs were the exception rather than the rule and that women really had nothing to prove. To duel over the affections of a man was rather demeaning; insults could be traded like for like if quick-witted enough and words could wound just as deeply as any bullet – if delivered at the right time and in the right company a woman could ruin another's reputation within the social circle of the upper class. As the author James Landale puts it rather succinctly in his book *Duel*: 'A woman can hold a pistol just as easily as a man. But women did not get involved because a duel, at its heart, was the defence of a very specific and very male conception of honour.' Yes, men and women do think very differently indeed.

7

SECONDS OUT

The Duties of a Personal Friend

By the very nature of the affair there were never usually many witnesses, but of all those attending a pistol duel the role of the second, and how he conducted himself, was every bit as important as that of the principal, for without his guidance the meeting could degenerate into nothing more than a gunfight. The presence of a second at a duel can be seen as an honour and a demanding challenge, requiring discretion of the highest magnitude and a stoic level-headedness. When a principal approached a friend with a view to requesting him to stand as his second in a duel, he was bestowing on him the mark of high esteem with which he held their friendship. Alternatively, it could be seen as asking too much from any friendship. If the role of second was accepted the elected friend would become privilege to details concerning the affair, such as the divulgence of the exact cause and the arrangements made up to the time of his appointment as second. This fact in itself implicated him in arranging a criminal act due to the illegality of the duel. One published work on duelling warned that to be selected as a man's second was 'the most awful responsibility that perhaps can fall to any gentleman'. It was a published opinion but also a stark warning at the same time. To accept the role of second without considering the duties expected of him was to act in haste, but a man did not want to let down a friend in his greatest hour of need.

A principal could ask any friend to stand by him, but a wise man would not select just anyone to act as his second, he would choose instead his most stalwart and long-standing acquaintance. The countenance was not always accepted and on occasion a principal had to choose someone else to escort him through his ordeal. In those instances where a man might find himself being challenged while visiting a town where he was not known to anyone, he may be advised to approach certain men who were unknown to him and he would have to trust their veracity. Seconds were not always willing parties to the task of assisting with a duel, such as William Millie who acted as second to David Landale in 1826. When first approached he declined the role. When pressed on the matter he reluctantly agreed to support his friend in the affair, even though he knew nothing of the duties. In fact, there was no reason why he should know. He implored Landale to release him from the task, but when the time came he stood by his friend as firmly as anyone could have wished and put aside all the trepidation which every second must experience.

Both principals usually appointed seconds and at some affairs there was more than one second in attendance to support each antagonist. In his meeting against Count Carletti in 1798, William Wyndham turned up with four seconds saying that he 'agreed to abide entirely by their counsel, and should consider myself no longer but an Instrument in their hands'. The presence of the second at the scene of the confrontation was much more than just to make up the numbers of observers. The second had to serve as a witness to see the duel was conducted in accordance to all the conditions pre-arranged by the principals through them, and to abide by the written codes. If at all possible he would try to extract an apology to end the affair before shots were exchanged. The *General Rules and Instructions for all Seconds in Duels* was the guide for the role and it appeared in 1793. It advises that a second 'is to try, and even rack his Invention, for any new and reasonable Light that can be thrown upon it; in order to reconcile the Party aggrieved.'

This was the European way of conducting a duel but in America, while the second had control over the affair, the policy was to shoot and get it over with. That is why duels were convened, because if a man did not intend to participate in a duel he should not have issued the challenge or accepted the challenge. A second was, then, in effect all at once a negotiator, conciliator and an umpire. He had to conduct himself with all the tact and diplomacy as if he were a head of state, otherwise a momentary lapse in protocol could lead to him being challenged to a duel for contravening guidelines, or exhibiting a demeanour which could be considered anything other than courteous to all present and certainly both principals, whom he had to treat with equal magnanimity. *The Art of Duelling* states: 'Unfortunately, few are aware of the great responsibility that devolves upon them, and from ignorance, inexperience and want of presence of mind, often commit serious mistakes.' That is when a second could find himself being challenged to a duel, and a man would be wise to learn from the cautionary words. Should the seconds find themselves involved to a greater degree than they would otherwise like, the Clonmel Rules covered the eventuality by stating: 'When seconds disagree and resolve to exchange shots themselves, it must be at the same time and at right angles.'

There were rare occasions when, on the conclusion of a duel, the second of the defeated duellist would then challenge the victor of the affair. This move was not regarded as the right thing and *The British Code of Duel* was specific in its condemnation of the practice by pointing out: 'It has happened that from some dispute in regard to arrangements, which are in themselves very simple, or on the conduct of a dissenting principal, seconds have become principals to each other. Nothing can be decidedly more wrong.' This was as it should be, for there had to be a limit on who faced who in a challenge, otherwise the duel could degenerate into a free-for-all as seconds and others could enter the fray; if this happened where would it all end?

It was a dangerous role in more ways than one, and a man risked sustaining injuries in the exchange of fire, especially if the adversaries were nervous or not experienced in handling pistols. In the worst instance a second could become a victim if one of the principals fired wildly rather than at his opponent. The nineteenth-century historian and author Andrew Steinmetz highlights this danger, when in one of his works he makes reference to a duel between two men known as Pierrot and Arlequin. During their affair these two men fired so wildly that each succeeded in killing his adversary's second, ending the duel with the deaths of two witnesses to be explained to the authorities. While there was a high risk of a second being hit because he was a close observer, he would place himself out of the way of the direct line of fire. For both seconds to be killed is outstanding odds indeed and utter carelessness on behalf of both principals. However, if the case referred to by Steinmetz is correct it was an unfortunate accident. But if one examines the names of the principals one cannot but come to the conclusion that they were pseudonyms used to fool the authorities, who may have attempted to halt the affair had their real names be divulged. The reason behind this assumption is because the names Pierrot and Arlequin (or Harlequin) can be found as characters in the Italian *Commedia Dell'arte* plays. It was a ruse which has kept the real names secret.

There were cases when a duel was conducted without a second being appointed. In 1749 Captain Edward Clark faced his fellow officer in the Royal Navy, Captain Thomas Innes in a duel convened in Hyde Park. The affair was conducted without a second being present and ended with the death of Captain Innes. Sixteen years later in 1765 Lord Byron shot and killed William Chatworth in a duel without the supervision of a second.

John Wilkes was a man who bucked the trend when it came to duelling, and on two separate occasions fought duels without a second. The first was in 1762 when he faced Lord Talbot, and the second time was the following year when he engaged with Samuel Martin in Hyde Park. Even as relatively late as 1809 duels were being fought without seconds, such as the case between Major Campbell and Captain Boyd in Ireland.

There were many reasons for a challenge to duel being made, some of which were for seemingly trifling matters, such as the behaviour of one's dog. Such an incident was the cause of the affair between Lieutenant Colonel Montgomery of the 9th Regiment of Foot (later to become the Norfolk Regiment) and Captain Macnamara of the Royal Navy in April 1803, as alluded to in a previous chapter. It began as the two men were riding separately in Hyde Park in London; as their paths crossed the two men's dogs began to fight. Montgomery shouted at Macnamara's dog to break off the fight or: 'I'll knock your brains out'. It was a strange statement to make, no doubt said as much out of frustration and anger, and one made without giving much thought to the words. Macnamara responded with his own words of threat, probably said with equal frustration: 'If you do, I'll knock your brains out.' The peaceful calm of the spring day in Hyde Park was ruptured as the two officers continued to exchange angry words. A duel was the only way of settling the affair and seconds were chosen and a formal challenge exchanged; arrangements were made for the officers to meet at Chalk Farm at 7 p.m., the same day as their confrontation. It was arranged quickly; ordinarily duels took a few days to prepare as letters were exchanged, and there was time for tempers to abate. The time of their meeting was also unusual, for duels were usually conducted very early in the morning. Macnamara was wounded in the duel, but in turn he hit Montgomery in the chest, who later expired. Other sources claim the words exchanged by the men varied slightly. One account has Montgomery opening the encounter with: 'Whose dog is that? I will knock him down.' To this Macnamara replied: 'Have you the impudence to say that you will knock my dog down? You must first knock me down.' The words may be different but the outcome still remained the same.

It was the antics of a dog, thirty-seven years later to the month, which caused another duel. Captain Fleetwood was exercising his animal in Hyde Park, as fate would have it, in April 1840 when the animal emerged from the waters of the Serpentine Lake, and as it shook off the excess water it dowsed two ladies who were taking the air in the company of a gentleman by the name of Brocksopp. Angry at being drenched by muddy water he lashed out at the dog with his walking stick, attempting to chase it off. Captain Fleetwood did not view this action kindly and challenged

Brocksopp to a duel. The two men met on Wimbledon Common and after exchanging shots without causing injury, honour was seen to be satisfied.

A verbal challenge to a duel gave notice of intent and prepared the challenged party to expect a formal letter to be delivered. Such correspondence was nearly always polite, and outlined the reason for the challenge and gave details of where the affair was to take place, the time and the date. The task of delivering the letter was one of the duties undertaken by the second. He could wait for a reply, either verbal or written, upon which the next step would be to try and resolve the dispute if at all possible. It seems strange to think that once a challenge to duel had been issued that men should then try to bring about a solution without resorting to pistol shots. But such was the protocol involved. Failure to reach a compromise and extract an apology meant the duel had to be seen through to its conclusion.

The many books on the conduct of duels had different opinions on how a challenge should be issued. For example, the Clonmel Rules drawn up in Ireland in 1777, states that: 'Challenges are never to be delivered at night, unless the party to be challenged intends leaving the place of the offence before morning; for it is desirable to avoid all hot-headed proceedings.' The intent here is well meant, but if someone was going to leave in order to avoid a duel, then the delivery of a note would not make him change his mind. If anything, such a note challenging him to duel would make him hasten his departure. A newspaper editor pinned a note to the door of his office with the details: 'Subscriptions received from 9 to 4, challenges from 11 to 12 only.' But levity aside, challenges were not to be issued lightly and were always taken seriously.

A man had to accept the challenge if he were not to lose his standing in social circles, but the exchange of letters between principals could continue for days as various points were clarified. Once a challenge had been issued and accepted there was no going back, the affair had to be seen through to the end. One way round this, if a man did not want to duel without losing face, was to leak details of the impending affair to the authorities. This was done anonymously, of course, but gave the precise information which allowed the authorities to arrive and break up the gathering. A second might undertake such a move if he feared for the safety and survival of his friend, and no one need be any the wiser for it could not be helped if the law intervened.

Seconds were not always inexperienced when it came to duels and there were many who had either served in the role several times before, or even been the principal themselves and so knew the intricacies involved. The French politician Georges Clemenceau, who served two terms as Prime Minister, is believed to have fought as many as twenty-two duels, but of this figure twelve is probably more correct, and of these he fought seven with pistols; he also stood in as a second. Even earlier, the prominent soldier General Sam Huston, who led the Texan forces during that state's War of Independence against Mexico, was a veteran duellist. Following the Battle of Jacinto on 21 April 1836, he was challenged to a duel. He made a note of it, appointing it 'number 14' with the coolest of remarks, saying the 'angry gentleman must wait his turn'. Among those other notables who served in the role of second at a duel was the American author Mark Twain, who acted as second to the French politician Leon Gambetta who faced fellow French politician Marie Francois Fourtou. Common sense, as much as anything else, played a part in the role of the second. In those cases where alcohol was the root cause of a challenge, the seconds might sit down to resolve the matter once the antagonists were sober, and therefore be amenable to a reconciliation and end the matter peacefully. The nineteenth-century author Abraham Bosquett wrote: 'I am confident that there is not one case in fifty where discreet Seconds might not settle the difference, and reconcile the parties before they came to the field.' Bosquett wrote of his personal experiences in duelling, claiming: 'I have myself been four times a Principal, and twenty-five times a Second.'

If no solution was forthcoming to whatever prompted the duel, the seconds would then be faced with the onerous task of making preparations for the duel itself, which included contacting a doctor to be present. Between them the seconds would agree the time, the place, which should be 'away from the haunts of men', the type of weapons to be used and the number of shots. They would also decide the distance at which the exchange of shots should take place for they would have to pace out the distance. They also had to load their principal's pistols in the presence of one another. The Clonmel Rules were most specific on that point by stating: 'The seconds load in the presence of each other, unless they give their mutual honours that they have charged smooth and single, which may be held sufficient.'

On rare occasions the seconds might collude between themselves, without revealing their intentions to anyone, and arrange that the affair, while conducted in accordance with the rules, did not end with a death or even a wounding. To this end they might load the pistols with a greatly reduced charge of gunpowder so that the bullet did not have the power behind it to inflict a wound. This is what happened during preparations for a duel between two young officer cadets, en route to join their posting for service with the Honourable East India Company. During their passage the two men began to argue over gambling and it was agreed they would settle the affair in a duel when the ship docked at the Cape of Good Hope. The seconds prepared the pistols with only powder charges and no pistol ball. The two principals faced one another and fired with one young man falling to the ground in terror. It was a lesson from which it was hoped the men would learn.

Another alternative the seconds could adopt was to arrange for the affair to be conducted on ground which was totally unsuitable for the purpose of the meeting, such as being either too wet and slippery or uneven so as to prevent good balance being achieved to permit accurate firing. The seconds acting on the part of their principals Cilley and Graves, members of the US House of Representatives, suggested the men use rifles in their duel. The distance between the two men was 80yd and the seconds stipulated the weapons be held at arms length. No doubt they believed with such conditions the men would not be harmed. Unfortunately it did not work out as planned and Cilley was killed in the affair.

Some of the advice given concerning the selection of seconds could be interpreted today as though duelling was being elevated to elitist status. For example, some works advise against choosing Muslims, while in *The Art of Duelling* the author advises against 'choosing an Irishman on any account, as nine out of ten of those I have had the pleasure of forming an acquaintance with, both abroad and in this country, have such an innate love of fighting, they cannot bring an affair to an amicable adjustment.' These were cautionary words of wisdom, because if a solution could be brought about without exchanging a shot, that was more sensible all round. But few duels were ever fully resolved by words alone and so it was not just the Irish who enjoyed the reputation of being pugnacious by nature.

Duelling in Ireland in the eighteenth and nineteenth centuries was actively pursued, indeed perhaps, if anything, with greater vigour than anywhere else. Sir Jonah Barrington, the well-known Irish judge, took to the field of honour and was regarded for his prowess with a pistol. *The British Code of Duel* suggested that the men acting as seconds 'should not be married or hold official position'. It is just as well that these recommendations were not valid and not held to be the letter of the law otherwise they would have been broken time and time again; lords, judges and other authority figures often stood as seconds to principals of equal standing and many of them were married men. *The British Code of Duel* continues that a second 'should be prepared to take a very active part in the duel should the need arise'. This point can be interpreted in many ways, such as simply offering words of encouragement to steady the principal or, in the other extreme, actually participating in the exchange of shots.

How the role of seconds came about is something of a mystery, but it is believed that it dates back to the period of the Middle Ages when tournaments and jousting was practised by knights. As the knights entered the 'tilt yard' where the opponents were to challenge one another in a trial of prowess, strength, skill and stamina, they would be accompanied by their squires, whose duties included making sure their masters were properly armed, prepared and equipped. And so it was only natural that a person engaged in single combat of a duel should be escorted by someone who, although present, need not necessarily participate actively in the affair other than to maintain order and give the signal to fire.

The role of the second should never be underrated, for it was he who would decide when shots should be exchanged. It was a responsible position, but some seconds shied away when the time came, as though wishing to distance themselves from the affair, lest they be implicated and later called to give evidence in court should the duel end in a death. In 1803 James Paull and Sir Francis Burdett met on Putney Heath in London accompanied by Mr Cooper and John Ker, who were acting as their respective seconds. John Ker gave the first command for the men to fire while standing at a distance of about 12 feet to the side, away from the line of fire but positioned midway between the two principals. James Paull's second, Cooper, it was observed, had taken refuge under a large tree some distance away from the duel itself. It was decided that a second round of fire would be needed and that Cooper should give the command. However, he was hidden so far away, and so well, that neither principal could see him and would probably not have heard him in his petrified state. Cooper's actions were cowardly and certainly betrayed the trust which Paull had invested on him as a supposed loyal and honourable friend. Secreted as he was, he would not have been able to intervene on his friend's behalf had Sir Francis Burdett failed to observe the rules of the duel. Furthermore, he absolutely refused to reveal any personal details such as his place of residence. His action was crass abandonment and a gross act of neglect.

The position of a second remains with us today and is a term familiar to anyone who has ever watched a boxing match where the referee declares 'seconds out'. The function still remains the same after all the centuries, which is to support and encourage and make sure their charge is prepared for the confrontation. Throughout the history of duelling with pistols, the role of the second was paramount and remained so right until the very last duel was conducted. The importance of their position can be judged from the fact that their names were recorded alongside those of the principals. To think of them as mere general factotums would be doing them a grave disservice.

8

DOCTORS

The Invisible Witness

Flintlock pistols during the eighteenth and nineteenth centuries fired a lead ball or bullet at relatively low velocities, somewhere in the order of around 1,000ft/second. The close distance at which duels were conducted, in most cases only a few yards, meant that pistol bullets, if aimed accurately, would hit within a fraction of a second. Understanding of the nature of gunshot wounds at this time was basic and the treatment of such wounds was, at best, rudimentary. Some medical men stemmed the flow of bleeding by applying a red hot iron to the wound to cauterise it, an age-old and proven method. Such treatment would have been almost unbearable to an already traumatised patient, but these outdated procedures were gradually replaced by remedial treatments devised by physicians, and this knowledge was passed on in their writings. These medical physicians gained invaluable experience because they accompanied the armies on campaign to treat the wounded soldiers.

There were many wars being fought during this period and, while destructive, there came from these conflicts a better understanding of wound treatment and advances in medicines and surgery techniques. Medical men such as Sir Charles Bell, Dr George Guthrie, Pierre Francois Percy and probably the most famous of all Dominique Jean Larrey, who served on many campaigns with Napoleon Bonaparte's Imperial Guard, all kept notes of their experiences and through their writings were able to pass on their ideas governing the treatment of gunshot wounds. These men and others, such as Thomas Gale and William Clowes, developed new methods which improved the treatment of wounds, including those inflicted by pistol shots fired at close quarters, leading to better survival rates and recovery times.

The speed at which pistol bullets travelled may have been slow, but the weight and calibre of these projectiles could be quite large and on striking a target the kinetic energy had to be given up and released into the victim. A typical pistol may fire balls weighing slightly less than half-an-ounce and have a calibre of any size; in fact, calibres of .67in, that is to say .67 of a full imperial inch, with some being larger or smaller, depending on the gunsmith's thoughts on the matter. In England, duelling pistols rarely exceeded a calibre of .57in (14.5mm) or 24 bore. (The term bore is given to mean that twenty-four such bullets would weigh 1lb or 454gm.) The effect such projectiles had on the human body caused wounds which could be severe as the bullet tore through muscle tissue, broke bones or punctured vital organs. Low-velocity pistol bullets could have a surprising effect on the human body and inflict wounds without actually knocking a person to the ground. Indeed, the accounts of eyewitnesses who observed duels told how injured men sometimes remained upright after being hit. For example, in May 1806 General Andrew Jackson received two broken ribs on the left side of his chest when his opponent Charles Dickinson fired during their duel using a pistol with a massive .70in calibre. Despite his wounds, Jackson retained his composure and fired at his opponent and killed him.

Wounds inflicted by pistol bullets were not always immediately fatal, even when delivered to vulnerable parts of the body. For example, an officer in the Hanoverian army survived being shot in the head on two separate occasions. He had lost most of his teeth and part of his lower jaw, but still lived an otherwise normal life. On the other hand, where the bullet ruptured vital organs and caused internal bleeding, the fatally wounded man could linger for hours or days after the duel.

In the Burr-Hamilton duel, Burr's shot struck Hamilton, entering his liver and causing him to linger for 36 hours before dying. Even if he had received the best medical treatment it is unlikely Hamilton would have survived because a wound so deep into a vital organ in the early nineteenth century was beyond the skills of even the most skilled doctors of the day. Penetrating wounds to the stomach or other organs caused peritonitis and were invariably fatal. If an artery was ruptured by a pistol bullet this could result in bleeding to death, but a good doctor might be able to stem the flow of blood through cauterisation or applying a ligature to tie it off.

All gunshot wounds received in duels had to be treated, with the wound being dressed if infection were to be prevented, which is why a doctor was almost invariably present at such fateful meetings. If the wound was a simple penetration, where the pistol ball had passed through muscle, a doctor might clean it by passing a clean silk handkerchief through the puncture to pull out any dirt. Such treatment would have been unbearably painful, but these harsh methods probably saved lives. If the attendant doctor was experienced and well versed in the latest medical developments, he would be capable of dealing with all wounds, except the most serious which would lead to death. In the cases where fatal wounds were sustained the doctor could at least make the dying man's last moments as comfortable as possible. One of the most simple, yet effective, processes to be developed as a result of the major battles was a method of cleaning non-fatal wounds known as debridement. This had been developed and was being practised by French surgeons such as Pierre Joseph Desault before 1780. The technique involved the doctor cutting away the dead and dying flesh around the wound and removing any foreign matter, such as material from clothing, dirt or anything which had been dragged into the wound when the bullet struck.

Dominique Jean Larrey was using debridement on wounded men during the French campaign into Egypt in 1799. For example, an officer hit in the throat by a pistol ball during the fighting was treated by Larrey who debrided both the entry and exit wounds and arranged for the officer to be fed through a tube made of gum elastic. Like the unfortunate lady shot in the throat by Laux Pfister almost 300 years earlier, this officer also survived the wounds to a vital part of the body. The pistol ball had entered the officer's jaw on the right-hand side, passed across the back of the throat, missing vital arteries, and emerged on the left side of the man's collar bone. The man lost his voice for a few weeks, but the incident does again serve to highlight the fact that not all pistol wounds were fatal, even at close range. But despite even the greatest of care and attention a wounded man could still develop gangrene, tetanus or septicaemia (blood poisoning), which could kill days or weeks after the injury.

And yet, for all their well-intentioned motives, doctors could find themselves being slighted by a patient who misinterpreted the methods of treatment they were receiving. For example, when Larrey was treating a Colonel after the Battle of Eylau on 8 February 1807, the doctor found himself being challenged to a duel. The Colonel had been shot in the foot by a bullet and as Larrey was preparing to operate, the patient's leg began to shake uncontrollably so that he could not perform the procedure. In an effort to calm the officer the doctor resorted to the shock tactic of slapping the man's face. Under normal conditions it would have been an affront to any man, but given that this was an extraordinary situation, and given the medical state of the officer, Larrey probably thought it warranted such harsh actions. The Colonel was stunned and shouted: 'Sir, you have taken advantage of my state in a most cowardly manner. I demand satisfaction.' From such an outburst, one cannot but help think the officer was not so terribly wounded as some of the other 10,000 French casualties from the battle. However, the doctor's action had worked and responded to the Colonel's demand for a duel by stating: 'Colonel, accept my apologies. I understand you and knew full well that such an insult would make you think of your honour and forget your wound. The operation is done and here is the ball I have removed. Give me your hand.' With that Larrey presented his patient with the offending ball which had been removed during the exchange of words, so quickly and deftly. It seems incredulous, almost to the point of ridiculousness, that in the heat of battle a wounded man should throw up a challenge to duel. But not all extractions of pistol bullets could be done with such skill as in this case with Larrey, and many were less straightforward operations.

In May 1833 George Guthrie, who had been a British medical officer with Wellington's army on campaign in Spain, presented a lecture on the subject of gunshot wounds caused as a result of duels. During the course of his talk he addressed his audience at Westminster Hospital in London on the difficulties of removing bullets:

> There is neither charity nor humanity in the manner of choosing pistols at present adopted. The balls are so small that the holes they make are always a source of inconvenience in the cure, and the quantity of powder is also so small that it will not send a ball through a moderately thick gentleman. It therefore sticks in some place where it should not ... to the extreme disadvantage of the patient, and to the great annoyance of the surgeon.

These opinions are not all necessarily correct, because some pistols balls were of large calibre and powder charges could force a ball to penetrate deeply and even emerge through the body. In the pages of *The British Code of Duel*, the advice offered on the matter of being wounded was that it was 'expedient that a surgeon should attend each of the parties; whenever possible, a gentleman should be selected who has had some practice in gun-shot wounds'. Few doctors, especially those with a rural practice, had first-hand experience in treating gunshot wounds, and most duels were attended by family practitioners. The pages of *The Art of Duelling* counselled that duellists 'should have been careful to secure the services of his medical attendant who will provide himself with all the necessary apparatus for tying up wounds or arteries and extracting balls'.

A doctor attending a duel would naturally wish to maintain a low profile so as not to cause undue alarm to either or both duellists. His presence was just in case his professional services were required. Doctors were usually summoned just before a duel was to be fought, and he could either be escorted to the meeting place or given instructions of where to meet. The task of arranging the presence of a doctor usually fell to the second, who on arrival at the duel's location should see to it that the doctor remained unobserved as far as possible. Messages were often conveyed in veiled terms, requesting a doctor to avail himself at a certain time at a certain place. On receiving such a note no doctor was in any doubt as to why he was being summoned. If he were to observe the proceedings he may be called on to give evidence, should the duellists be brought to trial, which did make some doctors decline any involvement with a duel. However, should he attend but not witness the shooting first-hand, then he could not give evidence under oath without perjuring himself; so by his very avoiding witnessing the act he was protecting all concerned.

Doctors were in effect the silent witnesses and, as one authority on the history of duelling put it, they were 'auxiliary to the duel but not its accomplice'. Some guideline pamphlets contained suggestions on the role of a doctor at a duel, and one counselled that doctors 'should turn their backs to the combatants so as not to see the firing; but as soon as they hear the report they should turn, and run to the spot as speedily as possible'. Good advice, but not all doctors were young enough or sprightly enough to run to an injured man's aid.

Should his services not be required the doctor could depart without anyone knowing he had ever been there, except for the person who requested his presence. Of course, a doctor treating a patient suffering from a gunshot wound was only obeying his Hippocratic Oath and saving a life, although the law would see it very differently and view him as an accessory, calling him as a material witness should the incident result in a court case.

In some instances the role of doctors at duels went far beyond their presence being requested. At the meeting between the Duke of Wellington and Lord Winchilsea in 1829, as has been accounted previously, it was Wellington's surgeon, Dr Hume, who not only procured the pistols used in the duel but also loaded them. His actions far exceeded what was expected of him and had it been brought to trial he would have been called as a prime witness in the case; a fact which could not be denied. Where only slight wounding had been inflicted which wasn't life threatening, the doctor could be called forward to pass an opinion as to whether or not the duel should continue. Some antagonists overruled the doctor's opinion if he decided the duel should be cancelled, and pressed ahead with the fight. In October 1783 Mr Green was injured in his duel against Captain Munro, a serving officer of the 16th Dragoons, but on his wound being examined he claimed the duel must be properly concluded or that Captain Munro apologise if honour was to be satisfied. The men had exchanged six shots, like the two officers on Jersey only the year before, and that should have been enough for any man. Despite implorations to end the affair and apologise to his opponent, the officer refused, saying: 'That, now, I will not do.' Green declared that the duel should continue, with the rather prophetic words: 'Then one of us must die.' They were the last words he uttered for with the next exchange of shots Green hit his man in the knee but was shot in return in the groin which proved fatal. Some accounts have Green being hit in the chest. How such an error could be made in distinguishing between groin and chest is anyone's guess. Had the men not been so adamant, it is possible both might have survived the affair.

The historian and author Kevin McAleer points out: 'The role of the doctor at duels was a delicate one … His purpose was not only to extract balls, if not too deeply embedded in tissue … but also consulted to see if a bout should continue.' No doubt some duellists were relieved when a doctor ordered the duel to be halted. Whereas Larrey had been lucky to evade the challenge of a duel by his patient, some medical practitioners were not so fortunate and found themselves facing the muzzle of a pistol. One such participant in a duel fought in America in 1844 was a Dr Marsteller who, on being wounded in the hip during the confrontation, showed great fortitude and instead of calling for aid, the physician removed the ball and dressed the wound himself. In 1830 Dr Smith faced his colleague Dr Jefferies at a distance of eight paces in their meeting in Philadelphia, thereby proving that medical men were prepared to shoot and take life if necessary.

Duels by their very nature were normally dour, sombre affairs conducted in a most sober and officious manner. The principals were supposed to always conduct themselves in a way which bore out the fact they were gentlemen with manners, and as such were meant to observe the formalities of a duel and not in any way ridicule the situation. However, despite all such observations, conduct at a duel did not always follow the guidelines and erratic behaviour could be exhibited. One such notable experience concerned the duel in 1806 between Humphrey Howarth, MP for Evesham, and the Earl of Barrymore, who had been enjoying one another's company at the Castle Inn at Brighton following a day at the nearby races. The conversation of the two men passed from being pleasant talk into a disagreement, probably over some trifling matter as was common, and fuelled no doubt by ample amounts of alcohol. They agreed to meet the following morning to settle their differences, with their seconds, doctors and some witnesses who had been present during the quarrel.

In his early youth Howarth had served on the medical staff of the East India Company, a trading company based in the subcontinent of India, but in 1806 he was an ageing and corpulent gentleman. Barrymore, from Ireland, was also used to a life of comforts and was no longer an energetic youth either. As he stood eagerly and ready to get on with proceedings on the morning of the duel, he was astonished at the sight of his opponent when he appeared. Howarth stood before him stripped naked to the waist, save for his underwear. The vision of a fat, elderly man in a state of undress holding a pistol was too much for the onlookers and they dissolved into laughter. Barrymore accused Howarth of mockery and failing to take the affair seriously. The MP declared he *was* serious and using his medical knowledge concerning the effect of gunshot wounds explained his reasons for disrobing, with the statement: 'I know that if any part of clothing is carried into the body by a gunshot wound, festering ensues … therefore I have met you thus.' Satisfied that the duel was still a serious matter the meeting continued and the men exchanged fire. In the end, Howarth's nakedness did not prove necessary as both men missed and another affair of honour had been satisfied. None of the pamphlets or larger tomes of the day, which offered advice on conduct in duels, appear to have taken into account the possibility that duellists might fight naked. But the point being made by Howarth about the ingression of foreign objects into a wound was valid and actually mentioned in *The Art of Duelling*, written thirty years after his duel. The book warns how 'cloth carried into a wound makes sad work'. In other words, infection would result and without antibiotics a dirty wound would almost certainly cause death.

The trajectory or path of the bullet fired from a pistol could be erratic and frequently had a tendency to fly far from true. It was not unknown for the impact of a seemingly slight wound to actually result in a fatal injury. The reason for this phenomenon was due to the round shape of the bullet which could, in some cases, be deflected. For example, if the lead ball struck a bone it could glance off in any direction, because a round ball hitting a round bone was apt to be deflected.

On 28 January 1837 the Russian poet Alexander Pushkin faced his wife's lover, the Baron Georges d'Anthes, in a duel to settle the issue of honour. Pushkin had written a particularly stinging letter to the man who was cuckolding him and the two men met in the outskirts of the city of St Petersburg. The first to fire was d'Anthes whose shot hit Pushkin in the thigh causing the poet to fall. Composing himself, he stood to return fire and struck his adversary causing wounding to his arm and chest. It was then discovered that Pushkin's wound was more severe than at first believed. The bullet had hit the thigh bone and glanced off, continuing its path to end up in his abdomen. Abdominal wounds, especially very deep ones, could not be treated and massive internal bleeding was almost invariably fatal. Pushkin was taken to his home where he lay for the rest of the day and through the night before finally dying the next day.

A duel fought in 1790 saw one of the principals hit in the wrist of his right arm as he held it up to protect his face. The bullet passed straight through and struck the man in the cheek, exiting through his neck. A study of modern ballistics shows that if a bullet follows a stable trajectory and hits the target in a stable manner, it will yield up between 10 and 20 per cent of its energy. However, if a bullet follows an erratic or unstable trajectory it will yield up 60–70 per cent of its energy and inflict a more serious wound.

In the nineteenth century there were few analgesics or sedatives and although infection was known, the exact cause was not clearly understood. The only forms of antiseptic were liquids such as vinegar or turpentine. The experience of doctors in treating gunshot wounds varied widely and for the most part many physicians would never be called on to treat such injuries. James McGrigor who served as Principal Medical Officer during Wellington's campaign in Spain believed that most medical officers were no more than 'druggists' apprentices', an opinion which could be applied equally as well to a number of civilian doctors. When dealing with the vast numbers of soldiers wounded on the battlefield time was a luxury surgeons did not have. They had to work quickly and as efficiently as possible if they were to try and save as many lives as they could. From these experiences, improved techniques in treating gunshot wounds were passed on and in peacetime civilian doctors, who did not have the same pressures as their military counterparts, could spend the time treating individual wounds with compassion.

There was no way of knowing how a man would react if wounded in a duel. Some would calmly walk away, their actions belying the severity of their wound; sometimes even the slightest wound could produce hysteria. There was advice on how to conduct oneself if wounded in a duel and one published work instructed:

If upon discharge, his adversary's ball has taken effect, he must not be alarmed or confused, but quietly submit the part to the examination of his surgeon, who should close round him, with his Second, the moment the discharge has taken place.

The pages of the instruction continue with further words of advice by emphasising:

I cannot impress on an individual too strongly the propriety of remaining perfectly calm and collected when hit; he must not allow himself to be alarmed or confused; but, summoning up all his resolution, treat the matter coolly; and if he dies, go off with as good a grace as possible.

Reasonable words, but clearly written by someone who had never been shot. When a duellist was shot the doctor would administer treatment to stem the flow of blood, then remove the wounded man to his home or some quiet premises where he could remove the bullet, if still lodged in the man. The doctor would in effect leave the scene of the duel in the same quite unassuming manner in which he had arrived.

In the case of the duel between Lord Camelford and Captain Best, as cited in a previous chapter, Best was uninjured but Camelford was hit in the chest and the man realised he was badly wounded. Calling the officer towards him Camelford said: 'You have killed me, Best, but the fault is wholly mine, and I relieve you of all blame.' The surgeon attending the wounded peer was Simon Nicholson, who would have noted that the bullet had broken the ribs on the right side of the chest, passed through the lobes of the lung and smashed into the sixth vertebra of the spine. The man was paralysed and his chest cavity filling with blood from internal bleeding. Even with such injuries Lord Camelford had enough presence of mind to motion Best towards him and said: 'Shake hands with me and forgive me, and then fly and save yourself from arrest.' It was a magnanimous gesture of deathbed exoneration towards the man who had killed him, but all said and done it was the peer's own tempestuousness which had brought on his own demise.

Once at the place where he was to perform the surgery to remove the bullet, the doctor might wish for the services of an assistant, who could be one of the injured man's friends. In most cases it would be necessary to restrain the patient as the doctor set about the painful task of locating the ball. This procedure involved the doctor using a long thin metal probe, rather like a knitting needle and sometimes with a slight curve to it, which he inserted into the wound to follow the track of the ball. It was a delicate procedure and not always simple, as the doctor might have to spend time probing for the ball, identified by its general hardness and metallic texture.

Once located the doctors used a special instrument to grip the ball and extract it from the wound. Care had to be taken if the wound was near an artery, making sure not to burst it. When William Richards, Mayor of Tenby in Wales, was shot in the groin by his opponent Henry Mannix, during their duel on 1 April 1839, his wound was not treated until some time after the affair. Normally most doctors preferred to treat gunshot wounds as soon as possible after being inflicted, but in this case it was almost a full week before Richards was operated on to remove the pistol ball. Newspaper accounts at first reported the Mayor as having been killed in the duel, but local newspaper the *Morning Chronicle* announced on 6 April that although seriously wounded it was believed Richards would recover. Almost three weeks later another local newspaper, this time the

Carmarthen Journal reported that Mayor Richards had been operated on and the bullet successfully removed. The reason for the delay may have been to allow the swelling in the groin to subside, particularly in the area where arteries are located. Three medical men treated the unfortunate Mayor in an operation which turned out to be more delicate than at first perceived.

From Pembroke there was the surgeon Joshua Paynter who was assisted by Thomas C. Jones of the Royal Navy and serving as Surgeon of the Royal Dock in Pembroke. There was also a local physician Dr Reid of Lamphey Park. Together the three medical men undertook the removal of the bullet which on examination had driven in deeply, lodging near the spine of William Richards. The projectile had also taken in fragments of fabric from the man's clothing which, if left unattended, could become infected with blood poisoning or tetanus at the least. The trio of medical men must have been working to the limits of their ability but finally they removed all the foreign matter from the wound and the bullet. Their patient would almost certainly have endured searing agony if he were not heavily sedated with alcohol or passed out through the pain. Remarkably he recovered from his ordeal and, even more amazingly, he lived for a further sixteen years and died in 1855 at the age of 60. No doubt the men were highly skilled, especially the naval surgeon, who would have known how to treat gunshot wounds. Such medical treatment would have come at a price and Mayor Richards was from a wealthy family with good connections which meant he was more than capable of paying for the best treatment available. In 1799 Samuel Fortune was not as lucky as Mayor Richards and when he was shot in Haverfordwest in Pembrokeshire in Wales he did not receive anywhere near the same type of medical treatment and died the following day.

Although the doctor's direct role at a duel may have been as the silent witness, his duties often went far beyond those of any other person involved, as seen in the case of Dr Hume at the Duke of Wellington's duel. The doctor's main role came after the duel in the care of the wounded. Some patients had to sometimes be dosed with liberal amounts of alcohol such as brandy, but that did not always work and the best that could be hoped for was the patient would pass out through the pain and in this inert state allow the doctor to perform his operation quickly. In the case of the affair between Lieutenant Henry Hawkey of the Royal Marines and James Seton of the 11th Hussars in 1845, the doctor did not perform his treatment as well as might be hoped. Seton was wounded and attended by the doctor, who made a mess of treating the man; he suffered excruciating pain for ten days before dying in agony. From the description of the duelling scene Seton fell clutching his stomach which would indicate an abdominal wound. Anaesthetics were still being developed at this time and chloroform, for example, would not be used until 1847; it is unlikely the doctor attending Seton would have brought a supply. Any attempt to remove a bullet from the abdomen could cause more complications, and if infection set in the patient would have been beyond any medical care. This is probably what happened in the case of Seton but eight years earlier the Mayor of Tenby could count himself exceptionally fortunate to have survived his operation.

Doctors were usually well-known figures in communities and could often be long-standing friends of a potential duellist. Through this intimate relationship one knew that if a doctor was requested to attend a duel, then whatever may be said a man could be confident in the doctor's integrity and complete discretion at all times. On being summoned to a duel, it was the usual practice to send a carriage for the doctor at an early hour in the morning so as not to arouse curiosity. The place where the duel was to take place might be some distance from the doctor's residence and if he were to walk anyone might see him, but in a carriage the shutters could be drawn.

In the duel between David Landale and George Morgan in 1826, each man arranged for his own doctor to be in attendance. George Morgan offered to take his physician, Dr James Johnston, to the site of the duel in his carriage. The doctor declined and said he would be at the scene at the appointed time. The good doctor's family were aware of the task he had been called to perform and did their very best to prevent him leaving the house, which included hiding his shoes and locking the door. Despite these delays Johnston left for the duel. David Landale used the services of Dr Alexander Smith who also travelled to the site of the duel in a separate carriage. On his arrival his was met by Landale who presented him with two letters, asking him that in the event he should be killed, the doctor would send the missives to Landale's brother and the other to a clerk in his employment. When Dr Johnston arrived he approached Landale's second, William Millie, and appealed him to stop the duel. Morgan told him to keep quiet, as a man in his position was not to become involved. Johnston in turn told Morgan to keep silent as he was not supposed to speak either. There was nothing to be done to prevent the fight and Johnston, who did not wish to be witness to the scene made to depart. As he did so he spotted his colleague Dr Smith, who was acting on behalf of David Landale, and moved towards him. Suddenly both men were startled by the sound of a pistol being fired. They looked towards the principals and saw that

Morgan was prostrate on the ground. Both medical men examined the body and pronounced him dead. Later, the wound was examined and it was discovered that the bullet from Landale's pistol had broken the fifth rib on the right-hand side, passed through both lungs and probably hit his heart in its passage before exiting under his left arm pit. After some delay the men arranged to have Morgan's body removed and he was later buried in Kirkcaldy in Scotland.

Penetration of two organs such as lungs or kidneys was a very serious problem and death would almost certainly result. The risk arose from the firing position of the duellist, which protocol insisted be side on to his adversary. It was meant to present the narrowest of targets, but the drawback was the high risk of double penetration of vital organs if hit. This was certainly the case in the Landale–Morgan duel. A wound to the abdomen was generally fatal, but some men did survive wounding in this region of the body. In 1852 Harry de Corcey, an American newspaper editor, was hit in the stomach during his duel and survived. On the other hand, Lieutenant Newman was hit in the nose and most of the proboscis shot away. It was not a life-threatening wound, but the young army lieutenant suffered great pain and could not eat properly. His remaining years were spent in great discomfort and he eventually died of malnutrition through not being able to eat anything of substance. Observations on the matter of being wounded during a duel were penned by an American writer in the nineteenth century and wrote:

> If a man could be sure of a ball in the right quarter, say the fleshy part of the arm, or of the thigh, or of a grazing shot upon one of the ribs, or not hit at all, it would be well enough. But it is not pleasant to anticipate [say] a bullet in the shoulder joint, occasioning infinite pain and a crippled limb for life: or a ball in the hip, badly scratching the femoral artery and bloating up into aneurisms; or in the articulation of the lower jaw, splintering bones of importance; or one in the lungs, producing great wheezing and weak wind for the residue of life; or in the stomach, allowing much gastric juice to escape and spoiling the thought of dinner forever.

This was gruesome warning indeed and penned with, no doubt, a certain amount of relish knowing that the more bloody a description the more widely it is likely to be read.

Thus it was that doctors were the reluctant but necessary observers to an act which went against their medical beliefs. So what prompted them to attend? In some cases it was the loyalty they believed they owed due to long-standing friendship. For others it was probably just the money they were being paid to provide a duty. No doubt each would have wished to be anywhere else rather than involved in a duel. Despite this, the presence of doctors saved the lives of some duellists which was what their training was all about. It was not down to them to moralise over the rights or wrongs of duels; in each case they had elected to attend and for that they cannot be seen to have done anything wrong. The law in those days saw things differently and would have held the doctor to account for his actions, but today with hindsight we have come to understand things so much better.

9

TOOLS OF THE DUEL

History of the Weapons

Before the advent of firearms, the choice for the duellist could be any hand-held weapon such as an axe, but more usually the sword was preferred. During the Middle Ages and the high period of chivalry when jousting tournaments and mêlées were held, swords, axes, maces and lances were used. The use of these weapons required skill and stamina which only came after years of training and experience often gained in actual battle. With the introduction of the handgun it became all too easy for the protagonists to arrange a meeting at a convenient location to resolve their differences by shooting at one another. That may seem like an over-simplification, but firearms rendered obsolete the need for true skill at arms. Those involved in an argument could settle their differences by firing at one another, having it all over and done with in a few moments and without the need for the physical exertion associated with duels where swords were used.

It has been opined by the author and historian Victor Kiernan that, 'a bullet's direction being less predictable than that of a sword-thrust, possibly some of the more religiously minded, or fatalistic, found it easier to see the hand of providence, or fate, on the trigger than on a sword-hilt.' One has to concur with these sentiments because, although anyone could pick up a pistol to shoot, one could not predict where the bullet might hit even if it was aimed. A sword point went where the user directed it, so although less personal, a pistol came to be the preferred weapon of choice for the duellist. Nevertheless, with guns one or both of the pair may be wounded or killed, but the end result reached the same conclusion, which is to say that honour was seen to have been satisfied.

With the benefit of hindsight we can look back over the years and see how a wide range of objects were selected and pressed into use as weapons by duellists, not all of which could be considered as natural weapons. For example, in France in 1843 an argument between two players erupted over a game of billiards, leading to the men consenting to settle their disagreement by hurling billiard balls at one another. At the time, billiard balls were made of ivory and due to their hardness, size and weight it meant that as missiles they could inflict severe wounds. The first man to throw did so with such speed, power and accuracy that he killed his opponent.

During the Napoleonic Wars Britain kept some French prisoners incarcerated on the moored hulks of obsolescent war ships. The captives were naturally denied access to weapons for obvious reasons. However, that did not always prevent prisoners from resolving their differences using improvised weapons, such as the pair who fought using scissors tied to the end of sticks. There would have been no finesse as the men hacked at each other with their extemporised primitive weapons. With prison guards being indifferent to maintaining order and the adversaries probably being goaded on by their fellow prisoners, the fight continued until one of the men inflicted a mortal slash across the abdomen of his opponent; the cut going so deep that the man's entrails were exposed. This incident was not so much a duel as a lethal brawl in a prison, but it does serve to illustrate to what lengths men were prepared to go to in order to settle an argument. The fact of the matter was, quite simply, that firearms made it quicker to settle such affairs.

Long arms or muskets which were fired from the shoulder had been developed relatively early in the history of firearms, but the length of these weapons required the firer to use both hands to operate them, and used a method of fire known as matchlock. These cumbersome weapons were loaded and fired in the same way as cannon, and some early firearms were called 'hand cannon' due to their size and method of operation. This was obviously a drawback because the length of the weapon made it unwieldy and awkward to aim properly; some were of such length they could not be used without the aid of a special forked rod on which to rest it.

Although gunpowder weapons had existed and been used in battle since the early fourteenth century, it was not until the sixteenth century that the first true handguns or pistols began to appear; the design of which used a method of operation known as wheel-lock. The first designs of these new type weapons were bulky due to the mechanism, but soon they evolved to become more compact and reduced in length. Italy is credited as being the place of origin of the pistol as a weapon and the term pistol is generally believed to have been derived from the town of Pistoia in Italy.

The wheel-lock was really a clockwork mechanism which used the stored energy of springs to impart a rotary motion to a disc of steel, which made contact with a piece of iron pyrite producing a series of sparks. These sparks would, in turn, ignite the gunpowder in the priming pan and the flash caused by the burning powder set light to the propellant charge and the pistol was fired. The mechanism was wound like a clock using a special key-like tool, and simply squeezing the trigger released all the stored energy to operate the weapon in a single movement. But the weapon was complex. An examination of surviving designs has revealed them to have had between thirty-five and fifty individual parts. As a weapon design the wheel-lock pistol was prone to failure due to the ingress of dirt into such a delicate mechanism or the breakage of springs.

One story behind the origin of the design claims it was devised in 1517 by a German clockmaker called Johann Kuhfuss (sometimes written as Kiefuss) from Nuremberg. However, there is no conclusive proof in the form of surviving documents that such a man existed and so the true origins of the wheel-lock are ambiguous at best. Furthermore, the date behind any claim that Kuhfuss invented the wheel-lock is discredited because there are examples of this type of weapon in museums dated *c.*1510, several years prior to the Kuhfuss story.

It is known that the artist and inventor Leonardo da Vinci drew designs for such a weapon between 1505 and 1508, and so it is quite possible that someone may have seen the drawing and been influenced by its design. What is certain, though, is that several years after the drawing is believed to have been created, a written account of a fatal accident involving a wheel-lock pistol appeared in a work titled *How Laux Pfister Shot a Whore in Constance*. It was contained in the writings of Wilhelm Rem, who included the incident in his work *Chronica newer Geschichten*. Not only is it a fascinating record because it tells us how dangerous wheel-lock pistols could be if not handled properly, and was no doubt intended to serve as a stark lesson to those who believed they knew better, but it does give us a precise date when wheel-lock pistols were in general usage. Rem's account begins:

In the year of Our Lord 1515, on the day of the Three Holy Kings [generally taken to put the date at the 6 January], there was a certain young citizen of Augsburg in Constance [this would be Laux Pfister] who invited a handsome whore. And when she was with him in a little room, he took up a loaded gun in his hand, the lock of which functioned in such a way that when the trigger was pressed, it ignited itself and so discharged the piece. Accordingly he played around with the gun and pressed the trigger and shot the whore through the chin, so that the bullet passed out through the back of her neck.

Miraculously the woman survived her injuries, which could have proved fatal had the bullet struck an artery or the lady's trachea in such a vital part of her anatomy. As for the young man, he came away from the incident very lightly and had to pay her compensation. The incident proves two things: Firstly, it illustrates that the design of the pistol was such that it could be easily carried and concealed. Secondly, this dated statement is two years before the Kuhfuss story, which again rules him out as the originator.

The reduced length of the wheel-lock pistols led to a number of measures being implemented in an attempt to regulate the spread of such weapons. For example, in 1523 the Italian city of Ferrara banned wheel-locks and issued the statement:

> … since an especially dangerous kind of firearms have come to be used, which are called stone guns [a reference to the wheel-lock mechanism] with which a homicide can easily be committed; in knowledge of this, His Excellency, knowing that these are devilish arms, prohibits … their being carried … without explicit authorisation, under penalty of having a hand publicly cut off…

This left no one with any doubts as to the consequences should they break the law. The town of Modena issued a similar law because 'these arms are being used more and more for murders and assassinations', and in 1547 the Duke of Florence banned the carrying of firearms short enough to be concealed about the person, with particular mention of wheel-locks and the newly developed flintlock design which was just becoming available. These proclamations are rather ironic, really, because here was the country where pistols had been developed, trying to impose an arms embargo, and it was use of these very pistols which led to Italy being identified as the birthplace of the formalised pistol duel.

At the time wheel-locks were in service the sword was still being used for duels, but in the space of little more than 100 years after the introduction of the wheel-lock, a new method of operation for firearms would be introduced and this was the flintlock mechanism. Firearms using the wheel-lock mechanism were expensive and pistols using this form of operation were usually reserved for the elite mounted troops serving as bodyguards to monarchs who could afford such weapons. Attempts to try and limit their use came to nought and certainly did not prevent the death of the Prince of Orange, who was assassinated by Balthazar Gerard using a wheel-lock in 1584 in Delft. The earliest types of these pistols were quite long and did not lend themselves to duelling because of their size, some of which could measure 24 inches long.

Gradually they became reduced in size and wheel-locks, while complicated in operation, were pressed into use in pistol duels, such as an affair in 1659 between two mounted riders in Switzerland who exchanged shots while on horseback.

It would appear that mounted duels at this time were not uncommon; perhaps a hangover from the early days when medieval knights engaged in tournaments or mêlées. A duel fought between an infantryman and a dragoon (a mounted infantryman) was recorded in the writings of Hans Grimmelshausen. The affair allegedly happened some time during the Thirty Years War, a European conflict which lasted from 1618 until 1648. From the writing, the author's reference to the 'glowing match' of the infantryman's weapon would indicate he was armed with a matchlock musket. The dragoon was carrying two wheel-lock pistols, which were common cavalry weapons at the time. At the command the two men approached one another; the infantryman on foot and the dragoon mounted. The infantryman had loaded his weapon in such a way that when he fired, the discharge gave the impression his musket had malfunctioned. The dragoon rode forward believing his opponent to be unarmed. It was then the infantrymen raised his musket and shot the rider dead.

Once the pistol had been developed, new forms of firing operation were established such as the snaphance (sometimes written as snaphaunce), which used flint striking against steel to produce the sparks needed to fire the weapon. These advances finally led to the development of the standard flintlock mechanism, a very simple and quite reliable method of operation, and it would be weapons of this type that would come to be used in duels.

The first flintlock designs appeared around the beginning of the seventeenth century and these new weapons changed warfare and the method of duelling. Pistols were still expensive, but the flintlock weapons were cheaper than the wheel-lock weapons and as such were more affordable to civilians as a whole. Cavalry troops were equipped with flintlock pistols on a wide scale, and in England during the Civil War the Parliamentarian army formed the New Model Army in 1645 under the aegis of Oliver Cromwell, whose troops were armed with these weapons. In the aftermath of battles, civilians would often descend on the battlefields and pick up all manner of items including pistols, and in so doing distributed such weaponry among civilians. Some were just collected for sale later as macabre souvenirs, but others found their way into the hands of criminals such as highwaymen. Cromwell may have given his troops the pistols for fighting battles but inadvertently he had also provided them with the means of fighting duels.

Cromwell did not approve of the practice of duelling, as we have seen in chapter 1; it was considered 'cavalier', and ordinances banning the fighting of duels were issued, indicating severe consequences for anyone sending or accepting the challenge to a duel. Even so, from around 1650 duelling with pistols continued to flourish, despite being banned.

Due to the short length of pistols they are inherently dangerous, because the user can inadvertently point the weapon in the wrong direction, which is to say away from the intended target, simply by a turn of the body. The inexperienced duellist unfamiliar with pistols could, in effect, present as much danger to himself and bystanders as he could to his opponent. If he fumbled his weapon then his second would be on hand to offer calming words of encouragement to settle any nervousness. If a man was unfamiliar with handling a weapon of any sort he was most likely going to be nervous, and the prospect of being killed would only compound matters and lead to the weapon being discharged prematurely.

By way of example to illustrate how dangerous pistols could be when not handled correctly, one only has to refer to observations made during the Second World War. A British Army officer recorded that he had seen thirty men shot with a pistol, and of this figure twenty-nine of the casualties were men under his own command who had shot themselves or comrades while handling pistols, either loading or unloading the weapon.

Handling a pistol is not as easy as one might think and it takes practice before it becomes familiar in nature. Pistols are designed to be used at close range and despite claims placed on a weapon's design by the manufacturer, the accuracy of any pistol ultimately lies in the hand and eye coordination of the user. The late military historian and small arms expert Ian Hogg, held the belief that pistols are not easy weapons to use. He was of the opinion that any person given a pistol would be 'highly unlikely to get their first shot into the target at all'. He went on to state that: 'To become even a passable pistol shot takes a good deal of training and constant practice, and these are not generally available in wartime or in peacetime.' Naturally he was referring to multi-shot pistols in military usage during the conflicts of the twentieth century. However, this opinion does apply equally well to the single-shot pistols of the eighteenth and nineteenth centuries and of the type used in so many duels. *The Art of Duelling* supports the above opinions by stating: 'Although it appears very easy to pull a trigger, and discharge a pistol, yet no one, until they make the experiment, can be aware of the difficulty in firing with accuracy and expedition.'

The revolver is but one form of a category of weapons known as pistols and is defined as having a revolving cylinder, from whence it derives its name, which can be loaded with six ready-to-use rounds of ammunition or bullets. This is a multi-shot weapon and the first reliable models to be mass-produced appeared at the Great Exhibition held in London in 1851 and were exhibited by the American firearms manufacturers Samuel Colt. At this time in America, pioneer settlers were moving into the vastnesses of the 'Wild West' and they saw in this weapon the ideal means to protect themselves from all manner of dangers. The cowboys working in this lonely, inhospitable wilderness took to the revolver instantly and it became an iconic part of their everyday lives. The revolver was a symbol of the frontier and came to be used by lawmen and the lawless alike. Indeed, when one thinks of the Wild West the most enduring impression one conjures up from this period is the scene of two cowboys facing each other to shoot it out to end an argument which in all probability started over a game of cards in a saloon.

While such scenes undoubtedly did happen for real, these encounters could hardly be termed duels. These were street brawls using guns, now termed 'gunfights'. Such exchanges of shots invariably happened spontaneously and in broad daylight, often in the middle of the main street in a frontier town. Nothing could be further removed from the logical, almost bureaucratic, method of conducting formal duels, played out with great ritual and often with a certain amount of aplomb which bordered on the ceremonial. The Wild West gunfight with revolvers, on the other hand, was over in seconds and even the celebrated gunfight at the OK Corral, fought in 1881 in the town of Tombstone in Arizona, is understood to have been concluded within 30 seconds.

Accuracy with any weapon does not come naturally, although a steady hand combined with a keen eye does help matters along. The British Army at the time of the First World War sought troops for training in the role of snipers, and recruited men from within the ranks who were 'of above intelligence, strong and tireless, have the makings of a good shot'. The point which stands out the most in this description is the fact that the potential sniper should only have the 'makings' of a good shot. Snipers use rifles to shoot over long distances, but the comments here can be taken to mean that with the right coaching and proper training anyone can become well versed in the fine art of shooting accurately.

Many duels were fought by men who had little or no experience of shooting whatsoever and had never seen a shot fired in anger. Prime Minister William Pitt, when challenged to his duel by George Tierney, had never had cause to handle a weapon in anger although he had participated in shooting as a sport. At this meeting neither man was injured, and it was later ridiculed in the popular press of the time.

In the case of so many novice duellists, the fact they hit their opponent can be seen as a lucky shot or, depending on one's point of view, an unlucky shot if that opponent is killed, in which case he could be tried for murder. A steady hand or a belief in oneself – however one chooses to explain such fortunate firing, fatalities at the hands of inexperienced shooters certainly did happen, much to the alarm of those in attendance who sometimes knew of a man's lack of shooting skills. The victim in those cases where only slight wounding occurred was not unnaturally shocked at being hit, and where a man later died of his injuries, witnesses could only express their surprise.

Despite the greatest care given to loading and preparing the pistols for the duel, there was the chance that a weapon could misfire, i.e. not operate properly and discharge. One cause of failure was the flint, which might not create sparks as it struck the steel to ignite the powder in the priming pan. A good flint could give sparks for thirty to fifty strikes, but there was no guarantee and misfires could occur. Problems could arise either due to the gunpowder not being up to standard and burning slowly, or from the damp caused by the moisture which hung in the air at the early hour of the meeting.

By the late eighteenth century the constituent compounds for the manufacture of gunpowder had been standardised, with a slight variation from one country to another. In the 1780s, for example, gunpowder in England was made using 75 parts saltpetre, 15 parts charcoal and 10 parts sulphur. Gunpowder for the Prussian States was slightly different and used 75 parts saltpetre, 13.5 parts charcoal and 11.5 parts sulphur. In England gunpowder was manufactured at special mills owned by the Crown at locations such as Faversham in Kent and Waltham Abbey in Essex; a similar practice was observed in other countries.

It was the question concerning the quality of gunpowder used by the British Army which in 1779 prompted a duel between William Adam and Charles James Fox, two outspoken politicians of the day. At the time, England had been engaged in the War of the American Revolution since 1775 and, after four years of fighting, during which time a number of battles had been fought on land and at sea, there was still no end in sight. The conflict led to questions being asked in the House of Commons and one of the leading protagonists making it very uncomfortable for the Prime Minister, Lord North, was Charles Fox, a Rockingham Whig, and fiercely opposed to the government's policy on war with the American colonists. Among Fox's criticisms was the efficacy of gunpowder used by English troops, and during a debate he declared it to be of poor quality. William Adam, a member of Lord North's Cabinet replied, doubting the veracity of Fox's claim and a row ensued. Fox was naturally tempestuous in character and refused to comply with Adam's demand that he publish an explanation of his remarks. Adam, a fiery tempered Scot, was indignant and he demanded satisfaction and challenged Fox to meet him in a duel. The two men agreed to meet in Hyde Park in London on 29 November 1779 in the presence of their appointed seconds. Fox was of rotund physique despite being only 30 years of age, and his attendance at the field belied his anti-belligerent stance. Once the formalities of engagement had been explained and pistols loaded and prepared, the two men readied themselves. The usual stance was for the duellists to turn side on with their shooting arm facing their opponent. Fox, however, faced full forward towards Adam, leading his second to advise he stand sideways. The instruction prompted Fox to reply: 'To what purpose, sir? I am as thick one way as the other.'

Adam fired and hit Fox in the chest inflicting a slight wound. Fox could have fired at his opponent but chose instead to discharge his pistol harmlessly into the air. The matter of honour had been satisfied. The men returned to Parliament where Fox was congratulated on his lucky escape. His natural talent for being able to pass an apt remark at the very moment it was needed came to the fore when he quipped: 'Yes, I am lucky to be alive … lucky that Mr. Adam's pistol was charged with government powder.'

Horace Walpole wrote of the affair:

> Of all the duels, on true or false record, this was the most perfect. So much temper, on a base of firmness and spirit, never were assembled. For Mr. Adam, I cannot describe him, as I have never extracted malevolence out of the fogs of the Highlands.

The affair was over, but eighteen years later Fox would criticise the government over its decision to go to war against France, the same year that the Prime Minister William Pitt fought his duel.

Military men were well versed in the art of shooting and could often keep their hand in by practising on some open ground. Likewise, landed gentry with large country estates might improve the accuracy of their aim by shooting game animals such as deer, rabbits and pheasants. Certain codes of conduct relating to duels strongly condemned any form of shooting target practice; as duelling was not legal such published rules were merely guidelines but some people stored great emphasis in them. These guidelines were often written by authors who wished to remain anonymous and published them privately. Such pamphlets or books, in some cases, contained stark warnings about duelling. Some contained anecdotal examples which served as lessons to others, such as the case of a young Englishman travelling across Europe, who for some reason found himself in a situation where he was challenged to a duel.

The affair was to be conducted indoors, which was most unusual. The men were armed with pistols and locked in a large room with all the lights extinguished, leaving the men to fumble around in the dark like some deadly game of hide and seek. According to the story, the Englishman's opponent fired first and missed. With his sense of fair play and not wishing to kill his now unarmed adversary, the Englishman felt his way to the large fire hearth and discharged his pistol up the chimney. There was a dull thud in the unused fireplace and on summoning assistance it was discovered that the Englishman had actually shot his opponent who had sought refuge in the fireplace. This is rather fanciful and does sound like an urban legend. *The Art of Duelling* by 'A Traveller' claimed the account contained much information which was 'useful to young Continental tourists'. Certainly this tale of the Englishman would have been warning enough for anyone to be on their guard against duelling in Europe.

In some countries it was frowned on to engage in any act whereby one tried to improve one's shooting skills. Despite these ideas and the published guidelines, establishments flourished where one could practise shooting skills, such as the elaborate Mardon's Shooting Gallery, the premises of which were located at Pall Mall in London. It was here, and at other establishments, that gentlemen could gather to fire for sport and no doubt wager on one another's shooting prowess. At these elegant and exclusive shooting clubs, gentlemen of means and army officers could spend time improving their firing techniques by practising indoors and shooting at targets, some of which were painted to resemble a life-size figure of a man to give the impression of facing an opponent during a duel.

Another way of preparing oneself for an ensuing duel was developed by a rather obscure figure called Dr Devilliers. He designed pistols which fired soft bullets made of wax rather than lead and as such were non-lethal. The firers wore long, loose-fitting top coats and a mask similar to that worn by sword fencers. With their shooting hands protected by a small shield fitted to the pistol, the firers could shoot at each other at a distance of approximately twenty paces. The heat from the powder as it ignited would have melted ordinary wax, so we have to assume that the wax used in Dr Devilliers's weapons was a special compound which became malleable and soft on firing, but which nevertheless would have stung on impact much like an early form of paintball shooting which is popular today.

Another suggested method of preparing oneself in the likelihood of being challenged to a duel was to rig up a life-sized manikin, which could be operated to fire a blank charge. Instructions on how to build this mechanical aid were given in the pages of a booklet of the period, along with advice on how to operate it to give the would-be duellist the maximum amount of training experience.

It was suggested that a life-sized wooden figure be built to include a strong bracket into which a pistol could be securely mounted. The pistol was loaded with a charge of gunpowder and made ready to fire, all except for a bullet, which was omitted from the loading process. A length of twine was attached to the trigger and the trainee duellist retired a distance from the contraption and attached the free end of the twine to his belt. Facing the target he would then assume his position and fire; at the same moment he should then lean back so as to place tension on the twine which would operate the trigger. If all went well the training weapon would fire its blank charge and the trainee would fire his loaded pistol at the manikin. The instructions claim that if this process was observed for some months then the trainee duellist should be capable of standing his ground and returning fire.

This all sounds fine, but the problem was that the training weapon did not fire bullets and, after several uses, a man would become inured to such practices and it would do nothing to prepare him for the real ordeal; that is, facing an opponent who is armed with a loaded pistol who can take precise aim rather than the jerky movements of a dummy. The author of these so-called useful instructions betrays the fact that he is an innocent when it comes to being shot at with deadly intent, otherwise he would not have been so ready to impart such foolish advice. Drawings from the period illustrate the device purportedly in the act of being used, but one has to question who was the most stupid in such a case. Was it the person who came up with the idea in the first place? Or, was it the person who actually believed such a device would work? It would have been far better for a man to visit a shooting gallery with all the attendant noise and smoke, and watch the motions of other shooters, such as Captain Gronow did, who exhibited his prowess with a pistol at the shooting galleries in Paris after the Battle of Waterloo. On one occasion, this officer of the British Army hit the chalk mark on a target – representing a Cossack – forty times in succession at a range of forty paces.

There can be no substitute for the real thing when it comes to shooting at a living being, and firing at a manikin was probably only intended for its novelty value. Even so, the person making the suggestion goes on to claim that with practice, and using his manikin, a would-be duellist should be capable of attaining a level of proficiency with a pistol to include loading, aiming and firing twelve shots at his target in the space of 6 minutes. This is quite extraordinary, because any self-respecting infantryman in any European army at that period could load and fire a musket two or three times a minute – and in the face of an enemy firing at him. This point rather makes redundant the author's claims and underlines the fact he cannot have ever seen a shot fired in anger. Such opportunities to train for a duel, however, were not available to all and for the average man who found himself embroiled in one, he just had to trust his nerve held and leave the rest to fate.

The general consensus agrees that pistols began to enter general use in duels around the mid-eighteenth century, although isolated incidents of pistol duelling are known to have been staged earlier. At this time the principals would have selected a fairly evenly matched pair of weapons which were offered for the encounter. The mass-production method of manufacturing weapons was still in its infancy and even in the late eighteenth century, pistols of similar weight, size and calibre, usually military pistols, would have been chosen and agreed on by seconds. It was a crucial point in seeing that both parties involved in the duel were as evenly armed as possible so that neither had an advantage.

In 1750 Captain Clarke shot and killed Captain Innes during a duel which some accounts say was fought as close as 12 feet apart. Captain Clarke was charged with murder and on inspection his pistol was declared to be better than that used by his adversary; such a declaration would indicate he had had the advantage. In the end he was an extremely fortunate man indeed, because the jury recommended he be spared. King George II granted clemency and the captain avoided the hangman's noose.

This same kind of attention to detail was something which was also strongly observed during duels involving swords. The blades of both weapons had to be of equal length and breadth and the weight of each sword also had to comply. If there was any doubt concerning the dimensions, the weapons would be rejected. The manufacture of firearms had always required attention to detail, but with improved machinery for boring, the tolerances could be more accurately measured. This in turn would lead to gunsmiths producing a range of pistols which were specially crafted for duelling. At first these would have been 'one-off' items, but gradually gunsmiths came to see an opportunity in the market and started to make duelling pistols available in matched pairs; they would be set in a lidded box containing all the paraphernalia for the loading and maintenance of the weapons, such as cleaning rods, powder flasks and tools, including screw drivers and spare flints or, in the case of percussion weapons, extra primer caps.

All firearms are expensive to manufacture and pistols, even though they are small, are not exempt, especially those of a bespoke design. In fact, if anything, they are among the most expensive forms of weaponry. An account of charges from 1631 listed as 'The Gun Maker's Rates', itemises a pair of snaphance pistols with accoutrements as costing £2. The cost for a pair of wheel-lock pistols at this time was £3 and standard flintlock pistols £2 for a pair. An invoice for the acquisition of weapons and accoutrements to equip an English militia unit, dated 1796, lists the price paid for various firearms: twelve carbines, short rifles for use by mounted troops complete with accessories cost almost £34, giving a comparable price per unit in modern currency of only £2.83 approximately. The document also lists eighty pistols purchased for the sum of almost £373, giving a price of £4.66 for each weapon in modern currency and showing how relatively little the cost had risen in the space of 165 years. Such weapons were produced by government arsenals and some private manufacturers under contract, and while the bulk was destined for the army a number of weapons were sold to private buyers.

Some gun-makers' names, specialising in the production of duelling pistols, stood out from the general list of gunsmiths, such as Jeremiah Patrick of Liverpool, Charles Moore of London, Henry Rowland, John Watson, Thomas Addis and William Graves. In 1631 King Charles of England established the Gunmakers' Company of London, a guild of skilled gunsmiths with great reputation and guaranteed workmanship. Over the years, the apprentices of such skilled men would continue the practice of producing quality weapons and this would culminate in the late 1700s with specialist duelling pistols being produced in England by men such as Westley Richards, Henry Twigg and the Manton brothers; in Ireland, Fowler of Dublin and the Rigby family stood out. In France Nicholas Boutet was the Directeur Artiste at the Manufacture à Versailles, where he enjoyed great respect for the quality of his elaborately embellished pistols, which were often given as presentation pieces to persons of esteem, including Napoleon Bonaparte. Boutet's duelling pistols, on the other hand, were simpler in style, with flush-fitting butt caps and plain mountings. Before the French Revolution Boutet had held office as the 'Gunmaker to the King's Light Horse', but his importance as a gun-maker meant he could serve the new regime equally well. Other countries such as Austria and Belgium had their share of leading gunsmiths, but it was in Britain and France that the art of producing fine pistols specifically for the purpose of duels developed into a virtual trademark of the gunsmith's profession. In America, among the leading gunsmiths to specialise in duelling pistols were Cooper of New York and Simeon North. Despite their reputation for producing pistols of quality in the English style, there remained something prestigious about owning a duelling pistol made in England. English firearms may not have been produced in the same quantity as in some other countries, but such weapons enjoyed a reputation for their excellent quality.

The flintlock pistol provided the opportunity for gunsmiths to show the full gamut of their skills when it came to producing extraordinarily fine pistols. This style of pistol produced by a select few for the purpose of duelling would evolve to incorporate a number of refinements, which would distinguish them from standard weapons intended for military service. One of the leading manufacturers of duelling pistols was Durs Egg, whose family business in London also produced firearms for the government in the late eighteenth century, and also for private purchase by gentlemen of means. Adding to the list of duelling pistol manufacturers was Robert Wogdon, whose name has unarguably become more closely associated with duelling pistols than any other gunsmith of the period, and has come to epitomise these specialised firearms. During his lifetime Wogdon's pistols were considered to be of unsurpassed quality and reliability, to the point they were even sold to clients in North America. If a case for libel or slander could not be settled in court, it was unofficially referred to as a 'Wogdon Case' meaning that only a duel could settle the matter, even though duelling was not legal.

In 1789 Frederick, Duke of York is understood to have been armed with a Wogdon pistol when he faced Lieutenant Colonel Charles Lenox of the Coldstream Guards in a duel. Other persons of high office who employed Wogdon pistols included the US Vice-president Aaron Burr, who faced the former Secretary of the US Treasury Alexander Hamilton in 1804. Further testimony to the reliability of these weapons, if it were needed, comes in a short verse composed by 'An Irish Volunteer', which appeared in 1782 and extolled the virtues of Wogdon's pistols:

Hail Wogdon, Patron of that leaden death
Which waits alike the bully and the brave
As well might Art recall departed breath
As any artifice your victims save.

In these four lines the writer leaves one in no doubt that Wogdon's pistols could be used to resolve all manner of problems and that the recipient of such vengeance should be fearful of anyone armed with a Wogdon pistol.

The new refinements to distinguish duelling pistols began appearing around 1770 and at first, there was not a great deal of difference between such weapons and, say, that of a high-quality officer's pistol privately purchased. These were normally 14 inches long, but some could be as short as 10 inches. Military pistols and those which could be purchased by civilians were virtually indistinguishable and were made in a range of calibres. The only real difference lay in the plain wooden stock of the military pistol and its robust construction so that it was reliable under adverse conditions and could withstand the rigours of the battlefield. The flintlock duelling pistol lacked most, if not all, embellishments and most were rather plain, apart from some cross-hatching on the butt to give a firm grip and prevent slipping, including those matched pairs made for presentation cases.

Gradually the so-called duelling pistol evolved with the butt or handle becoming gracefully curved, a shape which some refer to as 'hockey stick'. Some gunsmiths, such as Mortimer and Parker, both working out of London, would develop a form known as 'saw handle', from the similarity of the handle fitted to the carpenter's tool, which was soon copied. This style provided for a slight protuberance which extended back over the fleshy web of the firer's hand between the index finger and thumb. There was no reason why such a feature should be incorporated because it served no real purpose and may have been no more than a fanciful idea by the maker.

The anonymous author of *The Art of Duelling* did not hold with 'saw-handle' pistols, believing them to be clumsy. On this note he commented: 'The pistols I prefer for duelling should measure ten inches in length in the barrels.' He went on to write his approval of the more conventional style of pistol by stating they should be:

> … furnished with percussion locks [these came after flintlocks; see below for details] of delicate workmanship fitted into a firm stock bent into a curve that will fit the hand comfortably. To each barrel should be affixed two sights, one in the breech, carefully set for the centre, and the second about half an inch from the muzzle. I do not approve of silver sights for they are apt, when the sun glances on them, to dazzle and deceive the eye. Those of blued steel are best. The best pistol locks I have seen have been manufactured by Purdey in Oxford Street.

These observations were written after gunsmiths had begun to produce specialist pistols with 'dulled' fittings, and so the author was only passing on details of what was already in fashion.

The author was not alone in his disapproval of silver sights and would-be duellists and lesser well-known gunsmiths agreed with his thoughts when considering weapons for the purpose of duelling. Most pistol designs were fully stocked, that is to say the wooden frame holding the barrel might extend all the way to the muzzle. Later, refinements saw the stock finishing about halfway along the barrel and this style was popular in France and England. Mountings on the pistol, such as sights, were made of iron, but occasionally brass was used, although this was not as popular as the more dull metal. The barrels at first had the conventional smooth tube-like exterior, but over a period of about twenty years gunsmiths developed a distinctive octagonal exterior finished in a dull colouring of either 'blued' or 'browned' to prevent glare. The octagonal barrel form came to distinguish the duelling pistol and the style is accredited to the gunsmith John Twigg who may have been using it as early as 1775. The sights fitted to such pistols comprised of a 'V' type for the rear and a simple bead for the front or fore sight. The side plates for the locks were steel, as were often the butt plates fitted to the bottom of the pistol grip. Some gunsmiths, like Mortimer, fitted their pistols with rain-proof priming pan features to protect the powder and prevent it from becoming damp. These were really nothing more than covers over the priming pan which allowed rain water to run off; when one considers the length of time taken to conduct a duel, unless there was a torrential downpour, in which case the duel would probably be postponed, such items were frippery. In military usage, however, one could see the sense in such a feature where a soldier had to keep his powder dry and his weapon ready to use at a moment's notice.

Isaac Riviere of London patented an enclosed lock mechanism for pistols in 1825. This feature was designed to prevent the ingress of dirt into the firing mechanism, which could cause the weapon to fail, and was fitted to percussion-lock pistols made by the gunsmith. Duels were rituals and the published guidelines gave instruction on how they should be conducted. In the case where a pistol malfunctioned, either due to dirt in the mechanism, damp powder or the flint failing to create sufficient spark to ignite the powder, such misfires were deemed to be the equivalent to firing, because the duellist had pulled the trigger and had the intention of firing. It was through no fault of his own that a pistol misfired, and even had his second loaded the weapon satisfactorily there was no guarantee that it would fire. Even troops on the battlefield experienced this phenomenon with the same deadly consequences.

The wooden stock could extend along the full length of the underside of the barrel, as with some Wogdon models, but increasingly gunsmiths came to only 'half-stock' their weapons. That is to say the wooden stock finished halfway along the barrel and many makers, including Le Page of France, formed the butt and stock from one single piece of wood. The trigger guard on the first pistols were plain, but gradually a 'spur' feature was added so that the firer, particularly one with a nervous disposition, could rest their middle finger on it to steady the hand. This feature was used on English and French pistols, such as those produced by Le Page of Paris, Fowler of Dublin and Charles Moore of London. The short ramrod used for loading the pistol could either be included or omitted from the pistol design; since there was no hard and fast rule covering this item it was down to the manufacturer to decide whether or not to fit ramrods to their pistols. For example, English gunsmiths such as Perkins of Salisbury and Joseph Manton of London, included the ramrod on their pistols, as did the French gunsmith Nicholas Boutet of Versailles. However, the French gunsmith of Verney, working in Lyons, and his colleague Le Page did not always include ramrods in their designs, and Isaac Riviere of London also abandoned ramrods. When boxed or cased pairs of pistols were made the ramrods were included as separate accoutrements along with small screwdrivers to adjust the set spring of the trigger. The trigger spring could be set so that a slight pressure would be sufficient to fire the weapon and this was known as a 'hair trigger'. This meant that a reluctant duellist could fire without any great thought being given to his action. On the other hand, a nervous firer might unintentionally fire before the word of command was given, with potentially grave consequences. Indeed, there were a number of such accidental firings where a nervous duellist fired prematurely, so much so that by around 1830 this method of setting the trigger was being gradually abandoned.

One particular incident which highlights the dangers of lightly set hair triggers comes to us relatively late in the history of duelling and serves as an example of what may have happened many times. In September 1859, by which time duelling was no longer observed in Britain, the US senator David C. Broderick faced David S. Terry, a former chief justice of the Supreme Court, in a duel concerning differences of opinion relating to a speech on slavery. This abhorrent trading in men and women as goods had been banned in Britain and other European countries for many years, but in America the practice remained, although it did have its critics.

The two men, both from the state of California, agreed to use pistols in their affair and met at an appointed place. The weapons were fitted with hair triggers and on the signal to 'fire' being given, the men came up to the aim. Broderick, perhaps due to nerves, prematurely fired his pistol and the ball shot harmlessly into the ground. This left Terry to take his time and shoot his opponent dead. It was a lesson to be learned rather late in the day to save some, but was a stark reminder for would-be duellists in other countries where it was still practised. Such incidents led to a special 'locking bolt' being fitted to prevent accidental firing of the weapon until the hammer had been fully cocked to disengage the safety mechanism.

There were some internal differences between French and English pistol designs. The English duelling pistols lacked rifling and the plain surfaces to the interior of the barrel were referred to as 'smooth bore'. French gunsmiths, on the other hand, produced pistols with fully rifled barrels. Rifling comprises a series of spiral grooves cut into the interior of the barrel to impart spin to the bullet, giving it better stability in flight and thus improved accuracy. This feature on duelling pistols was frowned on in England as it was considered to give an unfair advantage. Indeed, one writer of the day claimed that rifled or even partially rifled pistols had no advantage over smooth-bored pistols at ranges of twelve to fifteen paces, and that they were better suited for long-range shooting. Considering the closeness at which duels were often fought the subject of rifling is an academic point. In England, when principals met at the place of the duel, pistols were often checked for the presence of rifling. Some designs had what is termed as 'half rifling' or 'blind rifling' cut into the lower portion of the barrel at the point closest to the breech. Sometimes called 'secret' rifling the feature was not obvious and could not be detected by simply looking into the front of the barrel which was left smooth. It is ironic to think that half rifling, which was considered 'not quite the thing', should be attributed to Joseph Manton, a leading English gunsmith manufacturing duelling pistols in a country where rifling was not accepted in such weapons. The only sure way of detecting such secret rifling was to insert a pistol ramrod used for loading and rub it along the inner surface of the barrel. Such pistols would be disallowed in English duels but were perfectly acceptable in European engagements. It was the duty of the seconds to detect such improprieties and ensure that each man was armed with pistols acceptable to the rules of duelling according to the country.

Even though the use of rifled pistols was frowned on in England, there were affairs of honour where such styles of weapon were known to have been used. Perhaps the most notorious incident was that involving James Brudenell, 7th Earl of Cardigan in September 1840. As recounted in chapter 1, Brudenell met with a Captain Harvey Tuckett on Wimbledon Common in London, where Tuckett was wounded. As a result, the earl was summoned to the House of Lords for trial where the most damning part of the charges ranged against him was the fact he had used a pistol with a rifled barrel. The trial collapsed, as many believed it would, because there was no charge to answer when it emerged the earl was prepared to allow Captain Tuckett to use the same type of weapon. Along with his social position it was deemed there was no case and the affair was concluded. Rifled barrels, it seems, could make all the difference during and after the duel.

As the trend for settling arguments among the gentry by means of duelling grew more formalised, due to published guidelines suggesting codes of conduct, the gunsmiths responded by producing evenly matched pairs of pistols in presentation cases to give each duellist an equal chance. The weapons themselves may have been plain and simple in style, but were made to such a well-balanced quality that on being raised in the hand such a pistol came onto the target. Even in their plainness such weapons were a statement of the gunsmith's art and capable of accuracy out to 'forty paces'. The carrying cases in which such pistols came were also a work of art, with small recesses for all the accoutrements required for shooting. One of the best known examples of such a cased set of duelling pistols was that owned by Earl Canning, not to be confused with George Canning who had fought a duel and been wounded in the leg by Viscount Castlereagh in 1809.

The set is dated 1834 and contains two pistols each with two barrels, and various other items including powder flask, bullet mould and tools. Of the barrels one form is smooth bore with a calibre of .47in (11.9mm) while the other is rifled and has the slightly smaller calibre of .455in (11.6mm). This set, with its inter-changeable barrels, could presumably be used either for the serious task of duelling or the pastime of target shooting.

Some sets of pistols were passed on as family heirlooms. The Irish judge Sir Jonah Barrington, who was given to fighting duels on occasion, inherited a pair of pistols from his father who had named the weapons 'Sweet Lips' and 'The Darling'. Sets of pistols often had a history of actual usage in duels, such as the pair of weapons purchased by David Landale in preparation for meeting his opponent George Morgan in 1826. Landale, who had never fired a weapon in his life, went to the shop of John Thompson in Princes Street in Edinburgh and chose a pair of pistols, without knowing anything about their use. The owner of the store informed him that the weapons had been used in a duel only the previous year and one had been used to kill a certain Captain Gourlay. Another victim then fell to one of the pistols, when Landale killed Morgan in their meeting.

Most authorities on weapons agree that a well made duelling pistol would be accurate in the right hands and that on raising the weapon it would so well balanced that it would come on to the target almost automatically and with only minimum effort. To aim deliberately was not accepted as convention in pistol duels and, besides which, the time lapse between the firers raising their arms and firing was so short it meant there was no time to take precise aim. The author and historian of firearms, Harold L. Peterson, in his work *The Book of the Gun*, opines that:

> It is a good test of such a pistol to hold it down at arm's length, then suddenly raise it and point it at a target long enough to check the aim with the sights. If it is a true dueller and well made, it should be right on target.

In the 1970s a series of trials were conducted using an English smooth bore pistol, that is to say one without rifling in the barrel, by firing against a man-sized target at a range of 85 yards. Given that the trial was conducted under controlled range conditions, and no duress placed on the firer that might otherwise produce attendant nerves, the target was hit three times out of four. This more than bears out an opinion of the time which held that a well-made duelling pistol could 'inflict a mortal wound at more than forty yards'.

The act of loading the pistol at the place of the duel was almost certainly the point of no return. Having come this far there was no turning back for either principal without being declared a coward. The pistols were almost invariably loaded by the seconds in the presence of one another to ensure fair play. Each man would have been familiar with handling pistols to some degree to permit loading. The first action on selecting the pistol was to insert the ramrod, sometimes taken from the pistol case or from under the barrel of the weapon itself, and use it to check the barrel was clear. One writer suggested that the barrel of the pistol be held up to the mouth and with a gentle and continuous breath blow down the barrel to check the touch-hole is clear. If it was blocked, the pistol would not fire, and so this simple test would ensure the correct function of the weapon. The pistol was then prepared by pouring a measured charge of powder into the barrel, followed by a lead ball wrapped in a wax patch and tamped down with the ramrod to ensure a secure fit.

The gunpowder was measured using a special copper or brass powder flask which usually came equipped in the case and this allowed the proper charge to be loaded. Powder flasks were sometimes divided into three sections and referred to as 'three way'. The main portion of such flasks held the gunpowder and the top was formed into a tube which gave a measured amount of powder suitable for the pistol it was designed to load. This was a feature of some but not all cased pistol sets and was meant to ensure there was no chance of foul play, because the measure of such an item was set and could not be adjusted. Another section of the 'three-way' flask held between three or four balls, which had been cast using the mould supplied with the case. This device operated like a pair of pliers, with the jaws of the implement forming a complete sphere when they were closed. A small opening in the mould allowed molten lead to be poured into the bullet mould to produce a ball of the correct calibre suitable for the pistol. When the lead was cooled the jaws of the mould were opened and the small protrusion or sprue was the only blemish on an otherwise perfect ball for the pistol. This slight sprue was caused by the residue from where the lead had been poured into the mould; it was easily removed by using the snipping edges which formed part of the handle of the mould, intended for this purpose. The last compartment on the 'three-way' flask was revealed when the base was unscrewed, and was where the spare flints were stored. These were necessary, for while a good flint might spark for up to thirty strikes, some might fail after three or four strikes and would need to be replaced before the duel could commence. Not all powder flasks were so elaborate; some were straightforward, containing only powder and fitted with a pouring nozzle. Others had two compartments for balls and powder.

The ball with which the pistol was loaded was usually slightly smaller than the actual calibre of the barrel in order to permit ease of loading. To prevent the ball from rolling out it was wrapped in a soft covering called a 'patch' and was usually a square of material cut from linen or soft leather. Some writers on the subject of duelling disapproved of the use of waxed linen patches which they believed left a deposit inside the barrel, 'to which some of the grains of powder could become stuck, thus reducing the amount of powder deposited in the breech'. This sounds reasonable advice, but anyone with a pride in his pistols, especially when being used for the purpose of something so serious as duelling, would ensure that his weapons were clean and the barrels free from any fouling.

Other writers advised the use of 'kidskin', very soft leather to wrap the ball, which should then be pressed into the barrel using the thumb and then firmed down with the ramrod. It was recommended that the ball should not fit too tightly and that when using the ramrod the thumb of the hand holding the pistol should cover the touch-hole to prevent any powder from escaping and reducing the charge. The hammer with the flint should be pulled back to 'half-cock', which was the safety setting on most pistols and prevented accidental firing of the weapon. Only when the hammer was pulled back to 'full cock' would the trigger operate and allow the hammer to fly forward, striking the flint on the frizzen steel and producing the spark to ignite the powder in the flash pan; this would fire the main charge and shoot the weapon. It was a method of operation that served well with muskets and pistols and would remain in service until a new method of firing was devised by the Reverend Alexander Forsyth of Belhevie in Aberdeenshire, Scotland, who patented his discovery in 1807.

The new method of firing a weapon used chemistry and although the principal was made known in 1807 it would take some time before it gained widespread appeal. The Reverend Forsyth was a keen shooter and enjoyed hunting, but he was frustrated at the delay between pulling the trigger and the weapon actually discharging. It may have only been a marginal delay, but was sufficient to make all the difference between hitting a moving target such as a bird in flight or missing it completely. Forsyth also dabbled in chemistry and, bringing his two interests together, he set himself the task of trying to develop a solution to the delay in shooting. He was not alone in this quest and many scientific minds were applying themselves to the challenge of how to gain instantaneous and reliable firing of a weapon as soon as the trigger was pulled. One of those involved was a man by the name of Edward Howards who was a member of the Royal Society. Around 1800 he discovered the properties of fulminate of mercury, a sensitive compound which detonated when struck hard.

Being a well-read man, it is possible that the Reverend Forsyth may have become familiar with the experiments conducted by Howards and taken his work to its natural conclusion, devising a special lock to replace the flint and steel frizzen plate arrangement. What Forsyth developed was a metal flask resembling a miniature bottle, a design which led to it being referred to as a 'scent bottle lock'. It was fitted to the side plate of a weapon in place of the flintlock and could pivot about on its own axis. This device was filled with an amount of fulminate of mercury powder, and when in the firing position lined up with a small hole connected to the chamber containing the propellant charge of gunpowder. A simple curved hammer was cocked back and on being released by pulling the trigger, it flew forward to strike a pin in the scent bottle lock creating enough of a blow to detonate the fulminate of mercury compound which in turn created a spark to fire the weapon. To fire the weapon again, one simply loaded the barrel in the usual way, inverted the scent bottle lock to permit a small quantity of fulminate of mercury to trickle from the reserve to the priming chamber, return it to the firing position, cock the hammer and pull the trigger.

It was satisfactory and the method of firing proven to work. Unfortunately, it now meant that a shooter had two types of powder to keep dry and this led to further experimentation, such as those trials carried out by an American dentist by the name of Maynard. He placed small amounts of fulminate of mercury on a strip of paper or linen and sealed it over. This was then coiled in a roll and the firer simply had to pull the tape to position a charge over the vent hole.

Following on from that development came percussion caps, which were small copper cups fitted over a fixed nipple into which was drilled a hole connecting with the powder chamber. There were no longer any moving parts, apart from the hammer which had to be cocked, and the fulminate of mercury was now contained in a sealed copper unit making it safer to handle, and was waterproof. There are several claimants to this development, including Joseph Manton and Joseph Egg, both of whom made excellent duelling pistols. Other claimants included the French gunsmith Prelat and the American Captain Joshua Shaw. Whoever was responsible, the fact of the matter remains that the development of an instantaneous form of firing a weapon had been successfully achieved.

The new system using percussion caps remained in use throughout the nineteenth century, being used by armies in wars such as the Crimean and the American Civil War. Former flintlock weapons were converted to the new method of firing, including duelling pistols, such as those made by Durs Egg and Boutet, from around 1800. Even the saw-handled style of duelling pistol, such as those made by Mortimer, were also converted because they were still useful. The new method of percussion caps spread with Jung of Suhl and and the French gunsmith Verney, both manufacturing target and duelling pistols with this type of mechanism.

The efficacy of the new firing method was trialled against the older flintlock to prove which system was better. An oft-quoted trial between the two was that carried out by the British War Office at Woolwich in 1834, with six flintlock muskets firing against the reliability of six percussion muskets, using the Reverend Forsyth's technique. Troops fired a total of 6,000 rounds through each type of weapon, during the course of which the flintlock muskets failed twice for every thirteen shots made; the percussion weapons failed only once in every 166 shots, making the new design the clear winner for reliability.

It would not be until the introduction of the brass cartridge case to make a complete bullet, as we know it today, which came about in the second half of the nineteenth century, which saw the next stage in improving the way weapons were fired. By that time, though, apart from hangover affairs such as the duel fought between the French politicians Georges Clemenceau and Paul Delroulede in December 1892, the high time of duelling with pistols was finished.

Today, duelling pistols, either as single items or matched pairs, are highly collectable. The most sought after are the cased pairs with all the attendant accoutrements which are often sold by specialist auction houses and can command exceptionally high prices. This can increase if the provenance shows their use in a real duel, or simply if the finish of the weapons is of superior aesthetic quality. The Reverend Forsyth probably never intended his invention to be put to use in duels, but such is the way of the world that it was inevitable. Pistols and duels were a natural combination when it came to settling points of honour. This is borne out in *The British Code of Duel* which states:

> Projectile weapons are consonant to the principle of duel, as relates to guarding against the false pride of strength or agility, since the most delicate sense of honour, and the utmost rectitude of mind may be found often unaccompanied by these qualities.

Museums often have flintlock pistols on display in cabinets, some of which are labelled as duelling pistols. There is no real way of knowing whether or not they were used in a duel, unless the history of the weapons is known, as with the pistols used in the affair between David Landale and George Morgan in 1826, which can be seen at the Kirkcaldy Museum and Art Gallery in Scotland. The typical octagonal shape of the barrel and other features which mark out pistols as being made for the purpose of duelling does not necessarily mean they were used to kill someone. But as items of mechanical ingenuity by the gunsmith, they have to be admired along with the quality of the workmanship which went into producing them.

10

THE END OF DUELLING

There had always been opposition to duelling, even from the very earliest times; Spain forbade the practice as early as 1480, and in 1563 the Council of Trent called for all forms of duellists to be excommunicated. Such factions against duelling had never been particularly vocal, and anti-duelling pamphlets which appeared in print were only ever read by a few people due to the fact that literacy rates were low among the working classes.

When the end of duelling came it was due to a number of factors, or so many would believe. However, it was never easy to stamp out something so deeply rooted and duelling never entirely went away. Almost everything has a time limit on it, which dictates how long it will be before the public tires of it and moves on to the next thing of interest. Eventually, the numbers voicing their sentiments against duelling gradually grew and attracted public figures to give credence to their cause. The Church had always been against duelling on moral grounds and the religious aspect won through; the anti-duelling body began to grow in numbers, collecting leading political and military figures as it went. As the historian G.M. Trevelyan has written:

> As the century went on, when growing humanitarianism, evangelicalism, and respectability helped to put down 'the ring' [a reference to boxing] they did the greater service of putting down the duel. The duel in the eighteenth century had been fought at the push of rapier; in the early nineteenth century it was fought with pistols...

G.M. Trevelyan went on to point out that duelling was beginning to wane in popularity in Britain in the second half of the nineteenth century, due to the fact that:

As the spirit of the age became less aristocratic and more bourgeois, less military and more completely civilian and more 'seriously' religious and, let us say at once, more sensible, duelling gradually dropped out.

This opinion is also true of Europe and into North America, beginning first with the northern states and then later the southern states as the country turned against duelling after the Civil War of 1861–5. The end came about over a period of time, as duelling became less and less used as a means of resolving differences and men realised that it was more profitable to sue someone through court actions instead of risking one's life at the point of gun, which was not only illegal but downright murderous in intent. If one looks at Britain as a whole between 1780 and 1851, when duelling with pistols was at its height, we find that the population increased from around 13 million to just under 27.5 million, which tells us that while the number of duelling incidents may have appeared high, the actual chances of being involved in an affair was relatively quite low. Most of the affairs were between the privileged classes, politicians and the military, which made for good newspaper coverage.

The public of any age is only interested in something for so long before it becomes jaded, and people start looking for the next exciting topic to engage their interest. Newspapers have always exerted a powerful influence, and through the pages of their publications could sway votes in governments or unseat unpopular politicians. During the nineteenth century both the local and national editions regularly reported on duels and their outcomes. Sometimes the nationals would pick up a story from a local newspaper and carry a report in an early form of serialisation, thereby spreading news of an occurrence. Over time, the public became so used to reading accounts of who had shot whom and for what reason, that the news of duels began to lose its sensationalism; instead readers became fascinated with the lurid reports of court cases involving litigation.

For example, John Scott, a practising lawyer in the 1780s who later became Lord Eldon and served as the Lord Chancellor, was challenged to a duel by a man called Macretti after he had lost his case for litigation against Scott's client. The lawyer, aware of the illegality of such actions, reported the matter to the authorities and Macretti was sentenced to six months in prison and fined £100. This amount was equivalent to a yearly income for some men and certainly more than a soldier received.

New titles were published to meet public demand, such as the *Petit Journal*, which appeared in France in 1863 and was instantly popular for the gossip it carried. In fact, the *Petit Journal* carried a front-cover illustration on its issue for Saturday 7 January 1893, showing the duel between the French politicians Deroulède and Clemenceau. They fought over the

Dreyfus affair, a so-called spying scandal involving a French officer selling military secrets to the Germans.

The new publications were interesting for their different content, and absorbed the readership with reports on scandals involving claimants seeking financial compensation; stories which replaced the trials of duellists. These articles were made more exciting because those involved in such court cases had their private lives made public and readers awaited the grand finale to discover what arrangements had been made for a settlement.

Some newspaper editors were more familiar with duelling than they may have liked, such as the French publisher Emile de Girardin, who had killed his opponent Armand Carrel, also a newspaper editor, when they fought a duel in 1836. With their first-hand knowledge, such men would have understood the mood of the public and reacted to their growing disinterest in duels, and to keep circulation high fed their new interest in gossip. By the 1880s the *Petit Journal* was selling around 800,000 copies, when only a few years before its rivals had been hard-pressed to sell even a tenth of that figure. Trials involving litigation for libel and slander were the new methods of duelling and going through the courts was certainly more 'respectable' and had better financial rewards. In 1843 Britain introduced the Libel Act which made such cases easier to conduct, but France had to wait a further fifty years before a similar law was introduced and even then it proved difficult to institute.

Many reasons have been postulated as to why duelling declined and what may have started it. High among those theories is public opinion; the law being enforced with greater effect; and, to a lesser degree, the political atmosphere in the mid-nineteenth century when a number of European countries experienced revolution, such as France and Austria in 1848. The truth is probably more down to earth than that, but the fact remains that duelling had lasted longer than many other trends. Its fall from grace was a gradual process so subtle that no one really seemed to notice that it was no longer of interest. From around 1840 in England, when Lord Cardigan was publicly heckled in the street following his duel with Captain Tuckett, other duellists found they were no longer being held in awe, and after 1850 duelling was virtually unheard of in England but it was still practised in countries such as France and America.

The act of duelling, either with swords or pistols, may have been universally condemned as being illegal, whatever the provocation, but even so, there was little, if anything, the law could do in order to prevent two men engaging in such an affair if they had set their minds on it. Under such circumstances the duel came to be tolerated rather than actually permitted, but that is not to say the law courts would accept duelling as an extenuation of circumstances as a means of settling disputes.

Duels were nearly always conducted in remote areas far away from public sites to avoid being observed by people passing by. In most cases the courts only came to know of the duel after the affair. Some seconds, in an effort to prevent the duel, would notify the police who would arrive on site to stop the action, but this was considered as being rather un-sporting. A principal's family may also take it upon themselves to alert the authorities of a duel being arranged in an attempt to prevent the affair from being conducted.

In the age when duelling flourished it was not only the courts which forbade the practice, there was also a small but vocal element in society which frowned on it, and over the years this faction grew in numbers as they sought to actively eradicate it. But the question always arose as to how something conducted in almost total secrecy, not ever known until *after* the event, could be prevented from being practised? Monarchs and heads of state might have joined the chorus calling for duelling to be stamped out, but how could they make any difference when so many prominent personages, like politicians, military officers and leaders of countries, engaged in the ritual? The public face of royalty, for example, may have frowned on duelling, but correspondence reveals that privately they sometimes expressed opinions which could be interpreted as condonation.

Wide-ranging threats against duellists did nothing to dim the practice even when relayed in no uncertain tones. In Russia, Tsar Peter I ordered that anyone even considering a duel should be hanged, and Tsar Nicholas I even prohibited the mention of duelling in the newspaper. In Prussia, duellists had been threatened with hanging and while such measures may seem 'Draconian' they were seen as necessary in order to break the murderous act. By contrast, the pugilistic sport of boxing can be viewed as a contest between two evenly matched men, but they are not deliberately setting out to kill one another when they set foot into the ring. Boxing was a sport in which men wagered money on the outcome, and even though such bouts were bloody and brutal, they were legal, something which duelling was not.

Even so, if two men were bent on duelling then they would commit themselves regardless, despite being aware of the illegality of their intentions and the consequences of their actions. Duelling in the eyes of the law was attempted murder and if one of the duellists was killed, then the surviving duellist was guilty of murder and, if arrested, would be charged with the crime. There may have been extenuating circumstances in some cases, but still, a number of cases were brought to trial with the accused charged with murder, or manslaughter at the very least. In some cases a verdict was not reached and a conviction not passed, which meant the accused could leave court with his reputation intact and his prowess as a duellist would see him elevated in social circles. Lord Cardigan's case was deliberated by the House of Lords for 5 hours before it acquitted him of all charges and he walked free. Some of the accused were not so fortunate and even if exonerated their personal reputation was ruined along with their professional career, as in the case of Aaron Burr.

While duelling was for the most part tolerated in all countries, there was an element which tried to at least restrain the affairs from being conducted in certain places. For example, duels were not to be fought near churchyards and neither were they to be fought on a Sunday. But like so many other thoughts on the matter the sentiments were ignored, and the English Prime Minister William Pitt fought his duel on a Sunday in 1798 which caused moral indignation.

Almost from the very beginning, when the ritual of formalised duelling with swords was established, the Church voiced its disapproval of the act. This disapproval naturally continued over to the time when pistol duelling became established. Under the various codes covering duels, the opponents had to meet in a quiet, out-of-the-way location to avoid chance encounters with passers-by who might witness the proceedings. There were clear stipulations concerning where duels could *not* be conducted, and the grounds near a church was one, despite the temptation.

Churchyards are consecrated places where people visit to pay respects, and if duellists contemplated breaking the code and fought their duel in the boundaries of a churchyard, they could be excommunicated. Some calls against the conduct of duellists went further, stating they did not believe that a man killed in a duel should be allowed to be buried in cemetery. This was but one opinion; the victims of fatal duels had to be buried somewhere and the natural place was for them to be buried in a cemetery, no matter how they had died. The Viscount Du Barrè is buried in the churchyard close to where he was killed just outside Bath; Thomas Heslop is buried in the cemetery of Llandyfriog Church near Newcastle Emlyn in Wales; and Samuel Fortune is interred in the cemetery at St Thomas' Church in Haverfordwest in Wales. These examples serve to show that no one really took any notice of the suggestion, and in most cases the headstones of those killed in duels do not give any clue to the deceased's cause of death. In the case of Samuel Fortune, he is surrounded by family members in an area of a churchyard without any mention of his demise.

Certainly in England, to be followed later by other countries, the whole logic behind the reason to duel came in time to be questioned. More and more the practice of duelling was being seen as an outdated anachronism which did not fit in with the progress being made at the time; it looked increasingly like a barbaric act trapped in an era where science, technology and engineering were making great strides in taking civilisation forward, medicine was improving health and social welfare was beginning to make progress towards better living standards. Newspapers changed their attitudes and instead of publishing accounts of affairs they started to print items calling for the end. The highly respected *London Times* joined in, and in 1840, following Lord Cardigan's duel, questioned his conduct as part of the editorial.

> What the effect upon society in general must be of letting it be understood that there is a crime which must not, or cannot, be restrained or punished because peers and 'gentlemen' think proper to commit it while the law declares it to be a felony, we leave to those to judge who know the power of example and the aptness of the lower orders to learn from their betters. We are firmly convinced that no more pernicious or anarchical principle than that of the defenders of duelling was ever broached by Chartism or even Socialism itself.

It was a wide appeal to all classes to think before getting involved in a duel, pointing out how wrong it was and that the more affluent had the opportunity to lead by example and break away from it. Two years later the Association for the Discouragement of Duelling was established and the following year, in 1843, the Anti-Duelling Association was created with 326 members including judges, lawyers, politicians and military men, all committed to finally putting an end to the practice of duelling. With the Libel Act being introduced at this time, the end of duelling in England was certainly drawing nigh. It had been a long time coming and although duelling had never been legal, it had been tolerated, but now action was being taken to enforce the law.

The Anti-Duelling Association, which was to be such a moving force in the final abolition of duelling, was formed as the result of a duel between two army officers, whose fight over a relatively insignificant dispute concerning property ownership could have been avoided had they exercised more self-restraint. The affair in question was conducted at Camden Town in London on 1 July 1843 between Lieutenant Alexander Munroe, serving in the Royal Horse Guards – also known as the 'Blues', an elite regiment of the Household Cavalry – and Lieutenant Colonel David Fawcett of the 55th Regiment of Foot (later to become the Border Regiment). The duel should not have taken place because of the disparity between the ranks of the two men. Three years earlier Lord Cardigan had broken that rule, and thereby set a precedent, when he fought Captain Tuckett, and so these officers could have cited that instance if called into question.

The two officers were also brothers-in-law and so the matter was more personal than most affairs of this nature. Lieutenant Munroe proved to be the better marksman and his shot hit Fawcett in the chest, inflicting a mortal wound. The stricken officer was taken to his home where he lay for two days before dying in the presence of his wife. Had the seconds been more decisive they could have prevented the tragic affair, news of which caused an outcry across London; it was obvious that something had to be done to kerb duelling. When news of the duel reached Buckingham Palace, and brought to the notice of Queen Victoria, it was certain that action would now be taken.

For eight months matters were debated until finally, on 15 March 1844, the Secretary for War, Sir Henry Hardinge, informed the House of Commons that Her Majesty Queen Victoria wanted a method of 'devising some expedient by which the barbarous practice of duelling should be as much as possible discouraged'. Sir Henry spoke with great knowledge on the matter for he had accompanied the Duke of Wellington as his second in 1829, and understood duelling from first-hand experience. It was decided to use the Articles of War to bring about change, and amendments were put into effect in April 1844 which made it perfectly clear that:

> … every officer who shall send a challenge, or who shall accept a challenge to fight a duel with another officer, or who, being privy to an intention to fight a duel, shall not take active measures to prevent such duel, or shall upbraid another for refusing or not giving a challenge, or who shall reject or advise the rejection of a reasonable proposition made for the honourable adjustment of a difference, shall be liable if convicted before a general court martial to be cashiered or suffer such other punishment as the court may award.

This left no one in any doubt that duelling in the military would not be tolerated in any shape, form or fashion, either directly or indirectly. In other words, there was no excuse for an officer to be caught up in a duel. The changes came too late to save the life of Lieutenant Colonel Fawcett, and had been ignored by Seton and Hawkey in 1845. The change in military law would have been known to Hawkey, and the final closing part where an officer engaging in a duel was to 'suffer such other punishment as the court may award', would have terrified him because it could mean hanging. He was a serving officer who had killed a former officer in a duel, thereby contravening military law; he had no excuse. The precedent had been set for hanging an officer who had killed another in a duel with the execution of Major Campbell in 1809, and faced with such a prospect no wonder he declared he was off to France, and was never heard of again.

Some fifty years after the changes in military law had finally put an end to duelling in the British Army, Germany, which had been unified and declared an empire in Versailles in 1871, also began to follow suit. The historian Heinrich von Treitschke wrote:

> The duel fell into disuse and disappeared completely; the riding whip ousted the sword and pistol and this victory of brutality was celebrated as a triumph of the Enlightenment.

It was the way forward, but some elements in Germany, i.e. the Junker Class, did keep sword duelling alive, with sons of old families proudly sporting scars on their cheeks. In the aftermath of the First World War this practice finally ended and, apart from a brief interlude under the Nazi regime, the practice of duelling in Germany ended in the twentieth century.

No one can say with absolute certainty when the last duel was fought, either fatal or non-fatal, any more than they can say when the very first such affair was convened. All that can be said is that when the end finally came, it put a stop to centuries of men having to be ever mindful of one's actions and words. No longer would a glance at an attractive woman at a social gathering automatically lead to a challenge to duel. Rather it was to be taken as a compliment to the lady's charms and fashion.

Duelling with pistols certainly did not end with the close of the nineteenth century. How could something which had been practised for over 250 years suddenly stop? With the coming of the twentieth century there was a profound change in attitudes which questioned why duels were fought. Duels were now being fought for convenience and any one of a dozen other contrived reasons. The true days of duelling were long gone but tradition dies hard and meetings were occasionally convened during the twentieth century. These later duels are outside the scope of this work, which has tended to focus on trying to understand the true meaning of duelling and its connotations during its heyday in the eighteenth and nineteenth centuries, when honour was the underlying force behind so many confrontations.

Those who fought duels at the turn of the nineteenth and twentieth centuries were seen as anachronistic, firing their pistols for reasons only they considered important and for something they still believed in deeply enough to risk being killed. The twentieth century would see many changes and, like it or not, the men prepared to fight duels had to change their ways also. Gradually the old duellists died and with them the stories of their encounters; all they left behind were the pistols they had used, as grim reminders, to be stared at in museum exhibits along with their written accounts.

This work has set out to chart duelling with pistols, and has attempted to give an insight into something which for a time, probably longer than necessary, was a social trend but never a sociable activity. Many thousands of duels are known to have been fought over the years it was practised, and it should be understood how impossible it would be to cover each and every single affair; each duel was, in itself, a unique event. What can only be achieved here is to provide a thumbnail sketch, looking at something which was a global phenomenon, and to leave any reader who wishes to do so, to discover more on a particular duel for themselves. By doing so, the history of duelling will not become distorted and we will have a better understanding of something we are still trying to fathom out years later.

BIBLIOGRAPHY

Anon, *The British Code of Duel*, Richmond Publishing, 1971.

Atkinson, John, *Duelling Pistols and Some of the Affairs They Settled*, Cassell, 1964.

Baldick, Robert, *The Duel: A History of Duelling*, Clarkson Potter, 1965.

Blackmantle, Bernard, *The English Spy*, Methuen, 1907.

Brereton, J.M., *The British Soldier: A Social History from 1661 to the Present Day*, Bodley Head Ltd, 1986.

Cormack, A.J.R., *The History and Development of Small Arms*, Profile, 1982.

Hague, William, *William Pitt the Younger*, Harper Collins, 2004.

———, *William Wilberforce*, Harper Collins, 2008.

Hamilton, Jill, *Marengo: The Myth of Napoleon's Horse*, Fourth Estate Ltd, 2000.

Hogg, Ian V., *The Illustrated Encyclopedia of Firearms*, Newnes Books, 1983.

Holmes, Richard, *Wellington: The Iron Duke*, Harper Collins, 2003.

Hopton, Richard, *Pistols at Dawn: A History of Duelling*, Portrait, 2007.

Keegan, John, *The Face of Battle*, Jonathan Cape, 1976.

Kelly, James, *That Damn'd Thing Called Honour*, Cork University Press, 1995.

Kiernan, V.G., *The Duel in European History*, Oxford University Press, 1986.

Landale, James, *Duel*, Canongate Books, 2006.

Neal, W. Keith, *Spanish Guns and Pistols*, G. Bell & Sons, 1955.

Newark, Peter, *Firefight!: The History of Personal Firepower*, David & Charles, 1989.

Peterson, Harold L., *The Book of the Gun*, Hamlyn Publishing Group, 1970.

Reid, William, *The Lore of Arms*, Purnell, 1976.

Richardson, Robert, *Larrey: Surgeon to Napoleon's Imperial Guard*, Quiller Press Ltd, 2000.

Rogers, Col. H.C.B., *Weapons of the British Soldier*, Seeley Service & Co, 1960.

Rothenberg, Gunther E., *The Art of Warfare in the Age of Napoleon*, Spellmount Ltd, 1997.

Rush, Philip, *The Book of Duels*, Harrap, 1964.

Traveller, A., *The Art of Duelling*, Richmond Publishing, 1971.

Trevelyan, G.M., *Illustrated English Social History*, vol. 4, Pelican Books, 1964.

Wilkinson, Frederick, *The World's Great Guns*, Hamlyn Publishing Group, 1977.

INDEX